Life begins at 65...

Life begins at 65

The not entirely candid autobiography of a drifter

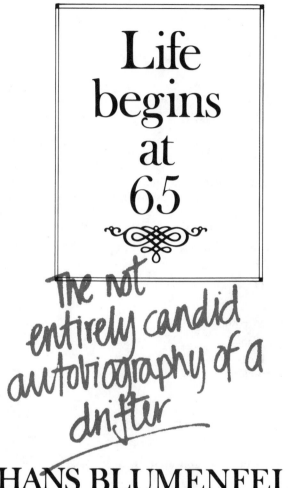

HANS BLUMENFELD

Harvest House

Deposited in the Bibliothèque Nationale of Quebec, First Quarter 1987

Typography and Cover: Joanna Gertler

Printed in Canada
First Harvest House Edition

For information address:
Harvest House Ltd.,
Suite 1, 1200 Atwater Ave.,
Montreal, Canada   H3Z 1X4

Canadian Cataloguing in Publication Data

Blumenfeld, Hans, 1892-
   Life begins at 65: the not entirely candid
autobiography of a drifter

Includes index.
ISBN 0-88772-034-X (bound).–
ISBN 0-88772-035-8 (pbk.)

1. Blumenfeld, Hans, 1892-   2. Architects —
Canada — Biography. I. Title.

 NA749.B49A2 1987   720'.92'4   C87-090027-7

Contents

*The publishers gratefully acknowledge
a publication grant from
the Canadian Institute of Planners.*

CHAPTER I

In the Nest

1892 – 1911

The lack of candor starts with the title. Life, of course, was far more intense and important before 65. What started after 65 was merely what is called "success": recognition, honors, more money than I need.

I have chosen the title as a declaration of war against the absurd tendency to divide life into three boxes: a first, in which one learns but does not work; a second, when one works but does not learn; and a third, in which one neither works nor learns. This has not been the story of my life.

In attempting to tell that story, I have relied almost exclusively on my own memory. I have never kept a diary, and not much documentation of any kind is available.

Memory is deceptive. The reader will find reports of cases where I clearly foresaw and predicted the course of events. No doubt there have been many more cases in which events have disproved my anticipations — these I have conveniently forgotten.

Goethe entitled his memoirs *Dichtung und Wahrheit* — putting poetry ahead of truth. I suspect that this is the appropriate title for this, as for any, autobiography.

ANCESTORS

According to family tradition, the families both of my father, the Blumenfelds, and those of my mother, the Warburgs, came from Venice to Germany in the sixteenth or seventeenth century. My paternal ancestors settled in Bad Mergentheim, in what is ethnically Franconia but now forms the northeastern corner of the state of Baden-Württemberg.

Mergentheim was the seat of the Grand Master of the Teutonic Order which also maintained an important establishment in Venice, so my ancestors probably received from the order the "protection" necessary for the survival of Jews. The order also owned a village by the name of Blumenfeld, near Lake Constance. Conceivably, my ancestors sojourned there on their way from Venice to Mergentheim and therefore assumed the family name when, in the eighteenth century, civil government took over the responsibility for registry previously incumbent on religious authorities.

My mother's ancestors settled in Warburg in Westphalia, from which they subsequently took their family name.

Toward the end of the eighteenth century both families moved again, further north: the Blumenfelds to Münster and the nearby town of Osnabrück, the Warburgs to Altona and to neighboring Hamburg. Both started a business in banking.

THE BLUMENFELD FAMILY

My great-grandfather, Nathan Blumenfeld, built (or remodeled) a house in the center of Osnabrück, opposite the bishop's chancellery. The ground floor was used for business, the second and the mansard roof contained the living and sleeping rooms. Nathan prided himself on the identity of his initials with those of Napoleon Bonaparte, and displayed them over the front door alongside the date of 1810. After the Napoleonic wars, when Osnabrück had become part of the Kingdom of Hannover, a British officer was quartered in the house and became a good friend of the family. On his recall to England he presented Nathan with a silver box for snuff, engraved on one side with Windsor Castle and on the other with the initials NB. I cannot help smiling when I look at this heirloom which has ended up in my hands.

My grandfather Aaron, who inherited the business, and a brother, who became a physician, married two sisters, Caroline and Henriette Maas. The Maases were a cultured Frankfurt family. I inherited part of the library of an uncle of my grandmother Caroline, which contained a 1792 edition of the complete works of Voltaire in 100 volumes, a handcolored forty-volume edition of Buffon, and other French scientific works of the eighteenth century. Only one of the Voltaire volumes remains.

Among the friends of the Maas family was Gabriel Riesser, a

leader of Reform Judaism and a member of the democratic left in the German National Assembly which issued from the revolution of 1848. The liberal-democratic traditions of 1848 remained alive in my father's family. The Maases were importers of Brussels lace. The crisis of 1837, in combination with a change in fashion, put an end to the family business. The Maases moved in with their in-laws in Hamburg, where my grandmother grew up.

I remember my grandfather well, though I was only five years old when he died. He was a tall, husky, happy-go-lucky man who took me on walks on the occasion of our annual Christmas visits to Osnabrück. He had never been sick in his life; when he was forced to stay in bed because of his terminal illness, he looked at the blossoms of the pear tree before his window and said, "Those pears I will not eat." Three days later he was gone.

My grandmother was just the opposite: small, deeply religious, and cautious. She managed the business as much as her husband did and probably saved it from bankruptcy by putting a brake on his inclination to take risks. She survived him by six years but sold the house to move into an apartment.

I remember lying in my bed in that house and listening to the deep sounds of the bells of the cathedral welcoming the twentieth century. No more than anyone else did I know what it held in store.

My father, Martin Jacob, had two brothers. The younger one, Louis, died as a student from a pulmonary infection which he had contracted by being drenched while helping to put out a fire in midwinter. An elder brother, Carl, took over the bank. He had four children; counting my brother and sister, the seven little Blumenfelds had great fun playing together during the Christmas season, which was celebrated in the traditional German manner in Osnabrück.

The surviving descendants of uncle Carl's line are now living in Stockholm. The descendants of my grandfather's brother live in Hamburg, where they still own and operate the Blumenfeld Line of ocean-going ships.

THE WARBURG FAMILY

In 1798 Moses Marcus Warburg founded the bank of M. M. Warburg & Co. in Hamburg. It is still in the hands of the family as one of the leading private banks in Germany.

Hamburg suffered greatly under Napoleon's Continental Blockade, in its subsequent annexation to the French Empire, and in its stubborn defense by Napoleon's Marshal Davout, which lasted beyond the fall of Paris in 1814. It is not surprising that the Warburgs did not share Nathan Blumenfeld's Napoleonic enthusiasm; in my grandparents' house in Hamburg the walls were covered with lithographs of the Cossacks liberating Hamburg from the French. However, their business seems to have thrived during this period, I suspect by financing the "patriotic" smuggling of goods from Helgoland — when it was under British rule from 1807 to 1890 — to Hamburg. In general, the Warburgs remained conservative in politics as well as in religion.

My great-grandfather Abraham married another Warburg, Sara. By all accounts Sara was a formidable matriarch, making all decisions for the bank as well as for the household. After her husband's death her two sons, my grandfather Siegmund and his younger brother Moritz, had to report to her every evening on the minutest details of their business operations.

Abraham's character was just the opposite. It is obvious that I inherited the genes for a strong inclination to put things off from him. An amusing story has come down in the family.

One night Sara aroused him from sleep, shouting, "Aby, the house is burning!" He put his hand to the wall, asserted, "It is not yet hot," and turned on his other side.

My grandfather, Siegmund Warburg, married Theophile Rosenberg from Kiev. The Rosenbergs hailed from Chotin in Bessarabia, situated at the point of junction of the three great early nineteenth-century empires of the European continent, those of the Habsburgs, the Czars, and the Sultan. It was an ideal location for smuggling, and it seems that financing this useful activity laid the foundation of the family fortune which paid, at least in part, for my education.

In any case, the Rosenbergs of Kiev, and the closely related Günzburgs of St. Petersburg, one of the very few Jewish families ever ennobled by the Czars, were very rich. The members of the Warburg-Rosenberg-Günzburg clans were closely knit by correspondence, frequent mutual visits, and numerous intermarriages; they had a much greater presence in my childhood than my father's relatives, who put much less stress on family ties.

Siegmund and Theophile had seven surviving children, two boys and five girls. The males, while both extremely kind, were no mental giants; the women were real personalities, most of all my mother. Inversely, my grandfather's younger brother and partner, Moritz, had two girls and five boys. The eldest, Aby M. Warburg, the founder of what is now the famous Warburg-Courtauld Institute in London, became a leading art historian. The other four became well-known bankers, Max and Fritz in Hamburg, and Paul and Felix in New York.

My grandfather Siegmund died two years before my birth, so I knew him only by hearsay. It appears that he was the first of the Warburgs who opened his mind to a broad humanistic view of mankind, which he implanted in his favorite daughter, Anna, my mother. Subsequently, she was confirmed in her world view by her history teacher, who was an ardent believer in the democratic ideals of the 1848 revolution, and to whose opinions my mother frequently referred in later life.

I often saw my grandmother Theophile, but cannot say that I knew her. She was a strong-willed woman, very much the Paris-educated grande dame. If I am not mistaken, her strict observance of Jewish laws and customs was less a result of religiosity than of bourgeois respectability. The Friday Sabbath eve and the Jewish holidays were solemnly celebrated. Christmas did not exist. After my uncle Carl died in 1905 and his widow and children moved from Osnabrück to Hamburg, it also ceased to exist for us children.

My grandmother lived in a huge house, five stories high, four windows wide, and almost 100 feet deep, with a large garden to the rear, the front facing the beautiful Alster Lake. She occupied it alone, but with a butler and four maids.

After her death the house, together with the faithful butler, Herrmann, passed to my mother's elder brother, Aby, who continued the orthodox customs, including our obligatory presence on Friday evenings and on holidays. On such occasions I had to rely on Herrmann to whisper into my ear the appropriate behavior at every stage of the ceremonies.

Our Nuclear Family

My father often said that he had wooed my mother for seven years, as his namesake Jacob had wooed Rachel. At the time of their engagement he wrote to my mother that, at the risk of losing her, he must tell her that he was not a believer. He was immensely relieved when she replied that she fully shared his views.

My father was a consistent atheist, a follower of the nineteenth-century German materialists Büchner and Moleschott. My mother considered herself a pantheist and liked to think in terms of a "religion of the future," or "of humankind," or of the "divine spark." I never prayed in my life, and I cannot remember a time when I believed in God. Certainly I was familiar with the Biblical stories from early childhood, but they must have faded into fairy tales as imperceptibly as did the stories of Cinderella and Red Riding Hood.

My atheism has not prevented a lifelong respect for, as well as fascination with, religions and their manifold manifestations, to which the world owes the better part of its man-made beauties. But I am firmly convinced that religion has nothing to do with ethics — except to sanctify whatever good or evil deeds human beings have set their hearts on.

I had two siblings, Franz, just one year older than I, and Margaret, two years younger. We were no longer children when my father died of leukemia in December 1908. As far as we were aware, our parents' marriage was perfect. When my mother's younger sister later said to Margaret, then in her fifties, "You know, of course, that your mother's marriage was not a happy one," she was deeply shocked and asked me if I had ever suspected it. I never had, though I was 16 at my father's death. Much later, in my thirties, I had involuntarily overheard a conversation of my mother with a friend; and to my subsequent question she answered, "I respected him but never loved him."

Most contemporaries may disapprove of parents going so far in hiding the truth from their children. But I am profoundly grateful to them. My confidence in them has certainly contributed to what is the greatest benefit — beyond all the advantages of a rich formal and informal education — of those who have been privileged, as I have been, to grow up in a family of secure wealth in the (apparently) secure pre-1914 world: an unshakable, if totally irrational, self-confidence.

MY FATHER

My father, in association with a friend, established a law office in Hamburg. In American terms he was a successful corporation lawyer. He explained to me that he always tried to settle cases by negotiation with the other party and, if cases went to court, regarded the judge as a mediator. He obviously was highly respected in the profession. A minister of justice of the Weimar Republic, who worked in father's office as a young lawyer, told me that it was from him that he learned the ethics of the profession.

One of my father's most important cases was a drawn-out fight of an independent oil company against the monopoly established by Standard Oil in conjunction with the powerful Deutsche Bank. This coincided with his strong adherence to the Manchester-liberal belief in free trade. When I asked him on the occasion of a big strike in the coal-steel region of the Ruhr which side he favored, he answered that in principle he was both against the cartel of the bosses and the trade unions, which he regarded as restraints on the freedom of trade; he admitted, however, that against those smokestack barons, the workers might have to organize.

I recall another story related to politics. On the occasion of a break with the Catholic Center party ("the blacks") the imperial chancellor, Count Bülow, had dissolved the Reichstag and managed to put together a coalition of Conservatives and Liberals. Thanks to mutual support of these hitherto hostile parties on the second ballot, they took a number of seats from the Social Democrats; so Bülow got his majority.

When I asked my father's opinion on these events, he replied, "Once, when I was a little boy, my father took me to a fair where I tried my hand at rifle shooting. On my first try I hit a red cock, to my father's and everyone's applause. I said, 'But, father, I did not aim at the red cock; I aimed at the black center of the disk!' My father replied, 'My boy, it is good that you are so honest, but you never will be imperial chancellor!' "

My father took his liberal-democratic views seriously. Once, on my question of how much income tax he paid, he named a sizable proportion, close to a quarter, but added that he would gladly pay more if the government would abolish indirect taxes and custom tariffs.

My father was very much a Victorian gentleman, going to the city in a top hat. He never showed his emotions, and I took it for granted that an adult gentleman never shows emotions, or indeed has any. I recall my surprise when, as a result of a tobogganing accident my brother lay unconscious, I saw my father white and trembling.

I guess that this attitude is responsible for my own inhibition in expressing emotion. I can count on my fingers the occasions when, as an adult, I raised my voice or broke down in tears. My father, like myself, kept late hours, morning and night. As a result, we never saw him at breakfast on school days. He had lunch downtown, followed by a visit to the stock exchange and a game of chess, at which he was very good. He did not come home before 7:30, and we children were sent to bed early to a relatively late age. So I saw my father mainly on Sundays and during vacations. Looking back, I have to admit that I really never came to know him well.

MY MOTHER

My mother was and always remained close to me. She was a remarkable woman, a strong personality. Without ever being aggressive, she almost always got her way.

Very beautiful, and a good and passionate horsewoman in her younger years, she was never in good health through the years I knew her. She had wanted to study medicine, but that was just not done in a patrician orthodox family. She was highly intelligent, always welcoming new ideas and new people. Her generosity was boundless, not only in terms of money, but of personal effort. While she never in her life held a "job," she led a very active life, displaying great initiative in many directions. She was active in organizations for charitable purposes and for women's rights and other progressive aims. Above all, she detested Prussian militarism and was an ardent pacifist. For many years she hoped that an alliance of Germany, Britain, and the United States could be brought about to establish and maintain world peace.

She regarded the present (pre-World War I) as a period of transition to a better, more just and humane world, vaguely sympathizing with socialist ideas. Her warm-hearted sympathy and wise counsel helped many people who found themselves in trouble. She was an indefatigable conciliator. My father said she had missed her vocation; she should have become a bankruptcy broker.

In a curious way, alongside her democratic, egalitarian ideals she retained a strong belief in people being of "good family"; in particular, she took great pride in her own Warburg family. Once an acquaintance said to her, "I met a relative of yours, a Mrs. Warburg from Magdeburg." My mother: "In Magdeburg there are no Warburgs." The acquaintance: "Excuse me, but she was from Magdeburg." My mother: "Oh, I know, those are not Warburgs, they are only called Warburg."

My mother formulated her philosophy as "creating as much joy and happiness as possible for oneself and others." Money had no meaning except to be spent for that purpose.

The celebration of joy included profound contempt for mere "amusement." It included celebration of true love between man and woman, including sex. Sex without love was unworthy of human beings. This approach dominated my attitude for many years, leading to curious feats of repression. This was certainly far from the intentions of my mother, who personally knew and admired Sigmund Freud, though she remained skeptical about his theories.

I never realized how deeply frustrated the life of my mother had been. It was only during her terminal illness that I learned that it had been dominated by two great loves, neither ever "consummated." The first, her mother's younger brother, Marc Rosenberg, started in my mother's early childhood and lasted throughout her lifetime. Marc Rosenberg was an art historian. He occupied a chair in that field at the Technical University of Karlsruhe and was the world's leading authority on the history of the art of jewelry. He was a remarkable personality of inexhaustible vitality. In his eighties, after enumerating to me all the blows of fate he had suffered — the death of his first and second wives and of his three highly talented children, the burning down of his beautiful house in the Black Forest, the theft and subsequent destruction of his unique collection, the loss of his fortune — he concluded, "And still I am a happy man." He, as well as his mother and two of his siblings, lived well into their eighties. If, as is likely, my longevity is conditioned by heredity, the genes must have come from the Rosenbergs. Her second love was Giovanni (Ivan) Stepanoff. Son of a professor of medicine at Moscow University, he had been sent to Italy as an adolescent for health reasons and became an Italian. After extensive studies in many disciplines, he became an art historian. My brother and he had become friends as fellow students in Freiburg, despite their difference in age.

My mother, who during her adolescence had spent several winters with her mother at Pegli, on the Riviera di Ponente, loved Italy and the Italians intensely, a love which I came to share. Whenever possible, she spent her winters in Italy. In 1914 she had given up our apartment in Hamburg, into which we had moved after my father's death, and planned to live permanently with Giovanni in the house he had built on Capri. The war destroyed that dream.

Both my parents strongly believed in the educational theories of Herbert Spencer that children should be brought up to be independent human beings, learn from their own experience, make their own decisions, and assume their own responsibilities. As far as I am concerned they certainly succeeded beyond their fondest dreams. A fierce refusal of any dependence on men, things, or habits, even on my own intentions, has always superseded all other considerations in my life. I like to say that, as a professional planner, I am willing to plan anything, except my own life. This is the justification for the "drifter" in the title of this book, even if for much of the journey I have drifted under my own steam.

One corollary of my parents' educational philosophy was to make us entirely responsible for success or failure in school; they never aided us in our schoolwork or allowed others to do so. My mother said all she cared about was that we would not have to repeat a semester; none of us ever entered that danger zone.

My Brother Franz

"Franz-und-Hans" was a unit. Probably, I have never been closer to any other person in my life. We always slept and lived in the same room and did everything together. When he started school and learned to read, I immediately used his schoolbook to teach myself to read. I shared his buddies, though he did not share mine.

We were very different persons. He and my sister were good children; I was difficult, pigheaded, and given to temper tantrums. He had no taste for physical activity; I loved all sports, without being good at any. He was outgoing and active; I was called "Hans the dreamer" and "Hans the silent one." It was always he who took the initiative, but never without asking my advice. My mother later told me that he often said, "I must ask Hans, Hans is so clever."

It was the classical relation between commander in chief and chief of staff. Much later in life I discovered, by analyzing my dreams, that this relation to my brother had irrevocably prefigured my relations to anyone with whom I collaborated in professional or voluntary work. I did not, and do not, shrink from developing policies and advocating them firmly, but I need an elder-brother surrogate to make the ultimate decision. It is certainly due to this prefigured attitude that in later life I have been able to work happily and successfully with "bosses" half my age: with Ed Bacon in Philadelphia, and with Murray Jones in Toronto.

My brother studied law, political science, and philosophy at several German universities, as well as at Lausanne and at Cambridge. At Cambridge he established a friendship with C. K. Ogden, who later became known as one of the founders of semantics and the inventor of Basic English. Ogden took him to the lectures of Bertrand Russell. Franz wrote to my mother, "I know it sounds silly, but I really believe he is a second Newton."

In the years preceding World War I, Ogden repeatedly stayed with us during summer vacations. In later years, I visited him a few times in London; he had the keenest intellect of any person I ever met in my life.

MY SISTER MARGARET

Margaret suffered from being the "little sister," called "Baby" for quite a number of years, who was excluded from the life of her brothers. This does not mean that we did not play together a lot, I with her dolls and she with my tin soldiers.

During a certain period, when I was about six years old, Margaret was the wide-eyed and unquestioning public of the tall tales I told of my heroic deeds in "the other world," where I was a great king and conqueror. My brother challenged me to explain just when I was absent from this more prosaic world. I answered that it happened during a second at midnight which extended over twenty-four hours in the other world, while the second after midnight there was equivalent to twenty-four hours here. My peculiar theory of relativity was greeted with no less skepticism than was Einstein's.

HAMBURG

Around the cocoon of the family lay the Free and Hanseatic City of Hamburg. Alongside its smaller sisters of Bremen and Lübeck and a few Swiss cantons, it was one of the last surviving medieval city republics. In the empire it was constitutionally the equal of the kingdoms of Prussia or Bavaria.

It was a proud city: proud of its history dating back to Charlemagne, proud of its wealth, proud of its role as "Germany's Gateway to the World."

In reading Thomas Mann's references to Lübeck, much reminds me of my childhood in Hamburg. The teacher who came once a week from Hamburg to Lübeck to teach dancing and ballroom manners to Tonio Kröger unmistakably is the same Herr Knoll who instructed me in these noble arts.

But while Thomas Mann refers to Lübeck as a "narrow city," Hamburg was wide open to the world, a very cosmopolitan city. My first buddy in school was born in Valparaíso, Chile; subsequently I shared my brother's chums, born in Colón, Panama, and in England, respectively. Later I formed a gang of three with a boy born in Amsterdam and one born in Cincinnati. I went swimming with the only Catholic in my high-school class, born in San José, Costa Rica, while our Protestant classmates sweated out their weekly hour of religious instruction. I did not have to wait for radio to teach me that I was living in a "Global Village," nor for space flight to discover "Spaceship Earth." I grew up with the notion of the unity of humankind, though with a definite Eurocentric bias.

While the Hamburgers were German patriots, they maintained their special identity very firmly. Dutch influence had been strong since the Middle Ages and still could be traced in such details as the size of bricks and the cross section of beams, which were identical with those used in Holland and different from those adopted in the rest of Germany.

When I grew up in Hamburg, the model for the way of life of the bourgeoisie was England, from the shape of houses and gardens, of dress and sports, to the swans on Alster Lake. Even first names assumed English form: my uncles were called Aby and George, and my sister was Margaret, not Margarethe. The Hamburg of my childhood was a carbon copy of London, down to minute details such as the location and equipment of wc's. We looked down on Berlin as a parvenu. There was more sympathy for Vienna, the old Imperial capital. It was from Vienna that Hamburg selected the head of its new dramatic theater, as well as the director and most of the teachers of its newly founded school of arts and crafts. A widowed aunt of my mother subscribed to the *Neue Freie Presse* of Vienna, which was passed on to us and which I read avidly.

There was no university in Hamburg, because the establishment was afraid of creating an "academic proletariat." While Hamburg was Germany's wealthiest city, it was also its reddest. From 1897 it always sent, by overwhelming majorities, three Social Democrats to the Reichstag, including August Bebel, the party's founder and leader. The government of the city-state, issuing from a complicated unequal ballot, remained generally conservative. But they were conservatives of the British type and had little in common with the Junker-dominated German Conservative party. Noblemen had been banned from the city in the Middle Ages and were never fully accepted. Bismarck, however, who lived in retirement in neighboring Friedrichsruh, was venerated.

Despite the absence of a university, there was no lack of intellectual life in Hamburg. There was first-rate music — for some time Gustav Mahler conducted the Hamburg Symphony — and growing interest in the visual arts.

Hamburg was and still is a very beautiful city, notwithstanding the complete absence of great architecture and an almost complete lack of any building antedating the middle of the nineteenth century. Water and trees create its unique image: "Qui peint cela?" exclaimed Monet when he visited it.

We first lived in a first-floor apartment just outside the "city" which remains clearly defined by the perimeter of its great walls of 1620, which had saved it from the devastations of the Thirty Years' War and thereby had laid the ground for its prosperity.

After my sister was born, my parents bought a house about a mile out of the city, in a district known by the medieval name of Harvestehude (fall pasture). It had been developed not long before as an upper-middle-class residential district on a large rectangular grid of broad, tree-lined streets. Most buildings were two-to-three-story single-family houses, but there were also two-to-four-story flats, some with shops in the basement or on the ground floor. On the way to the city I still passed cow pastures during my school years. Within five minutes walking distance from our house there were four well-treed parks, one of which bordered the Alster, where there were rowboats and sailboats for rent; close by were tennis courts which served as a skating rink in winter, a playing field for field hockey, an outdoor riding academy, and a velodrome: it was an ideal environment for a growing boy.

Our house had a well-treed garden in front and a large garden in the rear, in which we played by the hour, joined by the children from the neighboring gardens, who, characteristically, were born in Vienna and Mexico City, respectively.

The basement of our house contained a large tiled kitchen with scullery and cellar, two bedrooms, bath, and toilet for the cook and two serving maids. There were ten full-sized rooms, a bathroom, and two toilets on the upper two-and-a-half floors, with glazed-in verandas and balconies front and rear. The block was exceptionally deep, and from the rear windows one saw only trees, no houses.

The house is still standing, converted, like most of the neighborhood, to offices and flats, but visually unchanged. The neighboring house is now a "hotel-pension," and it is there that I stay on my visits. Hamburg is very much my hometown.

This was the environment in which I grew up. Ours was the typical upstairs-downstairs household of a cultured Victorian family. From time to time there were sumptuous dinners — we children peering down the stairwell from the second floor as the guests came in.

When our family dined alone, talk was of family and friends — gossip excluded — of public affairs, literature, and art. Money or food were never talked about. The only difference from London was that the food was better. In this respect the wealthy Hamburg merchants stuck to their original model, Amsterdam; almost alone in Germany, they ate well. When the leading Hamburg restaurateur and chef, named Pforte, opened a restaurant at the Paris World's Fair of 1900, it became a culinary sensation.

I was of course aware that not all people lived that well, that there were poor people whom we were obliged to help. Some of this help was just casual charity, which brings an amusing story to mind. One evening my father, coming home from work, met a man carrying a pair of boots. "Who gave you those boots?" asked my father. — "The lady of the house." — "How much would you have to pay to buy such a pair?" — "Three marks." — "Here are three marks and give me back my boots." To my mother's horror my father entered the house carrying his worn old boots, which were of course more comfortable than new ones.

"God is not almighty," Franz once remarked. "He cannot make old shoes."

My first real awakening as to how the other half — or rather nine-tenths — lived, came when I was about fourteen. It happened on the occasion of the Christmas appeal of a charitable organization which distributed castoff clothing and furniture to the poor. It was a tear-jerker, describing the plight of the unemployed. Looking at work as something to be shunned, I felt that it was a moral monstrosity that someone who did want to work was not allowed to do so. I still feel that way.

EARLY CHILDHOOD

I was not born in Hamburg. In 1892, Hamburg was ravaged by a cholera epidemic which claimed 8000 victims. My mother went to live with her in-laws in Osnabrück, and there I was born in the same house as were my father and grandfather, a source of silly but persistent pride.

Meanwhile, the cholera had abated. However, as Franz had caught the whooping cough, and my mother went to live with him in Cuxhaven on the North Sea, I was quartered, with a wet nurse, in my father's office in Hamburg. Unfortunately, this early association with the legal profession has instilled in me neither legal skills nor a profound respect for the law.

Some of my memories go back to my third year, but the most vivid one concerns the arrival of our English nanny, who replaced our German children's maid when Margaret was one year old and I was three. I still see her entering our large playroom, with the Irish stove glowing in the corner and the three of us seated on the floor. She was a devout Catholic, totally devoted to the children entrusted to her care. I loved her dearly and shed hot tears when my parents finally decided that we had long outgrown the nanny age; my sister was six and I was eight years old when she left. I certainly owe a good part of my education to her, even if she did not quite succeed in making me a perfect gentleman. Certainly it is due to her unfailing care and patience that my temper tantrums completely disappeared.

I also vividly remember my uncle Aby's first wife, Olga Leonini from Milan, who died early in my fourth year. It may have foreshadowed my future interest in architecture that I still retain clear images of two rooms in her apartment: a sunlit boudoir with a caged canary, and a rather somber dining room with a dark wooden panel crowned by a shelf which supported a collection of large faience ceramics.

Most vivid are my recollections of the annual summer vacations which we spent in the mountains or at the seashore. When I was five, we rented a house at Timmendorferstrand on the Baltic. At that age I rose early — a bad habit which by now I have overcome heroically. The neighbor's boy invited me on an expedition to a nearby chicken coop and ordered me to steal some eggs. I felt some misgivings, but if a big boy of ten said so, it must be all right. We sat down on the beach and started to consume the eggs. I had never eaten raw eggs and did not like the taste, so I went home. Meanwhile, the house was of course in an uproar over the missing child; as soon as I showed up, my nanny lifted me in her arms, with the egg yolk running down my pants. This was the precocious beginning of my criminal career.

EARLY SCHOOL YEARS

For the first three years I attended a private school five minutes from home. Learning was easy; I always occupied second place. I read avidly, including books on geography — I was fascinated by maps and globes — and history. Beginning in my second year, my classmates nicknamed me "professor." But I was anything but a bookworm. I organized a gang, whose main activity consisted in defending our turf in the schoolyard and invading those of other gangs. But my gang also had an esoteric, secret goal, which I revealed only to two most trusted chums: nothing less than the resurrection of the Hanseatic League and the transformation of Germany into a federation of city republics! I still consider it a good idea.

When I was eight, we spent the summer in Paramé, near St. Malo in Brittany. My father had found a hotel owned by a man from his hometown of Osnabrück. The hotel's small library contained German as well as French and English books. I discovered a small German handbook of pictorial statistics and was fascinated. I spent long hours studying the symbols representing the territory and population of the nations of the world, their merchant fleets, production of coal, steel, wheat, and so on. The interest in statistics has persisted throughout life and has served me well in my professional work. I am probably the only person alive who has played with statistics for over eighty years.

A document testifying to the curious mixture of childishness and adult interests has followed me to America: a copy of that handbook, with a handwritten supplement to the list of heads of state reading "Hans I, King of the Hanseatic League."

My fourth and fifth years were spent at another private school. One disturbing memory still haunts me. The boy seated next to me, K., a very sweet boy, was the youngest of five sons of a wealthy miller from a neighboring village. While I did not realize it at the time, the proprietor and headmaster of the school, though unwilling to forego the sizable income from five fees, resented the presence of these "low-class" kids in his prestigious establishment. One day, teaching in a classroom adjacent to ours, the headmaster, who was hard of hearing, continued his lesson beyond the bell. Meanwhile, we started to have fun as we usually did during our recreation period, and K. broke out into loud laughter. Furious, the headmaster entered and threatened K. with punishment for indiscipline; early in the next lesson he entered our class, called K. to the front, and caned him mercilessly. I was indignant that the teacher did not defend him and felt like crying out, "But K. has done nothing wrong," but could not bring out a word. To this day I feel ashamed when I think of my cowardice on that occasion.

This experience may have laid the foundation for my lifelong profound aversion to deliberate infliction of pain on a human being, as much as did the influence of my mother, who was passionately opposed to physical punishment. She later told me that in the early years of her marriage she had long discussions with my father, who believed that boys could not be brought up without an occasional caning. In practice, the question never arose at home; when I had my temper tantrums, my mother simply locked me in my room.

My aversion to inflicting physical pain did not mean that I shunned fights; I loved them. For a while I associated with a boy with whom I had nothing else in common but to start fisticuffs in the schoolyard. I cannot say when or why I terminated that phase; but I remember my profound shock when I saw a boy, whom I had knocked down, lying on the ground white in the face and writhing in pain.

Nor did I share my mother's opinion that a slap in the face offended human dignity. I did not mind occasionally catching one from my teachers, and frequently provoked them, which, of course, made me a hero in the eyes of my classmates. I excelled in torturing my teachers; "Still so small and already so fresh," one of them exclaimed in desperation.

I was always the shortest boy in my class and jealously proud of it. A short stature is indeed a tremendous boon. In school, where we were lined up by size to return to class after recreation periods, it extended my period of liberty. In World War I, it enabled me to walk upright in the trenches, while my buddies had to bend down. Above all, I am convinced that it is a decisive contributor to my almost-miraculous good health that I do not have to carry around, nourish, and keep in operation a superfluous mass of flesh and bones.

My brother Franz was of normal stature but in shaky health. My mother concluded that it would be good for Franz' health and my growth if we spent a winter in St. Moritz. We spent two winters there from December to March, under the marvelous high-altitude sun, joyously engaging in skating, hockey, skiing, and tobogganing. My father and Margaret joined us for shorter periods.

I also fell in love with the shape of the surrounding mountains, in particular those which I daily observed from my window: the Three Sisters and Piz Langard on my first stay, and the Piz Bernina on the second. Probably those two winters in St. Moritz were the happiest of the many happy periods of my life.

ADOLESCENCE

From my sixth school year on I attended the state-run Realgymnasium. My mother, an enthusiast of Classical Greece, would have preferred the Gymnasium, which taught Latin and Greek, my father the Oberrealschule, which concentrated on science and modern languages; the Realgymnasium, which taught Latin but not Greek, was a compromise. From my last school years on, I regretted my lack of Greek and at several periods made short-lived attempts to learn it. I never did; however, my attempts helped me somewhat to get along in Greece and also to clarify some sentences in the English text of Herodotus, whom I read much later in the bilingual Loeb edition.

As the years went on, I disliked school more and more. It did not oppress me, but it increasingly bored me. I felt that I was learning nothing. For my teachers I generally felt contempt; they raised their voices and got red in the face — they were not gentlemen. I had respect only for my teacher in mathematics and physics, Böger. He tried to introduce topology to the high-school curriculum, had written a textbook on it, and taught a course based on that textbook when he took over our class. I took to this new field like a fish to water, in particular as our previous teacher, with whom I had been at war, had given me the next-to-the-lowest mark. Böger was enthusiastic about this proof of the suitability of topology for high-school teaching. I soon disappointed him when it came to doing real work.

In his physics class, Böger once demonstrated an experiment which I remember vividly. He put a top on a scale; the scale stayed up. Then he spun the top and placed it on again; the scale went down. He remarked that perhaps weight and mass were a product of the movement of particles within atoms. Evidently he knew something of the budding science of nuclear physics.

I hardly ever did any homework. Only when I felt challenged by a problem in mathematics or the theme of an essay did I work late into the night.

Once our German teacher told us to present an essay-theme of our own choice for the following week. I gave no thought to it and when my turn came, I said, "Free Trade and Protective Tariffs." The teacher asked, "Do you know anything about that?" to which I answered "No," which, of course, evoked loud guffaws. The teacher ordered me to leave the class. No further word was spoken. I plunged into the study of books on my subject, wrote a lengthy essay, and received an excellent mark.

In fact, the subject was not far from politics, in which both my brother and I took a keen interest. We read the Erfurt Program of German Social Democracy and found ourselves in complete agreement.

I followed closely the wars of the time. I still remember the Spanish-American War, in which I identified with King Alfonso because he was a little boy like myself. Far more important was the Boer War, which gave me my first training in nonconformity and swimming against the tide. My classmates, like everybody in Germany, were for the Boers: sturdy farmers defending their land against the aggression of a bunch of millionnaires greedy for gold and diamonds. But a nephew of my beloved nanny was a British soldier in that war; that was decisive for me. I guess Emperor Willy and I were the only persons in Germany who sympathized with the British side in that war, both of us from personal loyalty, he to his granny, and I to my nanny.

In the Russo-Japanese War I was again on the unpopular side because of my Russian relatives. The subsequent Russian revolution puzzled me and surpassed my understanding.

Another extracurricular interest — in addition to sports and exploration of the city and its environs on foot and bicycle — was art and art history. With a beloved uncle and a cousin exactly of her own age, with whom she had grown up, being professional art historians, my mother was greatly interested in that field. There were many books on art and art history in my parents' large library to which we children always had free access, and I studied them intensely. But from an early age I was particularly interested in architecture. A great deal of building was going on in Hamburg at that time, and I observed it with a critical eye. I remember one relevant episode which occured when I must have been about ten or eleven years old.

My mother had a weekly *jour,* when ladies of her acquaintance came in for five-o'clock tea. I was often present on those occasions. Once, the ladies praised the products of "Jugendstil," the German version of Art Nouveau. I demurred and was asked which houses I liked. I mentioned four identical small houses which I passed on my way to school; they were extremely simple, straightforward creations of the "Biedermeier" style of the 1830s. I would still endorse that choice.

I read widely. As a result of my English education, I went through all the typical books, from *Ten Little Nigger Boys* through *Tom Brown's Schooldays, Black Beauty,* and *Little Lord Fauntleroy* to *Ivanhoe.* I was strongly impressed by Carlyle's *Heroes and Hero Worship.* Another — and lasting — favorite was the *World-Historical Observations* of the great Swiss historian Jacob Burckhardt.

I also had pleasure reading French novels in the original, in particular Anatole France, an author much in vogue at the time and now greatly underrated. His humane skepticism appealed to me, as did that of his greater countryman Michel de Montaigne, whom I read, however, only later, during World War I.

At school, our teachers of course tried to indoctrinate us in official patriotism. Once, a teacher, quoting the Roman *si vis pacem, para bellum* (if you desire peace, prepare for war), claimed that Europe owed its long period of peace since 1871 only to Germany's military strength, and, if the Entente nations claimed to be threatened by it, this was only a cover for their own aggressive intentions. I objected: what we considered defense, they inevitably saw as a threat of aggression, to which they had to respond by strengthening their own defense. The resulting arms race could only end in war; if you wanted peace, you had to prepare for peace by mutual agreement to limit arms.

Rejection of *si vis pacem, para bellum* has increasingly become a leitmotif of my life.

I organized a club for political discussion with a few of my classmates, opening the first meeting, which was held in a café, with a lengthy critique of all of the Kaiser's policies: internal, external, and cultural. When the school authorities got wind of our club, they prohibited it. We still had a few meetings at our house, but then the club went the way of most high-school associations.

There existed, however, a long-established fraternity called "Formica" to which first my brother and then I were elected. The obligatory beer-guzzling sessions were preceded by a "scientific communication" from a member. My first one was on the development of the British Empire; the second on "the shift of the center of history from warmer to cooler climates," a theory which I had grown on my own manure; the third on "the Hamburg office building," an architectural type which did not exist elsewhere in Germany.

In some respects, I was developed beyond my age when I finished high school at 18. A friend of the family, the painter Bruck, remarked that I had skipped adolescence, jumping from boyhood to manhood. He was only partly right: delayed adolescence haunted me well into my thirties.

CHAPTER II

Taking Off

1911 – 1914

EARLY UNIVERSITY YEARS: A MULE

My parents had always emphasized that, while they gave us the best possible education, we would be on our own and would have to choose and build our own careers.

Several years before finishing high school I had already set my mind on becoming an architect, but I waited until a few months before graduation to come out with that proposition; it was not welcome. Somehow it had been assumed, probably before we were born, that the male members of the family would enter M. M. Warburg & Co. in some form. The banker members of the family had already given up on Franz, who obviously was an incurable "idealist." But I was more worldly and looked like suitable material.

My father was no longer alive. My mother, whose attitude to life had been largely responsible for my choice, found herself in the role of the hen who had hatched a duckling. She doubted that I had the stuff to be a great architect, in which she was of course perfectly right. She showed me a letter from my great-uncle Marc Rosenberg, the art historian whose advice she had sought. Marc wrote, "As I know Hans, he will be better off if he goes to M. M. Warburg, where he will find a made bed." Knowing myself as the lazy bum that I was, I knew that I would immediately lie down in that bed — and considered it not a very worthy life goal.

The actual head of the house, my mother's cousin Max M. Warburg, spent a long evening trying to persuade me. Finally a compromise was arrived at. For my first term I would register as a student of law but would work as an apprentice in an architect's office. The husband of my mother's youngest sister, Dr. Otto Kaulla, who was a district judge in the little university town of Tübingen, was to make the necessary arrangements. The whole scheme was to be kept secret from my uncle Aby and the other partners of M. M. Warburg & Co.

Between graduation from high school in February 1911 and the start of university in late April lay a period during which I was what Germans appropriately call a mule, and I made the most of it. Herbert Knöhr, the Catholic boy with whom I had gone swimming during school classes in religion, told me that his parents had presented him with a trip from Hamburg to Naples on a boat going to East Africa and urged me to join him.

My mother had given up our apartment in Hamburg — I had stayed at my uncle Aby's during my last months in school — and lived in a hotel in Lausanne, where Franz was studying and Margaret was to perfect her French. I suggested to my mother that it would be only a slight detour to go from Hamburg to Lausanne via Rotterdam, Lisbon, Tangier, and Marseille, scheduled stops of the boat. My mother somewhat reluctantly agreed.

From Rotterdam I made a side trip to The Hague, where, in the Mauritshuis Museum, I discovered Jan Vermeer and the less known Carel Fabritius, whose works for me still represent ultimate perfection in the art of painting. But the great event was Lisbon. From the gray fog of Hamburg and Rotterdam I found myself suddenly transported into the full glory of a Mediterranean spring, with the magnolias in full blossom.

The site and architecture of Lisbon, with the azulejo-clad facades, the magnificent horseshoe of the Comércio Square, the fantastic decoration of Belem, and the cork oaks on the drive to Cintra, left a lasting impression. Equally unforgettable are the townscape of Tangier and a night in the Mediterranean, with phosphorescence illuminating the shapes and the wake of the dolphins who played around the ship.

There were several other young men on the ship, a Hamburg friend of Knöhr's, a Brazilian, and two Prussian Junkers from the Potsdam military school. They all were going on to Naples and urged me to pay the additional twenty-five marks to continue that far. I was easily persuaded and assented, borrowing some money from a fellow traveler.

From Marseille I made a side trip to Aix-en-Provence, through fields of almonds in blossom. Aix with its Cours Mirabeau enchanted me so much that I almost missed my boat, which was already afloat when I reached the quay at Marseille.

Three of us, Knöhr, the Brazilian, and I, together explored the sites and museums of Naples and Pompeii — where the guides were eager to show us the "secret" sections containing the erotica — as well as the beauties of Mount Vesuvius, Capri, and the Sorrento peninsula.

After a week in Naples, an English boat, returning from India, took me to Genoa, whence I took the train to Lausanne.

I stayed in Lausanne four weeks and started to learn Italian. I found it surprisingly easy. It seems that I repeated the millenary transformation of Latin into Italian in four weeks. Anyway, I have lost my Latin, but I feel quite at home in Italy.

My mother had taken Franz to Rome the previous year and had planned to make the same trip with me. However, as she was not amused by my Naples escapade, she decided to limit the voyage to Northern Italy. She had thought of Venice as the main destination, but I had preferred Florence.

Our first stop was Milan, where we spent an evening at the Scala in the Leonini family lodge, with Toscanini conducting Gounod's *Faust*.

Florence and the surrounding Tuscan countryside surpassed my expectations. On the first evening I went for a stroll. In the evening calm, not yet shattered by motorcycles, one heard songs accompanied by mandolins. The dim street lights yielded to the full moon. I had decided to leave the "sights" for the next day, but suddenly I found myself on the Palazzo della Signoria — and was overwhelmed. I have since found that spatial impressions are much stronger at night than in daylight and have developed a theory about this phenomenon. I have presented that theory as part of an essay on "Scale in Civic Design," which I published forty years later. That article apparently had more widespread impact than any other of my productions. Colleagues teaching at the universities of Budapest and Shanghai told me that they had it translated into their respective languages and made it required reading for their students.

After four unforgettable weeks we left Italy, my mother returning to Lausanne, and I proceeding to Tübingen.

Two years later my mother went with the three of us to Rome.

"Rome is the whole world, and the whole world is Rome," as Joachim du Bellay said in the sixteenth century. At the end of my stay in Rome, I went, alone, to Paestum. I arrived before dawn; it was utterly deserted, apart from some goats with a barefoot boy herding them. As the sun rose, the temple slowly awakened to life and intoned its solemn melody, majestic like a Bach fugue. It was the most unforgettable architectural experience of my life.

TÜBINGEN

Tübingen was at the time a town of fewer than 20,000 inhabitants which had largely preserved its medieval image. I stayed at my uncle's house and worked at a local architect's office. Mr. Staehle was a genial man and a fairly competent architect. He introduced me to all aspects of the profession; I liked them all and felt that I could cope with them.

I did not study law, but I took time off to take courses in art history, literature, and economics. Economics was taught by Robert Willbrand, the only socialist who occupied a chair in that discipline in Germany. He was a remarkable man who later became the first minister of economics of the Weimar Republic.

One day my uncle Aby came to visit the Kaullas. His first question was, "Where is Hans?" "At his architect," answered honest Otto — and the cat was out of the bag.

I returned to Tübingen the following year to work as a carpenter's apprentice. Among the German middle-class youth of my generation there was a strong rejection of the bourgeois pursuits of money, prestige, and "careers," expressed by the "Wandervogel" (migrating bird) movement, which glorified "return to nature" and community with the "Volk," with peasants and workers. In Hamburg, first my brother and then I, following in his footsteps, had already worked in a settlement house. I wanted to share the life and work of the working class for a while. I figured that I could kill two birds with one stone — also learning something about architectural design — by working on a building site rather than in a factory.

As I did not know how to find that kind of job, I turned to Mr. Staehle, who easily found it for me. I enjoyed those two months, but as far as my dual purpose was concerned, it was a failure. Carpentering did not make me a better architect; and while my workmates treated me with smiling indulgence, I never became one of them.

During these two summers in Tübingen I also explored the beautiful Swabian country. It was not unknown to me. My uncle George, who had studied agriculture, had bought a farm of about 500 acres, called Knight's Estate Uhenfels, on the Swabian "Rough Alb," and we had spent several summers there. Five minutes distant from the farmyard, the brother of the former owner, a sculptor, had built himself an imitation of a small medieval castle, very attractive and livable, on a rock with a beautiful view of the valley 300 meters below. It is in this little castle that we stayed.

Uhenfels is connected for me with the memory of Friedrich Huch, who spent one summer vacation there with us.

After "nanny" had left, she was followed first by a young English girl and then by a lady who was a descendant of French Protestant refugees and a professional teacher of French, in order to improve our knowledge of foreign languages.

We were old enough by then not to need a special person to look after us, and my parents had no intention of hiring anyone.

However, my mother had read and liked Friedrich Huch's first novel, *Peter Michel.* Huch lived in Hamburg as the tutor of the sons of a widow, Mrs. Laeisz, who owned a large shipping line. Straight-laced Mrs. Laeisz felt that a man who wrote novels glorifying a love affair between two unmarried persons was not a good influence for her boys and fired him. Aby M. Warburg, the art historian, told my mother of Huch's plight. My mother's reaction was, "On the basis of that book I would hire him." Aby M.: "Why don't you do it?"

My mother, who, as her sister Elsa said, "never was one to do anything by halves," did just that, with my father, as usual, consenting. So Friedrich Huch moved into our house, where he stayed for about two years. The only condition of his employment was to keep hands off our schoolwork. Instead, he swam and played tennis with us and instructed us in botany and zoology, which were not taught at the Realgymnasium.

Friedrich Huch belonged to the circle of the poet Stefan George, which played a considerable role in the intellectual life of Germany in the early decades of this century. Through him, my mother, and subsequently I, met several members of that circle in Munich.

MUNICH

I had chosen the Technical University of Munich for my studies because Theodor Fischer taught there, an architect hardly known outside Germany but whom I still greatly admire both as an architect and as a human being. It did not work out as I hoped; Fischer taught only studio work for the advanced students. I skipped the courses in mathematics and other auxiliary sciences and concentrated mainly on studio work. But I also followed the lectures on Renaissance and Baroque painting by the great art historian Heinrich Wölfflin at the university.

My mother stayed in Munich during my first months. She asked Ludwig Klages, one of the founders of graphology, to analyse my handwriting. He found that I had high aesthetic sensitivity, but that inhibitions between brain and hand would prevent me from becoming a creative artist. He had actually hit the nail on the head, but at the time I was unwilling to accept his conclusions.

The year in Munich was a rich experience. Several of my classmates from Hamburg had also come to Munich, in particular Richard Tüngel, who at that time studied painting but soon switched to architecture. We had endless discussions over glasses of wine about everything under the sun; and on weekends we went hiking in the Isar Valley or boating on Starnberg Lake.

During the winter I went skiing in the Alps and plunged enthusiastically into the month-long carnival — sometimes combining skiing and dancing through the night in a 24-hour sequence.

I spent much time in Munich's rich museums and art galleries. In that era the Munich art world was stirred by Kandinsky's works and writings pioneering nonobjective art. The concept was not new to me. In Hamburg I had discussed it with Gertrud Bing, a second cousin on my father's side who was my age and shared my interest in art; she later became the secretary of Aby M. Warburg in Hamburg and of the Warburg-Courtauld Institute in London. We had agreed that painting, in its movement away from interest in the "object" and its significance, was bound to follow music in developing into "pure" art. That has happened since that time, and the experience has made me modify my view. Nonobjective art certainly is real art, but it has limited possibilities. It seems that visual art, like Antaeus of the Greek myth, loses its strength if it does not touch the earth from time to time — study visible nature.

With my mother I also visited the "salon" of the poet Karl

Wolfskehl, a member of the George circle. I was engaged in conversation there by a lady of strange ascetic beauty, Anna Maria Derleth, who invited me to visit her and her brother Ludwig.

The Derleth siblings were devout Catholics. Ludwig was a poet who, like Friedrich Nietzsche and Stefan George, looked with contempt on modern "progress" and worshipped the "heroic" life. I spent long hours in talks with him, which left a lasting impression.

Ludwig never tried to convert me, but Anna Maria urged me to make a pilgrimmage to the sanctuary of Altötting. I had long admired the Catholic church on two accounts: the great art which it produced during one-and-a-half millenia, and its (apparent) ability to bridge the division of classes. I went to Altötting and knelt before the alter in an attempt to pray for receiving faith. Suddenly a loud noise disturbed the sanctuary: the big sketch book, which I had hidden under my coat, had fallen on the marble floor. I suddenly realized that I was playing a comedy to myself, got up, and left the church. It was my first and last attempt to "get religion."

I visited Ludwig Derleth again in January 1919. He in no way shared my hopes for the socialist revolution, but was deeply pessimistic. He described with amazing accuracy what since has become known as the totalitarian state. I still see the expression on his face as he, with his eyes focused on the distance, slowly said, "Scheusslich, scheusslich!" (disgusting).

Karlsruhe

My uncle, Marc Rosenberg, who was just retiring from his chair at Karlsruhe, described to me the course in design which Friedrich Ostendorf had started there. It was exactly what I had been looking for, and I decided to continue my studies in Karlsruhe.

Ostendorf was not a great architect, but he was a marvelous teacher. He believed in renewing the great tradition which went from Roman art through the Italian Renaissance to the French architecture of the eighteenth century and had been interrupted by eclectic historicism. He rejected attempts to create a "new style," stating, "One does not need a new language to express fresh thoughts"; the language of architecture would gradually change in response to new building programs and building techniques. The goal was always the greatest possible unity and simplicity.

My uncle's successor was A. E. Brinckmann, the first art historian to teach a course on city-building at a German university. In contemporary America his subject would be called "Civic Design." I owe much to these two teachers.

The curriculum required passing a preliminary examination — there were no others — after the first two years. I had originally intended to do without a degree but on Ostendorf's advice decided to go through the mill. But this did not result in changing my habit of skipping classes which did not interest me. So when the exam approached, I took some intensive tutoring classes, giving up most other activities.

THE LAST SUMMER OF PEACE

However, on the last day of carnival, I felt entitled to one night of dancing. The crowd was appallingly philistine; two sisters in similar costumes attracted my attention, and one of them much more than attention. We danced, and she then led me to her table and introduced me to her husband. I must have made a rather stupid impression; I had estimated her age at 17, but she was actually almost 24, two years older than I.

Gertel Stamm and Oscar Hagemann were both painters. They had married a year before to protect their relationship, agreeing that each would remain as free as before.

Gertel was a remarkable person. Very small but perfectly proportioned, she had a beautiful, radiant face and the hands of a Gothic madonna. Her origins were unusual: her father, a high-school principal, came from a line of Rhenish Protestant clergymen and civil servants; her mother was the daughter of a peasant boy from the Black Forest who, through his remarkable artistic as well as managerial gifts, had risen from apprentice to owner of a ceramics factory, after marrying the boss's daughter. They had met when her father, an excellent violinist, together with some fellow students, had given a concert in the Black Forest village in which the factory was located.

Gertel's mother was a deeply passionate woman, "boundless in her love, and boundless in her hate," as Gertel put it in a poem. Fortunately, she included me in her boundless love for Gertel, her favorite among her four children.

Gertel could not tolerate school so, after a few weeks, her parents took her out and educated her entirely at home. It was probably due to this unusual upbringing that she preserved a spontaneity and freedom from inhibitions rarely to be found in the modern world. She was overflowing with love to all creatures, animals as well as man. Clock time did not exist; she lived by her own rhythm.

She was endlessly creative; her hands were rarely at rest, producing drawings, silhouettes, paintings, or sculptures. She also sang, played the flute, and wrote beautiful poems. Her fine and lively intellect followed its own ways, which were not those of conventional logic. No wonder that she became the one great love of my life, up to and beyond her death.

At the carnival ball, Oscar and Gertel invited me to visit them the following Sunday, the invitation to be confirmed by mail. As no mail had arrived by Saturday night, I left early on Sunday morning for an excursion with a fellow student. When I came home in the evening, I found Gertel's invitation. (There was Sunday mail delivery in those days.)

I was in despair, thinking I would never see her again. But two days later, while I stood on a streetcar platform at a stop, Gertel discovered me and invited me for the following Sunday.

Oscar and Gertel lived in a wing of a sixteenth-century castle at Grötzingen. When I came to the door, I was received by a male servant, their factotum. He told me that I was expected and asked me to wait for the return of my hosts. I had leisure to look around the house, which was full of beautiful old furniture and minor works of art, mostly of peasant origin. There were two huge Danish dogs and a parrot which moved around freely. After a while Gertel came home, we had dinner together, engaged in some hours of animated talk, I could not say about what, and agreed to see more of each other.

Grötzingen castle was not unknown to me. It was owned by the Fikentschers, a couple of middle-aged painters. Together with their two boys and two girls, who were about my age, they had made it a community center for youth of the "Wandervogel" persuasion, with a bit of a "Völkisch" bent. Later, in the twenties, this developed into anti-Semitism, but at that time there was none of this. They rented out parts of the sprawling castle cheaply, and one of their young friends and tenants was Walter Schwarz from Hamburg, who was Jewish and had grown up a few blocks from my home; he became a good friend.

I had learned about Grötzingen castle from Walter Koessler of Strasbourg, my closest friend among my fellow students, who had urged me to move there. I had hesitated because of the distance to the university, but my encounter with Gertel put an end to my hesitations.

Shortly after I had moved in, I went to a performance of Beethoven's "Missa Solemnis" with Gertel. Oscar, who was hard of hearing, did not attend but was to meet Gertel later in front of the concert hall. I was very surprised when Gertel obviously was in no hurry to take leave of me and delayed meeting her husband. I felt so happy that I did not shut an eye all night and got up at dawn for a long walk in the woods.

With my thoughts on Gertel day and night, preparation for my exams took a back seat and, not surprisingly, I failed several subjects. With the requirement to repeat my exams making it necessary, and Gertel's presence making it more than desirable to stay in Karlsruhe, my location for the summer term was fixed. However, I was not willing to renounce my previous plan to study that term in Munich with Theodor Fischer.

I knew that it was illegal to be enrolled at two universities at the same time. I presented myself at Munich, asking to resume my studies interrupted one-and-a-half years before. To the registrar's question as to what I had been doing in the meantime, I replied, shamelessly lying, that I had been traveling. He insisted that he needed a document and finally suggested that I get a certificate of good behavior from the police of my hometown. I wrote to the police of Osnabrück, requesting the desired certificate, carefully enumerating all details concerning time, etc. of my birth, adding that I had spent the first three weeks of my life in Osnabrück. I promptly received the requested documents, containing all the details which I had submitted, including the three weeks, with the added sentence: "During this period the said Hans Blumenfeld has not been guilty of any criminal act, and nothing unfavorable about him has become known." When I gave this paper to the registrar, he said, "There we have got something," and immediately admitted me. Glory and praise to bureaucracy!

I rented a room in the center of Munich and commuted weekly, making detours to visit architectural monuments, primarily the glorious churches and monasteries of the South German late baroque period. The work in Fischer's studio was very much worthwhile.

One morning in June, when I went on my customary walk with

Gertel and we had sat down on the grass, she told me that, at her husband's request, she had to ask me to stop my visits. She was taken aback when I flatly refused. I prevailed, and our life went on as before.

The summer of 1914 was a lovely summer.

During part of my time in Karlsruhe, Franz studied in Freiburg, where I repeatedly visited him on weekends. We shared the concern about the deep rift between the "common people" and the "educated" class. Franz, and subsequently I too, participated in the "student worker's instruction courses" in which student volunteers taught evening classes on various subjects. Once, on a skiing trip in the Black Forest, I remarked to Franz that, while these courses might build a bridge to the workers, we had no contact with the peasants. Courses of instruction obviously were not the right approach to them; I suggested a traveling student theater. Franz took up the idea and organized such a group, which successfully performed in a number of villages near Freiburg.

Franz was a very capable organizer. He said this role required the observance of two principles: first, never do anything yourself; delegate every task to someone else; second, what you do not do yourself will never be done. I have not encountered a better formula.

CHAPTER III

War and Revolution

1914 – 1919

CLOUDS OF WAR

In the early years of this century, as the division of Europe into two antagonistic blocks hardened, talk of war increased. Several crises were settled by compromise, but every compromise left a bad taste; hardliners on both sides claimed that the other would have caved in, if only their own diplomats had "stood firm."

During the second Morocco crisis, in 1911, my uncle Otto Kaulla shared his colleagues' insistence on firmness. I disagreed, feeling that good relations with France were infinitely more valuable for Germany than was Morocco. The conflict had started because a German consortium wanted a concession to exploit the iron ores of the Rif. My brother Franz, at the same time, asked another uncle who, as the head of a firm which dealt at wholesale in steel, was a member of the consortium, if the matter was really that important. His answer was surprising. "We don't care," he said. "If it is German, we will establish an *aktiengesellschaft* in Berlin; if French, a *société anonyme* in Paris. To us it makes no difference; we make all that noise only because the government wants it." In this case at least the relation between big business and national government was the reverse of that assumed by Leninist theory.

We frequently discussed ways of preventing the threatening war. Once, when we were sitting together with our common friend Fritz Solmitz in a beer garden in Freiburg, Franz said that the soldiers ought to turn their rifles on their officers. Fritz countered that German soldiers would never do that. I agreed with both: the soldiers should do it but would not.

Fritz Solmitz later became editor of the Social-Democratic newspaper in Lübeck. Lübeck was the only city in Germany where the Social Democrats responded to the Communist call for a general strike when Hindenburg appointed Hitler to be chancellor. The Nazis arrested Fritz and, after months of torture, murdered him in prison in 1933. After the fall of the Third Reich, the prison guards guilty of that crime were put on trial. The judge found that he could not identify the person who had actually committed the murder, and the "lesser" crimes were covered by the statute of limitations; so they went scot-free.

Somewhat later, Franz, C. K. Ogden and I discussed the possibility of stopping a war by a general strike in all the countries involved; this was the policy adopted by the Socialist International at their Stuttgart Congress, largely at the urging of Lenin and Rosa Luxemburg. Ogden felt that a war would mean the end of German social democracy. I disagreed, saying that they would join the war effort; to which Ogden countered, "That would be their end."

A few months later the "Zabern Affair" erupted. In the Alsatian garrison town of Zabern (Saverne) a lieutenant drilling his men had shot dead a young worker who jeered at the performance. In the evening the citizens of Zabern assembled in peaceful and orderly protest. The colonel commanding the garrison had them rounded up and locked up for the night in the basement of the barracks. A storm of indignation broke loose in the Reichstag and in the press from all parties — except the extreme right — demanding punishment of the guilty officers. In the end, the colonel was transferred to another garrison, and the lieutenant was acquitted as having acted in "putative self-defense." Within two weeks all but the Socialists dropped the case in the interest of "upholding the honor of the army."

I saw the whole performance as a test mobilization of public opinion for war, testing how far it could be swung around by waving the flag, and was alarmed. For the first time in my life I went to a public meeting called by the Social Democratic party. The speaker, a lawyer and member of the Reichstag, dwelt exclusively on the legal aspects of the case, with no word on its political meaning. The large audience, mostly workers in their Sunday best, seemed satisfied. I was not. To my great surprise I found that I was more radical than the Social Democrats.

The shots of Sarajevo touched off a wave of demands to punish the Serbian government. Few listened when I pointed out that there was no conclusive proof that they were involved. (They were, in fact, and later boasted of it.)

In the summer of 1914, my mother, as well as her sister Rosa from St. Petersburg, stayed at Travemünde on the Baltic, where their brother Aby had built a house and bought a neighboring house for his guests. When, at the end of the summer term, I boarded the train to join my mother, an acquaintance whom I found in my compartment tendered me a newspaper displaying the Austrian ultimatum to Serbia. "That means war," he said, "and we will be in it."

As previously planned, I stopped in several small towns on my way to Travemünde to look at works of architecture. Everywhere there were excited crowds at the stations, singing patriotic songs; in several towns horses were being mustered by the army. War was in the air.

A few days later the "state of war" (not actual war) was proclaimed. The three women of the family all appeared at dinner in black dress. It was not a concerted action; they just felt the same terrible pain.

My uncle, reflecting the views of the business community, thought the war would be over by Christmas; I said it might well last two years. To his question, "Where is the money to come from?" I replied that money spent would flow back to the government through taxes and loans; as long as men and materials were available, the war could continue. I did not think that it would last more than two years, because then war losses would far exceed any conceivable gains of victory. I did not yet understand how infinitely more difficult it is to end a war than to start it. Governments, having imposed unconscionable sacrifices on their people, dare not tell them that it has all been in vain.

A group of my fellow students from Karlsruhe, under the guidance of one of my teachers, completed a study tour of Baltic towns at Lübeck. I joined them there for dinner. To the professor's remark, "You will of course also volunteer," I replied rather sharply, "I don't know that yet."

The next evening the group came to Travemünde. I was so disgusted with their noisy flag-waving that I left. On the boardwalk

I met my Alsatian friend Walter Koessler and a Swiss fellow student; we were the only three dissenters.

Germany declared war on Russia on August 1, 1914, and on France on August 3; Britain declared war on Germany on August 4. My mother's reaction to this second event was, "Also verloren" (So it's lost). Incidentally, the Kaiser's reaction was the same; his marginal note read, "Edward the dead defeats me the living."

FRANZ AND I VOLUNTEER

My mother wanted me to go to neutral Denmark. I refused. I felt that, having done nothing to prevent the war, I could not wash my hands of it; I had to share the fate of my people. Either I actively opposed the war, publicly calling on the soldiers to mutiny, or I had to become a soldier myself. The first option looked entirely quixotic. I had no contact with any group which opposed the war. I did read reports in the papers — probably distorted — of the stand taken by left-wing socialists, such as Rosa Luxemburg, against the war. But their interpretation of the war as a class war of the capitalists went counter to everything I saw with my own eyes. The workers were jubilant in the streets, while my mother and my two aunts, both wives of big bankers, grieved. I also knew that Albert Ballin, head of the Hamburg-American Line and one of Germany's leading capitalists, was in deep despair.

There was an additional reason: but for class privilege, I would have been a front-line soldier. German boys were drafted at age nineteen for two or three years of service in the armed forces. Boys who had successfully completed nine years of high school were "one-year volunteers" who could choose their own regiment; if they attended university, they could claim deferment up to six years. I had made use of that privilege. High school in Germany at the time was strictly a class school. Parents had to pay a fee; more importantly, workers' families could not make ends meet without the help of their boys from the age of fourteen. Consequently, in German high schools there were no sons of the working class and only very few from the lower middle class. It would have been disgraceful to use this unjust class privilege to save my hide while millions of fathers of families put their lives at risk.

I had to admit to my mother that less noble motives, such as love of adventure, contributed to my decision. She also reminded me that being a soldier meant willingness not only to risk one's life, but to take the life of others. I countered that the same reasoning that prompted me also applied to those on the other side. In fact, I was quite concerned that my Russian cousin Fedya Günzburg, who at the time was in Germany, get out in time to do his duty to his country, as I did to mine.

Franz, who was politically much more mature and active than I — he had enthusiastically participated in the international peace meeting in the Basel cathedral during the Christmas period of 1913 — had also decided to volunteer in Freiburg, for essentially the same reasons, except for love of adventure, which was foreign to his serious nature.

Gertel, who had found herself accidentally swept up by a prowar demonstration in Heidelberg, was temporarily carried away by the general enthusiasm. To her letter relating that experience I replied that I in no way shared her feelings. The war, I said, could result only in the ruin of Germany: material ruin if we lost, and moral ruin if we won. I felt then, and continued to feel, that the least harmful outcome of the war would be a stalemate, a peace without victors or vanquished.

War enthusiasm swept not only Germany, but all countries involved in the war, even Russia. Bertrand Russell, who observed it in London, was profoundly shocked, interpreting it as a primitive drive to aggression breaking through the thin crust of civilization. I am not sure that his interpretation was quite correct. My brother may have come closer to the truth. Franz wrote, "What appears to most people as extraordinary is the deeply serious background, the feeling of community with the entire people and the consciousness of bearing a great responsibility." He added that he was not enthused by the war, because he had always been fully conscious of community and responsibility.

Probably the main root of war enthusiasm was the feeling of being important.

When, many decades later, I read William James' essay on "The Moral Equivalent of War," it struck me as a realistic view of the attitude of many of the best of European youth in 1914: contempt for the philistine goals of wealth and comfort and a longing for the heroic life and for self-sacrifice. "The will to sacrifice is more important than the cause for which the sacrifice is made," wrote my brother at the time. In this, I now know, he and I were misguided.

I enlisted in a field-artillery regiment at Bahrenfeld, a suburb of Hamburg. Practically all deferred students volunteered, as did many high-school kids. There were also almost two million young men who had not been drafted, because during the preceding ten years the number of men of draft age had exceeded the scheduled strength of the armed forces. The army could not cope with this flood. There were not enough beds in the barracks, so we were welcome to provide our own accommodation, and I rented a pleasant room. Training was sketchy, to put it mildly. Artillery soldiers were divided into two categories, "cannoneers" and "drivers." There were five cannoneers under a sergeant for each gun, and three drivers to ride the six horses which drew each of the four cannons and four ammunition carts. The mechanism of the cannon and of the harnessing of the horses were demonstrated to us; but as I was short and the crowd was large, I never saw anything of it. But I enjoyed the occasional ride on horseback and I learned to take care of horses.

Coming from similar backgrounds, we volunteers got along together very well. Only two roughnecks who had volunteered to get out of jail stood apart. Town leave was granted freely. So the months at Bahrenfeld were a quite idyllic and pleasant time but in no way a preparation for front-line service.

My brother had joined another field-artillery regiment at Freiburg and was sent to the front in November of 1914. He was terribly shocked by the rudeness of his comrades and wrote, "I am afraid of losing my faith in human beings, in myself, in everything good in the world. What does it signify if all bullets and shells spare me, but I suffer damage to my soul? This is how one would have once expressed it." Later his relations with them improved, but he was appalled by the slaughter. He wrote to my mother, "You know that I have always been opposed to war, but now that I have experienced it, I have decided to devote all my life to work for peace, if I ever come back."

He never came back. On the eve of Christmas of 1914 a letter from his sergeant informed us that he had been killed by an exploding shell at Contalmaison on the Somme River.

When in the 1960s I tried to find his grave, which the sergeant's letter had described, I found it had disappeared under a cemetery of Canadian soldiers killed later in the war.

Toward the end of the war, a professor of literature at Freiburg published a collection of letters from students killed in the war.

In the 1920s the *Nouvelle revue française* reprinted some of them, including all those written by Franz. André Gide added a comment, dealing almost exclusively with my brother's words, which had profoundly moved him.

"War swallows the best," Aby Warburg, the art historian, wrote to my mother. "We are stoking the furnace with pianos." For my mother it was a terrible blow, a wound that never healed.

First Battles

Barely two weeks later I was sent to the front in East Prussia and was immediately thrown into battle. It was bitterly cold, and we got little sleep, but the worst was the hostility and contempt of my comrades. Of course, I could not cope with my tasks as a rider; they shook their heads at my abysmal stupidity and understandably resented the fact that I did not pull my weight. I could not stand their insults when standing in line for chow and added hunger to my other deprivations. I was so utterly exhausted that I registered the many corpses and burnt-out villages without any feeling.

Those three weeks were the hardest of my life. They ended in a most unheroic way: in cutting bread I had cut my hand, and the wound became infected. The battalion physician ordered me to see him the next day to operate on it. But for several days we were far away from battalion headquarters, and by the time he saw me again my whole arm was swollen and he sent me back to hospital. I got rides on military trucks to the small Polish town of Augustovo. The field hospital had been established in the synagogue, where I found hundreds of wounded soldiers. I turned away in horror, and for the first time in my life I took advantage of my being Jewish. I asked a Jewish tailor to put me up for the night, which he did with loving care. The next day I reached the hospital in Rastenburg. The surgeon operated immediately; he told me that twenty-four hours later it would have been too late.

In Rastenburg I learned that the Russian occupation had been very civilized. The soldiers had scrupulously paid for everything they took, and the only thing destroyed was the crockery in the officers' casino, which the Russian officers had smashed in a drunken spree on the eve of their retreat. The 1914 war was probably the last one based on the rule that only the armed forces were the enemy, not the civilians. We were strongly indoctrinated with that rule. The only case I heard of a German soldier being shot by court-martial was of a man who had raped a Polish woman. The only case I personally witnessed, later in the war, was a man in my outfit who had robbed a store owned by a Russian woman; he was sentenced to hard labor. When we were quartered on inhabitants, we did not evict the inhabitants — we squeezed them into narrow corners — and took only food and fodder. When we were quartered in abandoned houses, we also took blankets and other things we badly needed but did not "liberate" other goods. Certainly this was not true everywhere but, in general, Prussian militarism, with all its harshness, was not Hitler's Third Reich.

After recovery, I was sent to Schwerin in Mecklenburg, a city embedded in a beautiful landscape of lakes and forests. In Schwerin, and later in the camp at Zossen near Berlin, I came to understand the ways of my proletarian comrades, and I increasingly identified with them. Both my mother and Gertel visited me at Zossen, and Gertel gave me two small silhouettes, one of herself and one of my mother, which I carried on my chest throughout the war years. I came to look upon them as a kind of protective talisman; I still have and treasure them.

LATVIA

Around the first of November 1915 I was again shipped to the front, near Dvinsk in Latvia. I became cannoneer number four of the fourth gun. I was immensely lucky; my sergeant, Hannes Clausen, was one of the most admirable characters I ever met: straight as a bolt in body and soul, without the slightest grain of falsehood or meanness. Thanks to him, the fourth gun was always a happy family.

This was not necessarily true of the entire battery. Our battery was known in the entire division for its skill in stealing from other outfits; when we were in the neighborhood they doubled their guards.

It struck me then and since how little time it takes for a group of men, however casually thrown together, to form an "in-group" versus all "others." I later came to call this apparently deeply rooted human trait "a-noi-ism," after a poster I saw in Mussolini's Italy early in 1930. The poster showed a young fellow slouched against a wall, obviously not knowing what to do with himself, and a marching band of young Black Shirts waving to him with the printed shout "a noi!" (to us!). They felt they were somebody.

From Dvinsk we were shifted to another position, where the provisions, generally still plentiful in 1915, failed to arrive; probably they were stolen by some "rear-area swine" for sale on the black market. We survived by stealing the molasses meant for our horses. I dreamt of steaks and kicked myself for allowing my stomach to dominate my mind. But the experience taught me no longer to look down on my comrades because of their endless talk of food.

When our horses started to collapse en masse, we were withdrawn for rest to a Latvian village. Subsequently, I was assigned to a group putting up listening towers to determine the location of enemy artillery by acoustic triangulation. The work also included setting up tripods in front of the trenches. As soon as these appeared, there was machine-gun fire from the other side. I barely escaped a beating by the infantrymen in the trenches, who were furious because I had disturbed their informal armistice. They never shot at the Russian soldiers who were engaged in harvest work on the other bank of the Dvina in plain view.

Nobody hated "the enemy"; our enemies were our officers; even more hated were the rear-echelon swine and the war profiteers at home; most hated of all were the journalists and clergymen who continued to glorify the war. To us it was anything but glorious. Nobody ever talked of "this war"; it was always "this shit-war."

There is a myth around that Germans are "born soldiers." In our battery, the best soldiers on each level were non-German. On the officer's level it was a Lithuanian. Because, as a worker, he had never passed the "one-year-volunteer" exam, he was barred from being an officer; his title was "officer-substitute." But our captain, who was a career officer, wisely left it to him to lead the battery, in combat as well as in the daily management; both tasks he performed brilliantly. On the sergeant's level it was a Frenchman from Lorraine. He kept up his spirits when everyone else's were down. Everybody loved him; he was killed in battle. On the men's level it was an Alsatian, a class-conscious metal worker.

Later we were stationed opposite Riga, and every evening I watched from a lookout the spires of that old Hanseatic city, so similar to those of Hamburg.

RUMANIA

Winter was approaching, and we were glad to be put on a southbound train which, in glorious September weather, slowly rolled through Poland, Moravia, Hungary, Serbia, and Bulgaria to Varna on the Black Sea. From Varna we marched northward through the Dobruja to participate in the battle of Constanta. We were then shifted to Svishtov, on the Bulgarian side of the Danube and crossed the river without a hitch — probably the Rumanian commander had been bribed — to march on Bucharest.

During the fighting in Rumania, one evening, we had fired a few shots from a hilltop, then went to sleep in the safety of the valley behind the hill. The hilltop was in full sight of the enemy, and our officer-substitute wanted to move the guns to another position. But a stupid young lieutenant, who was in command while the captain was on leave, thought he knew better and ordered the guns to stay. The next morning, when we returned to man the guns, we all knew what was in store. Hannes Clausen immediately ordered us to dig a trench, unload the ammunition, and bury it in the trench. A minute later a grenade hit the ammunition wagon behind which I crouched. Clausen's foresight had saved my life, but two others were killed. One died on the spot, with a smile still on his boyish face. The other writhed in pain; I tried to carry him to safety, but his body was too heavy, and he told me to run. After the firing stopped, the medics carried him down to the valley. I held him in my arms, with his guts hanging out. He repeated incessantly, "My poor wife, my poor children."

This event brought home to me the utter criminality of war. *This* was what I was doing to my fellows on the other side.

Before we reached Bucharest, I was struck by a light case of hepatitis and was sent back to hospital at Nis, Serbia. At that time the debate about unlimited submarine warfare was raging in Germany, and the newspapers strongly advocated it.

It is a strange phenomenon that states at war, when victory eludes them, challenge a power even stronger than their present adversaries. When Germany could not defeat the Entente, it provoked America; when Hitler failed to conquer Britain, he invaded the Soviet Union; and when Japan could not subdue China, it attacked the United States. How utterly unrealistic are the scenarios which assume that nations in the heat of war will swallow conditions or compromises which they were unwilling to accept in a more rational atmosphere before the start of hostilities.

I returned to my battery, which was then stationed in Moldavia. In the spring I, with three other Germans, was sent to serve with a Turkish antiaircraft battery to convey telephone messages between them and the headquarters of the German division to which it was attached. I spoke no Turkish, and the battery commander, a lieutenant of Armenian descent, knew no German. We communicated in French; he treated us Germans as gentlemen, a welcome change. I also liked the Turkish soldiers. They were very goodnatured; quarrels and shouting matches, so frequent among my German comrades, never occurred. But they were also very passive. I had come to admire the initiative and inventiveness of my German comrades in building our dugouts, making them comfortable, and landscaping the surroundings. The Turks were satisfied with any hole in the ground.

Our battery was most primitive, consisting of two field-artillery guns mounted on wooden supports; they could not be raised higher than 60 degrees. Once a plane reached the area directly over the battery, we were just defenseless sitting ducks. That happened once; bombs exploded all around us, but miraculously no one was hurt. As I wrote to my mother, who of course constantly feared for me, "There is so much more space elsewhere."

However, this attack had a tragic aftermath. The Turkish soldier on guard duty, who had failed to notice the plane in time, was punished by a brutal bastinade which horrified me. The next day he disappeared; rumor, probably true, said that he had deserted, had been caught by the military police, and had been shot.

We were stationed a few miles from Braila, where one of my mother's Russian cousins was married to a Rumanian grain merchant. I visited their house frequently. When the armistice with Rumania was concluded, their son came over from Galati, where he served as an officer in the Rumanian navy, whose long-range guns had made my life with the Turks quite uncomfortable. He was indignant that I was not an officer.

My mother had subscribed to *The London Times*, Clemenceau's *L'homme enchaîné*, and the Italian *Secolo* for me. These "enemy" papers were faithfully delivered to me by the German military mail. A Turkish officer of Greek descent regularly visited our battery to pick them up.

In the fall I had to take leave from the Turks, with regret and the decoration of the Red Half Moon. I had learned to speak some Turkish and to brew Turkish coffee.

I returned to my battery but soon fell ill with a neuro-rheumatic disease which crippled my legs. I was sent to a hospital in Bucharest, where I quickly recovered. On release I was classified as "unfit for front-line service" and sent to serve as a guard in a prisoner-of-war camp at Buzau, also in Rumania. My duties included registering ins and outs and listening to prisoners' complaints. I found that a civilian, an elderly Rumanian peasant who had worked for the German army, had fallen ill and had been sent to the prison hospital. The hospital had released him weeks ago, but he was still kept in the camp because no regulations had been issued for such a case. I finagled his release.

I soon struck up a friendship with the Russian interpreter, an Ukrainian-Jewish student of medicine. He was a Menshevik, I favored the Bolsheviks, and we had long discussions. I took him to town to visit his girl friend, discreetly waiting in the anteroom.

It was the top sergeant's duty to notify the military police of prisoners' escapes, which were frequent; but he preferred to spend his time with Rumanian girls and left this duty to me. I always delayed notification by twenty-four hours. For the Rumanians, who invariably returned straight to their home village, it meant just a night with their wives or sweethearts; but four Russians who had managed to procure themselves German uniforms were never caught.

In Buzau I also had my first prison experience. I had repeatedly mediated messages between my second cousin in Braila and her mother in Geneva through my mother. After recovery from an illness, she suggested that her mother would drop her worries about her health if she saw her handwriting. So I included her handwritten letter to my mother. The letter was opened by the military censor, and I was sent to the klink for five days. I hid Kant's *Prolegomena* in my left sole and a homemade game of chess in the right one, and had a glorious time lounging in the sunny prison yard.

The Russian Revolutions

As the war dragged on, opposition increased. I had followed with interest the International Meeting of Socialist Parties opposed to the war in 1915 at Zimmerwald in Switzerland. At that meeting Germany was represented by the Independent Social Democratic party (USPD) which had seceded from the "Kaiser-Socialists," the Social Democratic party (SPD).

My mother, with her hopes for a life in Italy with Stepanoff shattered, had resumed her earlier dream of studying at a university. She had established herself in a good hotel in Heidelberg and attended seminars held by Hans Driesch, the leading proponent of the "vitalist" theory in biology, and by the well-known philosopher Karl Jaspers; both became personal friends of their unusual student.

My mother was in touch with several antiwar organizations and received literature from them. She found herself in agreement with a pamphlet calling on the soldiers to refuse to serve. She discussed it with her coiffeuse and left it with her. Another client noticed it there, questioned the coiffeuse about its origin, and promptly denounced my mother. A police investigation ensued. My mother was ordered by the military authorities to return to her hometown of Hamburg and not to leave it.

The following year my sister Margaret studied in Heidelberg. She joined a student antiwar organization headed by the poet Ernst Toller. She was also expelled from Heidelberg and continued her studies in Berlin, concluding them after the war with a doctorate in economics.

The overthrow of the Czar in February 1917 encouraged revolutionary antiwar movements in other countries. In the summer of 1917 the Austrian Navy mutineered at Cattaro (now Kotor) and the German Navy at Wilhelmshaven; there was also a serious mutiny in the French Army. All three mutinies were put down; but while Clemenceau had hundreds of French soldiers shot, only the two top leaders of the Wilhelmshaven mutiny were sentenced to death, the others only to hard labor.

In Russia, the provisional government under Kerenski continued the war. The Bolsheviks, after Lenin's return to Russia, promoted the slogan, "Peace without victors or vanquished, without annexations or separations, based on the self-determination of nations." I was happy that now a powerful party had adopted my goal of a "Peace without victors or vanquished," and strongly sympathized with the Bolsheviks, without agreeing with their goal of the "Dictatorship of the proletariat."

When the Bolsheviks seized power in November 1917 and, as their first act of government, broadcast an appeal "To All, to All, to All!" to put an immediate stop to the war, and unilaterally dissolved the army, I was enthusiastic. When the German government responded by concluding an armistice and entering into peace negotiations at Brest Litovsk with the young "Socialist Republic of Workers' and Soldiers' Councils" ("Soviets" in Russian), I was overjoyed. So much greater were my disappointment and indignation when it turned out that the Kaiser's government interpreted "self-determination of nations" as the right of the Germans to establish puppet governments in all parts of the Czar's empire which they had occupied, and even beyond. They broke off the Brest Litovsk negotiations and invaded the Soviet Union.

This finally and forever ended my hesitations. This certainly was not a defensive war; it was naked criminal aggression, and I had to act against it. I wrote two letters to my sister — one mailed in Buzau, and the other by a soldier on leave in Germany — asking her to register me as a member of the USPD. Of course, the letters never arrived; Margaret's mail was censored.

I made a feeble attempt to organize a mass refusal of service. I talked to about a dozen fellow soldiers. Only one agreed — on condition that I got at least ten others to join. None did. They were glad that their hides were safe in their rear-echelon position and did not want to risk them.

CRIMEA

In the spring of 1918 my health status was reviewed. As I had a heart murmur, the doctor seemed inclined to prolong my exemption from front-line service. I assured him that the murmur was harmless, as indeed it was; I did not want to be a permanent rear-echelon swine. I was directed to rejoin my outfit at Simferopol in the Crimea and, as a private-first-class, I was entrusted with taking along two other men. One of them was an idiot and the other a criminal, which suited me perfectly.

My Braila cousin gave me two addresses in the Crimea: of her sister in Feodosiya, and of the German manager of the vast estates owned by the Günzburg family in the Crimea, who lived at Simferopol. At Simferopol I visited the manager and questioned him about the time under Bolshevik rule, which he, of course, strongly opposed. I was surprised that luxury shops and cafés were operating, with no plate-glass windows smashed; he confirmed that they had not been disturbed. I was also surprised that the railroads which had been owned and operated by the Russian state continued to function; when I asked who operated them, the answer was, "The railroad." They told me that they had lived in fear under the Bolshevist regime; but when I asked what happened to them or to people they knew, there was nothing. This experience was later repeated many times; everybody told horror stories, but they always had happened somewhere else.

The manager asked me to take a ham to Feodosiya, which a tenant had brought as a present to the lady of the estate. I did. The son of the family, who was a Russian officer, politely avoided me, but the mother and daughter received me with great warmth. They said that with the aid of their devoted old "nanya," they had survived the Bolshevist period quite well; it must be horrible in Moscow and St. Petersburg. Fifty years later I met the daughter in Israel; she remembered our encounter as vividly as I did.

In Simferopol we were informed that our outfit had moved to Evpatoria, on the west coast of the Crimea. I proceeded to Evpatoria with my two "subordinates," only to be informed that it was now stationed at Armyanske Bazarskoye, on the north coast of the Crimean Peninsula. We were in no hurry to get there; we swam in the Black Sea, and I was impressed by the beauty of the town's Turkish-style mosque. We proceeded in leisurely fashion to Armyansk, being driven from one German village to the next. In one village the farmers were not German, but Czech. Surrounded as they were by Tartars and Russians, they identified with the Germans on the basis of their common Protestant faith and Central-European culture.

The well-to-do German farmers were of course hostile to the revolution. But they all said that the Bolsheviks had not been too bad; they had suffered from inroads by the anarchists and by the "Krasnogartsi" (Red Hearts), an otherwise unknown group. Once, however, I met a poor German farm hand who said the Bolsheviks had done much good. He looked anxiously around him. The Germans, who had established a puppet "Tartar Republic" in the Crimea, ruthlessly persecuted the "Reds." Once, a charming Tartar boy of sixteen glowingly told me how he had cut off their heads. I could not hate him. He was as innocent as a lion devouring a gazelle; he did not know what he was doing. But I almost came to blows with a German soldier who gleefully reported how the military police had beaten up a "Red."

In Armyansk I was assigned to the telephone exchange. Others were assigned to control the smuggling between the Ukraine and the Crimea, both of which now postured as "independent states." My comrades divided the spoils honestly with the smugglers.

After some weeks of this idyllic life we were moved again, marching through the whole length of the Crimea to Yalta. In Yalta many wealthy "White" Russians had taken refuge and shared in the typical life of an elegant spa. In the midst of this I was posted with my gun on the promenade overlooking the Black Sea.

One day a German officer approached me and very politely asked permission to look through my telescope. I had, of course, been instructed to permit this to no one, but I cared a damn about regulations. This officer had introduced himself to his fellows as "Prince Reuss" and had been feted at the officers' casino as a scion of one of Germany's ruling dynasties. When it was discovered that he was a "Red" spy, he tried to escape on a motorcycle but was felled by rifle shots.

I had taught myself some rudiments of Russian, and a good deal of my time was taken up acting as an interpreter in the black market deals of my buddies.

In September we marched to Sevastopol along the beautiful coastal road. The first night we were quartered in the Czar's palace at Livadia, which later became famous as the seat of the 1945 "Yalta Conference." We guzzled the exquisite wines from the imperial cellar.

When I rejoined my old outfit, I reproached my buddies for fighting the Bolsheviks with whom most of them sympathized. They replied, "We did not fight them; all we ever did was to fire a few shots across the bow of two Russian navy ships which tried to escape from Sevastopol." The ships had promptly returned to the harbor and had been impounded by the Germans, but they remained under the command of their elected Sailors' Soviets. Curious, I hired a rowboat to have a closer look, and was impressed by their spick-and-span maintenance. When, in the thirties, I tried to find out from Russian Communists what had happened to those ships, they all staunchly denied that any ship of the Red Navy had ever surrendered to the Germans; they had all been blown up at Novorossiysk to prevent them from falling into enemy hands. That's what the Party line said, and my eyewitness account meant nothing.

MACEDONIA

After a short stay at Sevastopol we were loaded on a ship. We thought we were bound for the Caucasus, where the Germans had landed with the connivance of the Menshevik government of Grouzia (Georgia), intending to march on the Baku oilfields. But we were unloaded at Varna and shipped by rail to Macedonia.

Against my wish, my mother had obtained my exemption from battle service on the grounds of my being the only son of a widow. The captain called me and asked me if I was willing to voluntarily renounce this privilege. I refused. So I had to leave my family of the fourth gun and was put in charge of the water wagon, to be assisted by my two old friends, the idiot and the criminal. It is questionable whether driving my wagon across open fields exposed me to less enemy fire than being at my gun. Certainly there at least I was not in danger of being beaten up. At the wells, which were few and far between, there were always hundreds of thirsty Bulgarian soldiers who got mad at a German water wagon blocking access. I had to display all my diplomatic skills to appease them.

Soon the Bulgarians disappeared, as their government had concluded a separate peace. The few German and Austrian units had to beat a hasty retreat. Near Vranje we were encircled by the French; I later met a French hero of that battle in Montreal. I managed to get my top-heavy water wagon on the road, but three gun crews had to abandon their cannons. The fourth gun with my "family" was missing. I feared that they were dead and hoped that they had become prisoners of war.

Our horses had survived and were pulling empty carts. I got fed up with the long marches and, relying on my heart murmur, asked the doctor for a certificate that would allow me to ride the carts. To my great surprise he sent me straight to a hospital in Germany. I suspect that the officers, fearful of the threatening revolution, were glad to be rid of that subversive fellow.

Overcrowded trains carried me to Elbing (now Elblag) in Western Prussia. As I was in perfect health, I was released after a few days to go to the army camp at Zossen. On my first leave I went to Berlin to apply for membership in the USPD. I also went to see Otto Freundlich, a painter who was a friend of my mother's. He was convinced that the revolution was already under way. He was a Communist who had shared his first studio in Paris with Picasso. In fact, that very day, November 4, 1918, the sailors of the Imperial Navy had taken power in the city of Kiel, establishing a Workers' and Soldiers' Council. Three days later, Workers' and Soldiers' Councils had taken power in Hamburg, Brunswick, and Munich.

On November 8 a soldier from my battery whom I met again at Zossen told me that plans were under way for a Soldiers' Council to take over the camp the next day; was I willing to help? I certainly was.

On November 9 thousands of soldiers assembled on the parade grounds to elect the council. While the speeches were still going on, the news came through that the Kaiser had abdicated. The news was greeted with earsplitting jubilation.

As far as Germany was concerned, the war was over. The Allies concluded the armistice only on the eleventh. Thousands of soldiers on both sides were killed during those two days.

I had survived the war without a scratch. The soldiers on the Eastern Front suffered much less from enemy action than those in the West; they suffered more from cold, hunger, and lice.

Lice had interfered with my reading, for which I had ample time during the war. I read Kant, Schopenhauer and Montaigne, but also novels by Flaubert, Dostoevsky, Strindberg, Heinrich Mann and others.

When I read a new German translation of Homer's *Odyssey*, I was surprised that a buddy, a farm hand from Mecklenburg with only six years of schooling, borrowed it from me and read it with great pleasure. He read it as a smashingly good adventure yarn — which indeed it is.

I had learned some things in the war. I had learned to read, as well as to sleep, in the midst of noise. I had learned to counter harassment by putting up a stoic front. *"Du hast die Ruhe weg,"* (freely translated: "You sure are damn cool") said my buddies. Above all, I had learned the meaning of class struggle, which I had experienced in its simplified form as the struggle of men against officers. From then on I identified with the working class. I was, however, aware that my education had given me a different culture which I by no means intended to give up.

The worst of the war was boredom. When, after the war, I saw antiwar films, I felt that they could not achieve their purpose of deterring men from war. Young men feeling their oats are attracted by danger, however terrifying. If only one could turn out a picture showing the boredom of war! . . . But then, people don't go to the movies to be bored.

FINDING MY WAY

I had no doubt that a revolution was justified and necessary to end the war and overthrow militarism. The Russians had shown the way; we, as well as the Austrians and Hungarians, had followed, only too late. But what was the new society we were going to build?

It had to be both socialist and internationalist. But which came first? For a short while I toyed with the idea of "Internationalism first, socialism later." I feared that an economy owned and managed by a nation-state would produce a nationalism much more virulent than had a "laissez-faire" economy. Subsequent developments in socialist as well as in capitalist countries — in all of which the role of the state in the economy has also greatly increased — have shown that my fears were only too well justified.

However, I soon realized that a peaceful capitalist international order was a pipe dream. This insight was confirmed for me by Lenin's *State and Revolution* and *Imperialism,* the first Marxist literature I ever read apart from the *Communist Manifesto* of 1848 and *The Erfurt Program.* I decided that socialism had to be built immediately, alongside the development of international solidarity. This was also the view of the USPD, of which I was now a member. Beyond this there was a wide range of opinions in the Party, from the revisionism of Eduard Bernstein to those of extreme leftists. I welcomed this diversity and the ensuing lively discussions within the party. I was and still am convinced that it is essential for the health of a socialist party, in power even more than in opposition.

There was a particularly lively discussion in the USPD about who should manage the economy, the political authority of the Workers' and Soldiers' Councils, or an independent federation of producer (including farmer) and consumer cooperatives — the producers represented by the shop councils and industrial unions — with central planning and local administration. I preferred and at heart still prefer the second option. With most of the USPD, I regarded the Workers' and Soldiers' Councils as a provisional government, to be replaced by a freely elected multi-party parliament.

On November 9 there had been a huge antiwar demonstration in Berlin, in which my sister also participated; Karl Liebknecht had proclaimed a German Soviet Republic from a balcony of the Imperial Castle, and the "Kaiser-Socialist" Scheidemann had proclaimed a German Republic. An assembly of Workers' and

Soldiers' delegates gathered to elect a government of "People's Commissars."

Karl Liebknecht and Rosa Luxemburg were the leaders of the Spartacus League, which had originated within the USPD, but had seceded to form a third party, soon to be renamed the German Communist party (KPD). The assembly wanted a coalition of the three socialist parties, but the Spartacists refused to have anything to do with the "Kaiser-Socialists," the SPD. So the Council of People's Commissars was formed out of three leaders of the SPD and three of the USPD, with Fritz Ebert, the leader of the SPD, as its chairman.

I admired Liebknecht and Luxemburg, who had opposed the war from its first day and had been jailed, as martyrs of the revolution. But I was repelled by the language of their paper, *Red Flag*, in particular by a statement saying "Mistrust is the first revolutionary virtue" (actually a quote from Marx). I was and remain convinced that mistrust is the main factor responsible for war, even more so than lust for power and pelf.

For a long time I doubted the accusation of the Communists that the SPD had betrayed the revolution at the end of the war, as they had betrayed internationalism at its beginning. However, several years later Ebert proudly reported that his first act after his election was to call Hindenburg's headquarters in France, on the secret wire, asking his help in "restoring order" in Germany.

"Order" was indeed restored in the early months of 1919. *The Kaiser Goes, the Generals Remain,* to quote the title of a book describing these events by Theodor Plivier, a sailor who had been one of the leaders of the Kiel mutiny. In the army retreating from France under Hindenburg's command, the old lines of authority were maintained. In the armed forces in Germany and in the East, and also in civil government, authority had been assumed by Workers' and Soldiers' Councils.

This was indeed "the smashing of the bourgeois state" which Lenin had proclaimed. It had not involved, as I had feared, the smashing of skulls and of property. What had been "smashed" were the lines of command.

The "smashing" had, however, been far from complete. In civil government, and even more so in private enterprise, the authority of the Workers' Councils was in most, though not in all, cases purely nominal. An uneasy balance prevailed.

I had been keenly aware from the beginning of the danger of

the restoration of militarism. Immediately after the big meeting in Zossen on November 9, I urged my fellow soldiers to establish contact with nearby units, in order to organize an army for the defense of the revolution. They laughed me off; militarism was dead for good. They were more interested in the supplies of food and drink in the officers' casino.

I did not share their optimism. I knew that the revolution and socialism can only survive if its adherents are willing to risk their lives for it, if necessary in armed struggle.

I stayed in Zossen and tried to protect army supplies from being stolen for sale on the black market. But everything was falling to pieces, and after three weeks I shed the hated army uniform and returned to Hamburg, where my mother lived in a comfortable *pension*. I contacted the local USPD, propagated its program, and made a few converts. But this was clearly not enough.

SCHWERIN

A friend of a friend of my mother's, the writer Ernst Fuhrmann, told me of a group of young people in Schwerin who were preparing some action for Christmas. I traveled to Schwerin, found, on questioning, that they had little support, and concluded that they were a bunch of adventurers. I returned to Hamburg. Nothing happened in Schwerin at Christmas. I learned from Fuhrmann that the action had been postponed to January 6, 1919. I was plagued by doubts. The Schwerin group were putschists; but who else was doing anything? I asked the advice of the editor of the Hamburg USPD newspaper. He wanted me to go to Schwerin, but mainly to obtain a firsthand report for his paper. I remained undecided until the afternoon of the fifth; I finally made a decision and took the train to Schwerin. By a strange coincidence I overheard the woman taking the tickets at the station exit whisper to the man before me, "200 Volksmarines at R," a suburb of Schwerin. This increased my confidence.

The "Volksmarine Division," under the leadership of Navy Captain Paasche, was the most important of the revolutionary armed units which had been organized here and there in Germany.

I contacted one of the conspirators, B., a lawyer. He told me to return early the next morning. The putsch had succeeded during the night, and B. charged me with supervision of the telephone exchange. I put on a red armband and took command of the exchange, unarmed. I listened in on all long-distance calls and also reported to the Hamburg paper.

Not surprisingly, the success of the putsch did not last long. I heard rifle and machine-gun shots coming closer and realized that it had failed. But I stayed on, continuing my supervision; I had learnt that a soldier never leaves his post.

Some soldiers entered the exchange and arrested me. Some civilians, and later a soldier, wanted to beat me up, but my guards did not permit it. They brought me to a barracks basement where I found myself in the company of two-score men of the Volksmarine Division. I avoided talking to them, but felt badly when I heard later that two of them had been killed.

I realized that my situation was not without danger. As the only civilian and a student, I might be taken for the "intellectual author" of the putsch and shot on the spot. After several hours we were led out into a long hallway crowded with civilians. I managed to melt into the crowd, jumped out of a window, and walked toward the nearby forest. Soon shots rang out, but I succeeded in reaching cover.

Being familiar with the Schwerin area, I knew that I was on a long island, stretching from south to north for about twelve kilometers. One could leave the island only by the two bridges; if the authorities wanted to recapture me, all they had to do was to post a soldier at each bridge; I expected them to do this. I considered my best bet was to spend the night in the woods; by morning things would have calmed down and the danger of on-the-spot shotgun justice gone. Nobody stopped me when I crossed the northern bridge. I walked to the next station and took a train to Hamburg.

Probably as a result of spending a cold January night in the woods, I ran a fever. On the first evening I came down for dinner, two gentlemen met me, identifying themselves as members of the Schwerin police, and showed me a photo of B. I confirmed that I knew him and, on further questioning, said I had met him at Fuhrmann's. I took it for granted that B. had been arrested and was confident that Fuhrmann knew how to deal with the police.

As it happened, B. had escaped and was hiding at Fuhrmann's house, where he was arrested. The next morning the story, including my name, was in the paper. My poor uncle Aby was deeply embarrassed when his friends at the stock exchange peppered him with questions about his red nephew. But I was more embarrassed about my stupidity and of having thought only of saving my own hide. I still feel ashamed of having betrayed B. The consequences were not as serious as I had feared. In Schwerin justice was still in the hands of the Workers' and Soldiers' Council, and after a few weeks under arrest B. and other arrested leaders of the putsch were acquitted.

Without knowing it, I had been a participant in the historical Spartacus Revolt. At Christmas, government troops had evicted the Volksmarine Division from the Imperial Castle, after some fighting. On January 6, the Spartacists had stormed and occupied the building of the *Vorwärts,* the central organ of the SPD. The *Vorwärts* was the property of the Berlin organization of the SPD, which opposed the war. During the war the prowar Central Committee had stolen it from them, with the aid of the military authorities; the Spartacists reclaimed it for the revolutionary workers of Berlin.

The Spartacus Revolt was put down at the cost of several thousand lives. Rosa Luxemburg and Karl Liebknecht, who had opposed the revolt but had submitted to the majority of their party, were found a few days later and brutally murdered. This was the turning point of the German Revolution; from then on restoration proceeded apace.

MUNICH

I had planned to leave Hamburg for Munich a few days later; the visit by the police speeded up my departure. I went first to see Gertel, whom I had not seen for three years. German front-line soldiers were entitled to two weeks' home leave every nine months; but I had only one leave in three years. I had firmly intended to visit Gertel after seeing my mother, but unforeseen circumstances had interfered. Gertel wrote me a letter full of bitter disappointment. The letter had made me both sad and glad; sad because I had missed seeing her, and glad because it showed how much she still cared for me.

Oscar and Gertel Hagemann had left Grötzingen shortly after the outbreak of the war and now lived, with Gertel's elder sister, called "Tinny," and a maidservant, alone in another sixteenth-century castle in Sommerau, in the Spessart, a beautiful, scarcely populated area of forested hills located in the large loop of the Main River. Sommerau castle was a very romantic place; surrounded by a moat, it could be approached only by passing through a tree-lined driveway, over two bridges, and through three gates. Gertel could indulge her love of animals there with a pony, a donkey, a dog, and two parrots, supplemented at various times by other four-legged or feathered pets. I stayed for an enchanted week.

Tinny, Gertel, and I also spent two days in Frankfurt. As on later visits, we stayed at the "Baseler Hof." In the evening I sat for hours at her bedside, talking and occasionally stroking her soft golden hair. It did not occur to me to "go further." Incredible as it may sound, at the age of 26 I was still "innocent"; my sexuality was still asleep.

In Munich I resumed my studies, including attendance at Theodor Fischer's studio. In Bavaria, power was still in the hands of the Workers' and Soldiers' Council, with an USPD-SPD cabinet headed by Kurt Eisner, the leader of the USPD. There was still a revolutionary atmosphere, with mass meetings and demonstrations in which I participated. There was also a fairly large and lively socialist student group, which made me one of its delegates to the Workers' and Soldiers' Council. Among the speakers invited was the sociologist Max Weber, who was not a socialist but one of the founders of the Democratic party. I disagreed with almost everything he said but was greatly impressed by the person of this great mind.

Eisner, a firm believer in parliamentary democracy, called elections. They resulted in a crushing defeat of the USPD. Eisner, with his abdication speech in his pocket, was shot down by a right-wing fanatic. This set off a mass movement of protest; the Workers' and Soldiers' Council suspended parliament. There were long and heated debates in the council, with the Communists demanding the proclamation of a Soviet Republic. They were voted down by a strong majority of SPD, USPD, anarchist, and nonparty delegates.

I had agreed to meet Gertel at the home of one of her friends in Pforzheim, near Karlsruhe. I now called her, saying that in this critical situation I felt I could not leave Munich. She came to Munich and took a room in one of the best hotels; so did I. That night we became lovers.

I said to Gertel, "Now you must come to live with me." She was surprised; the notion struck her as fantastic. I insisted that she tell her husband; at our next meeting she said that she had not done so, but that he understood. Oscar and I really liked each other, but fate had made us rivals and I kept a certain distance, feeling that, "Whom God has separated, men should not unite."

In Munich tension mounted, and the demand for a Soviet Republic gained support; finally even the SPD delegates were for it. Now it was the Communists who opposed it, to the great indignation of most of the delegates, including myself. In fact, the Communists were simply more aware of the situation outside Bavaria, in the rest of Germany, as well as in Hungary and Austria, which in the past month had greatly deteriorated.

On April 7 the Bavarian Soviet Republic was proclaimed; its chairman was the anarchist Gustav Landauer, a pure idealist. When I received the news, I immediately got in touch with other members of the socialist student group at the Technical University. We went to see Landauer and received a document empowering us to establish a Revolutionary University Council. I approached Theodor Fischer, asking him to head the professors' section of the council; I hoped that he would seize the opportunity to put into practice his ideas for the reform of architectural education. He simply replied, "I am not a revolutionary." I was disappointed but respected his decision. A professor of engineering accepted the role.

We called a student meeting to ask them for a mandate to represent them. It was a stormy meeting. When in my speech I used the expression, "Our people," there were shouts of, "Which people?" Anti-Semitism was on the rise. I said, "As my person seems to be an obstacle, I resign." To my surprise, this turned the assembly around; the socialist candidates were confirmed by a substantial majority.

We had assumed that the support of the SPD delegates of the Workers' and Soldiers' Council implied that the SPD government would hand over power. Far from it, they moved to Nürnberg and called on troops from other German states to help them subdue the Munich "Reds." I realized that the "Bavarian Soviet Government" was stillborn and hoped for its peaceful liquidation. On a Sunday morning I learned that it had been overthrown by a right-wing putsch.

Gertel had invited me to spend my inter-term vacation at Sommerau. If I failed to respond a second time to her invitation, I feared that she might give up on me. So I boarded the first northbound train. I experienced unprecedented happiness; the weeks in Sommerau passed like a dream.

In Munich, on the afternoon of the same day, the Communists had mobilized the workers and had reestablished Soviet power under their own more militant and realistic leadership. I was torn; I felt my place was in Munich, but I could not tear myself away from Sommerau.

I arrived in Munich the day after the Soviets had been overthrown in bloody battle. The White Terror started. Train service into Munich had not yet been restored, and I walked five kilometers to my quarters, being stopped for identification by soldiers about half-a-dozen times.

The USPD was still operating legally. I went to party headquarters to offer my services. They were being flooded by stories about misdeeds, including murders, by the "Whites," and asked me to investigate and report. My first report, immediately published in the party's paper, was on Gustav Landauer, who had been brutally clubbed to death. The reply of the military command, published the next day, was the strangest denial I have ever encountered: "It was not a club, but a heavy stick, and it was swung not by an officer, but by a sergeant."

Complaints poured in from many sides. I established a "Legal Aid Office of the USPD." We needed money to rent an office, to support people in need, and to hire lawyers. I had inherited money. A quarter of it was in mortgages. I was convinced that their value would soon be eaten up anyway by inflation, and I instructed my bank in Hamburg to sell them immediately and to send me the money. Very reluctantly, the bank complied. I used the money to finance the legal aid. I also got minor financial contributions and some volunteer assistance from the USPD and the now illegal KPD.

It was full-time work. When the university, which had remained closed for about six weeks because many of the students served as volunteers in the White Guards, reopened, I had no time to attend.

I obtained official recognition from the "commissar" who had been put in charge of work similar to mine by the Social Democratic government, and I was allowed to visit the prisons where the political prisoners were held. I found their conditions were quite fair, apart from the food, which was very short everywhere in Germany. I could talk freely to Ernst Toller, the anarchist poet Erich Mühsam, and other leaders of the Munich revolution. But I also found that many men were being held without charge.

When I submitted a request to release the prisoners held without charge to the military commander in control of political prisoners, a Major Seisser, he seemed inclined to agree; respect for due process was not yet dead in Germany. But after he saw his assistant, a Captain Roth, energetically shaking his head, he refused. Much later, in 1934, when Hitler "liquidated" many of his inconvenient conservative supporters as well as the leadership of his own storm troopers (SA), Seisser was one of his victims. Roth made a brilliant career under the Nazis.

This case illustrates clearly the fundamental difference between conservatives and fascists, a difference too easily overlooked or at least underestimated by many of my left-wing friends.

In all of Germany the proletarian revolution had been defeated. The basic power structure had reasserted itself: the landowners, the captains of industry, the military officers, the civil servants, the judiciary, the academic barons. The USPD members had resigned from the "Council of People's Commissars"; the rump government consisting of the three SPD members had called an election. The new Reichstag, still fearful of the revolutionary workers of Berlin, met at Weimar and adopted the constitution of the Republic and the colors of the 1848 revolution, Black-Red-Gold. A coalition government was formed by the SPD, the Democrats, and the Catholic Center party.

The Weimar Republic was not the Kaiser's Empire. The reforms achieved in the first months of the revolution could not easily be abolished. They were those that had been pioneered by the Russian Revolution: the eight-hour working day (previously found only in Queensland, Australia), unemployment insurance (previously only in Great Britain), and paid vacations for workers. Most important was official recognition of the labor movement: shop stewards, factory councils, and trade unions. Also, cultural life, which had been budding strongly during the two preceding decades, burst into flower during the Weimar Republic.

The question "Reform or revolution?" is a false question. Substantial reforms are conceded only when revolution is feared. On the other hand, the work of a revolution consists in carrying out reforms which, at least in principle, could have been implemented without it. But revolutions greatly accelerate reforms; they are, in Marx's words, the locomotives of history.

The right-wing opposition, which was unwilling to accept Germany's defeat and longed for the full restoration of the Kaiser's Empire, gained adherents by ranting against "the shameful Treaty of Versailles." But their main weapon was terror. Liebknecht, Luxemburg, Landauer, Paasche, and Eisner were not their only victims; there were many others, including Hugo Haase, the leader of the USPD. The press in the Western countries paid little attention to the terror; after all, only Reds were being murdered. Only when a leader of the Center party, Erzberger, who as minister of finance had introduced a federal income tax, was murdered, did they take notice. But it was then and there that the seeds of Nazism were planted.

Bavaria was — and is — the most reactionary of the German states; Hitler got his start in Munich. At the time, he took his meals in a vegetarian restaurant named "Ethos," where I also took most of mine. I probably have seen him more than once, but he left no impression.

THE "MURDER CENTER BLUMENFELD"

I lived in a furnished room in a small apartment in a workers' quarter of Munich. My landlady, an elderly widow, was a devout Catholic. One day in August 1919, to the good lady's horror, a policeman came to arrest me. At police headquarters I was fingerprinted and questioned, then sent to Stadelheim Prison, on suspicion of "participation in murder."

What had happened? Among the many people to come to our Legal Aid Office for financial support, one of the most assiduous visitors was a certain Blau. One of my aides, H., had become suspicious and, in searching Blau's luggage, had found conclusive proof that he was a spy in the service of the "Guards Cavalry Rifle Division," one of the right-wing armed outfits that had sprung up in Germany in 1919, in gross violation of the Treaty of Versailles but with the tacit support of the "democratic" government of the Weimar Republic; it was later revealed that this division had employed over 400 spies!

On the day after my arrest, the *Bayerischer Kourier,* organ of the then-ruling Bavarian wing of the Catholic Center party, carried a big headline: "Communist Murder Center Uncovered!" The center had been headed by a student named Blumenfeld, now safely locked up; the good burghers of Bavaria could go to sleep quietly.

So did I. "Participation in murder" was punishable by death, but I was unconcerned. Due process had in the meantime been restored in Germany, and the whole story was absurd. H. had told me that he was accompanying Blau to Berlin on the latter's insistence. Somewhat later, at a meeting of Communist Youth, Blau had been unveiled as a spy and had been killed. H. had reappeared in Munich, had told me of Blau's death, and said that he was under suspicion, though he had nothing to do with it, which I believed, knowing him as an honest and decent man.

The story of the accusation was that I had planned and organized the murder of Blau, using H. as a middleman. While I was held in prison, I was called to see the Berlin judge who was in charge of investigating the Blau case. He confronted me with a man called Schreiber, who had also been one of the clients of our Legal Aid; I had even put him up one night on the couch in my room. Schreiber testified as follows: "I had hired him and five other men to serve in the Red Army in Hungary; I had made them swear allegiance in the light of a red flame burning on a tripod." I told the judge that my landlady could testify that there never had been a tripod in my room, and that I never had more than one visitor at a time. At the end of my testimony the judge took my oath. Under German law no witness can be admitted to oath if there is any suspicion that he might be involved in the crime under investigation.

It was evident that the murder charge was a pretext; the purpose was to stop embarrassing revelations by the Legal Aid Office. That purpose was achieved: the Legal Aid Office ceased to operate; it had remained basically a one-man operation. When my lawyer asked the police president for my release, the answer was, "We will release him if he ceases his activities." My lawyer countered, "You mean his activities as a murderer?" There was no reply.

After five weeks I was released but ordered to leave Bavaria within three days and to stay out. There was, of course, no legal basis for barring a German citizen from any part of Germany. I overstayed the three days. On the fourth a policeman appeared, ordered me to pick up my belongings, and accompanied me to the railroad station, where I was put on a train to Darmstadt.

Prison is never a pleasure, but the five weeks at Stadelheim were not too bad. The prison guards treated me correctly, even politely. I suspect their reasoning was as follows: "One never can know which way the wind will be blowing; the USPD had just achieved great success at the elections to the Munich City Council; the pendulum might swing back. Less than a year ago they had held a man who soon after became minister of justice; maybe this fellow Blumenfeld would become their next superior."

Whatever the reason, I was treated well. My sister, who had come to Munich, was allowed to see me and to bring me clean underwear, some food, and books. At long last I had time to read Marx's *Capital;* I was impressed by the sweep and depth of his thought. I also read Oswald Spengler's *Decline of the West,* which contains many pertinent observations on aspects of history which have nothing to do with the title.

CHAPTER IV

Last Student Years

1919 – 1921

DARMSTADT

I had chosen Darmstadt, an institution in the state of Hesse, not because of its faculty, but because of its geographic location. It was close both to Sommerau and to Heidelberg, where my mother had resumed her studies. I was 27 years old and felt that it was time to graduate as soon as possible and to start practical work.

I continued political work. The local organization of the USPD put me on its executive; I was also chairman of the small socialist student group which cooperated closely with an equally small democratic group; there was also a somewhat larger group of Catholic students. But the great majority of students supported a right-wing group.

It so happened that the only participants in a seminar on art history were the leaders of the right-wing and Catholic groups and myself. It is characteristic of the relatively civilized atmosphere that still prevailed at most German universities, despite the greatly heightened political tension, that our relations were very friendly; in private discussions we honestly tried to understand the others' views.

The Kapp Putsch. In March 1920 the right-wing "Kapp Putsch" erupted. General Lüttwitz, the commander of the Berlin region, had occupied Berlin and proclaimed a "Government of Experts," headed by the ultraconservative president of Eastern Prussia,

Kapp. The loyalty of army commanders in other regions was in doubt. The Social Democratic government of Hesse of course supported the Weimar regime, but the situation was tense.

As soon as news of the putsch arrived in Darmstadt, a meeting was called at the trade union hall. It was decided to form a "Workers' Defense" force with a unified leadership consisting of three representatives of each the SPD and the USPD and one of the KPD, which had only seven members in Darmstadt. The latter proposed their local leader, a man kicked out of the USPD because he had stolen party funds; he was, of course, not acceptable to the assembly. Carlo Mierendorff, a Darmstadt member of the USPD who was studying in Heidelberg, whispered to me that Theodor Haubach, who also studied in Heidelberg, was at home in Darmstadt. I proposed that he be elected to represent the Communists; this was accepted by the assembly.

Haubach had written a brilliant pamphlet debunking the legend promoted by Ludendorff, who had been the chief of staff of the Imperial Army; the legend claimed that the war had been lost because the "victorious German Army" had been stabbed in the back by traitors at home: Communists, Socialists, and Democrats, all allegedly led by Jews.

It turned out that Haubach was far from being a Communist, as I had assumed; he said to me, "Bolshevism is a purely Asiatic affair." Anyway, the leadership now consisted of seven members: three SPD, three USPD, including myself, and Haubach. It was headed by SPD member Leuschner, who was the head of the Trade Union Federation of Hesse; I was impressed by his ability.

Mierendorff and Haubach later became members of the Reichstag; Haubach became the founder and leader of the "Reichsbanner Schwarz-Rot-Gold," the paramilitary organization of the Weimar coalition.

It was these three men from Darmstadt, Leuschner, Haubach, and Mierendorff, who represented social democracy in the "Kreisauer Kreis" around Count Moltke, which tried to create a democratic Germany to replace Hitler. After the failure of the attempt of the General Staff of the German Army to overthrow Hitler, all members of the "Kreisauer Kreis" were arrested by the SS and executed.

At the time of the Kapp Putsch, a group of ten, including Mierendorff and myself, all unarmed except Mierendorff, who had an old Browning, requisitioned a dozen rifles from a post of the "Heimwehr," which was manned by three men who offered no resistance. The "Heimwehr" had been organized all over Germany, with the approval of the Weimar government, to defend "law and order" against the "Reds." Their members came from the middle classes; most, though not all, of them were right wing and certainly not prepared to defend the Republic against the Kapp Putsch.

Other groups of workers proceeded as our group had. By evening a Workers' Defense Force of more than 300 men, all armed with rifles, was in being and occupied critical points in the city.

Similar Workers' Forces had been created all over Germany and, in places where the situation had been more critical than Darmstadt, were instrumental in defeating the putsch, which collapsed within a week. As soon as it was again in control, the Weimar government turned around and ordered the Reichswehr generals, many of whom had shown an ambivalent wait-and-see attitude when the putsch started, to disarm the workers. The SPD and Haubach were willing to comply; we of the USPD mistrusted the Reichwehr. While our discussions were still going on, the question became moot. The French army occupied Darmstadt, and we agreed that the workers had to turn in their arms.

The members of the USPD managed to scratch together enough money and material — I contributed, in the form of a loan, an electric motor to drive the printing press — to start a weekly newspaper called the *Workers' Newspaper for South-Hesse*. An engineer, Fritz Löw, edited it in his spare time. Soon after, Löw was offered a much better job in another town and left Darmstadt. The party asked me to take over. It was quite a job; we were often short of suitable material, and in some issues I filled the four pages almost entirely with my own writing.

Lenin had founded the Third International, "Comintern," and there was strong feeling within the USPD to join as a sign of solidarity with the Russian Revolution, which had succeeded against hell and high water where we had failed. Many others were opposed, because they could not accept the top-down centralized structure; joining the Third International meant joining the small German Communist party (KPD). I wrote a number of articles analyzing the arguments of both sides. When I visited the offices of the Frankfurt paper of the USPD, one of the editors asked me, "Are you for or against joining?" "Did you not read my articles?"

I said. She replied, "That's why I am asking!" I, like most members of the USPD, preferred its more democratic decentralized structure but felt that international solidarity was the overriding issue.

In December 1920 the National Congress of the USPD met at Halle. Zinoviev, then the leader of the Comintern, made important concessions as to party structure. A substantial majority voted for fusion with the KPD; the minority continued for about two years as the USPD and then merged with the SPD.

Just before the Halle Congress the business manager of our Darmstadt newspaper had absconded with several thousand marks, leaving the paper deeply in debt. It had to be liquidated. This was the end of my career as a journalist. I reclaimed my motor to install it in a farmhouse which we had just bought, and where it drove the pump previously operated by hand.

BRUNSTORF

Since we had given up our Hamburg apartment in 1913, my mother had been living in hotels or *pensions*. With inflation rapidly evaporating our inherited fortune, I feared that she would not be able to continue this lifestyle for long. I wanted her to be assured of a permanent, comfortable home, as well as of adequate food, and considered ownership of a farm to be the only solution. I also thought of farming myself if the prospects for architectural employment continued to be as bleak as they were at the time.

My mother was not enthusiastic about my proposal but finally consented. I traveled to Hamburg, talked to an agent, and visited several farms in the Hamburg area which he had listed for sale. I found the right one at Brunstorf, 32 kilometers east of Hamburg, at the eastern edge of the large and beautiful "Saxon Forest" which in the early Middle Ages separated the Saxons from the Slavs. The farm included four acres of that forest, in addition to fields and pastures which were scattered around in various locations, following the inherited medieval pattern.

My farm was one of the eight "full-peasant" holdings in Brunstorf. The "peasants" looked down on the "craftsmen," who owned smaller amounts of land; they in turn looked down on the landless workers. The reverend was included in the peasant clubs, the teacher in the craftsmen's! The class structure in the village was much more rigid than that in the city.

The only city people among the some two hundred inhabitants of Brunstorf were the family of the retired army captain from whom I bought the farm. He had greatly improved the house, installing a bathroom and — in terms of 1920 Germany — "modern" kitchen equipment.

The dwelling was a typical "Lower-Saxon Peasant House," probably about a hundred years old, built of half timber and brick, with a huge thatched roof; as in all these houses, only the eastern part, protected from the predominant, often stormy, west winds, was used for human habitation. The much larger western part was reserved to the animals, the cows occupying one side and the horses, plus the pump and some farm implements, the other side of a large space into which the hay wagons were driven. The hay was unloaded through a trap in the ceiling into the huge space under the roof. The inhabited rooms, three on the first and two and a half on the second floor, all faced east, onto the large garden, with many trees and shrubs — some of them fruit bearing — flower beds, and a pavilion surrounding the lawn. Along the south side ran a street; to the north was the farmyard with pigsty and chicken coops.

I found a competent and reliable farmer, Mr. Graff, who already operated most of the church lands, to work the farm. Our contract did not stipulate a monetary rent, which I knew would soon lose its value; it called for the annual delivery of specified amounts of rye, potatoes, milk, butter, meat, and eggs. Later, after the mark had been stabilized, we converted the rent into equivalent money terms. We shared the house with the Graffs. They occupied the ground floor and we the second. I added three bedrooms and a bath on the north side of the second floor, lit by a long dormer window fitted into the thatched roof. I never put a line on paper to convey my design to the building craftsmen but designated everything to them on the spot and participated in their work. I was well satisfied with my first architectural creation. This happened, however, only in 1921, after the previous occupants had moved out.

SOMMERAU

In 1920 I was still in Darmstadt. Most of my weekends were spent with Gertel in Sommerau. We went for long walks together and for horseback rides. Gertel loved it when I read to her while she worked. We also made overnight trips to neighboring old towns and beauty spots. With my knowledge of art history, I was a knowledgeable guide, but she experienced beauty much more deeply. We visited Tilman Riemenschneider's altar at Creglingen near Rothenburg, a masterpiece of woodcarving; when we were alone in the little village chapel, she broke into tears. "If only I could make that," she sighed. She had started, on my urging, to carve in wood; but as she simply used a kitchen knife, she found the work physically demanding.

Gertel also invented a new technique of painting. For a while she had been collecting Bavarian peasant paintings. They consisted of a single layer of paint on the backside of glass. Gertel applied the multilayer technique of oil painting to painting behind glass. It is a difficult technique because the top layer has to be put on first, but she mastered it easily, thanks to her marvelous imagination, which was as exact as it was imaginative and dreamlike.

Many of these pictures now hang on the walls of my apartment in Toronto; Gertel was always generous in giving them to her friends, but she cried as for a lost child when one was sold.

One day, when I came back to Darmstadt, I found a letter from Tinny, Gertel's elder sister. She said that she was alone at Sommerau and sick, and urged me to come immediately. When I called, Gertel, who had meanwhile returned, replied that there was no need for me to come before the weekend.

For some time Tinny had been taking less and less food and had dwindled to a skeleton. One evening, a few weeks after her letter, she asked Gertel to sing Schubert's "Death and the Maiden." Gertel sat down at the piano; I turned the pages. When I glanced back at Tinny, I was frightened; Tinny was staring wide-eyed into infinity. When she left to go to bed, she asked me to come to see her, after I would have left Gertel. When I entered her room, she asked me to sit down at her bedside, and she said, "Promise me to never leave Gertel." I could not imagine a life without Gertel and gave her my promise. She then asked me to sit down at her bedside for the night. I was surprised but agreed. When Tinny noticed my eyelids drooping, she said with a sigh, "You are tired; go to bed." I left, went to bed, and slept soundly.

When I came down the next morning, the house was in alarm. Tinny had died, alone; I had failed her in her last hour. Nobody had noticed her death; only Gertel's little green parrot was sitting at her bedside, something which he had never done before. Do animals have deeper feelings than humans?

Tinny had suffered from no disease; apparently she had deliberately starved herself to death. Why? Years later, when I reread her strange letter and pondered all I knew about her, I realized that she had loved me. Had she left this earth in order not to interfere with my and Gertel's love? Was I the cause of her death? I will never know.

In the fall, Oscar and Gertel gave up Sommerau and moved back to Karlsruhe. I drove Gertel's pony wagon to Karlsruhe, a three-day journey through the autumn landscape.

1921, YEAR OF CRISES

The "March Action." I was now a member of the newly united Communist Party of Germany (KPD). For the first few months this changed nothing, as the old KPD had very few members in Darmstadt.

In central Germany, the main stronghold of the Party, many workers had retained their arms. When the Weimar government ordered the Reichswehr to disarm them, armed struggles erupted. The KPD, on urging by the Comintern, called for a general strike. The Darmstadt leadership, fearing arrest, went into hiding and asked me to take charge of the Party in South Hessen during their absence. I traveled to our main strongholds in the region, including the big Opel Auto plant in Rüsselsheim, with my rucksack stuffed with leaflets. Everywhere the workers refused to move; they had sense enough to understand that the "Action" was bound to fail and would backfire. So did the leader of the Party, Paul Levi, who had opposed it from the beginning and criticized it sharply after its collapse. He was excluded from the Party. His attitude was shared by another leader of the Party, Clara Zetkin. She was one of the historical leaders of the international socialist movement, highly respected by everyone, including Lenin. When Fritz Heckert, in the name of the leadership of the KPD, asked Lenin's consent to Zetkin's exclusion, Lenin is reported to have replied, "I would lay your head before your feet — if you had one." This was not quite fair to Heckert, whom I later met in Moscow. He certainly was not an intellectual giant, but I found him to be an honest man, totally dedicated to the cause of the working class.

Maulbronn. During my winter term in Darmstadt, I often visited Gertel in Karlsruhe; we also continued to make overnight trips. In April 1921 we went to Maulbronn, a medieval monastery. Gertel's friends had invited us to spend the following night with them at Pforzheim. When we arrived, Oscar awaited us at the door, asked me not to enter, and went in with Gertel. Gertel's friend came out and advised me to wait until morning. I took a room in a hotel next door. It so happened that from my window I could look into a room of the house, where I observed Oscar and Gertel engaged in serious quiet conversation, Gertel from time to time nodding or shaking her head. When I went to the house the next morning, I learnt that they had returned to Karlsruhe. I took the next train to Karlsruhe, rented a room in a hotel close to their home, and penned a letter to Oscar which was delivered by an employee of the hotel. I wrote to Oscar that I understood his feelings but asked him to have a talk. He came to my hotel room. He said, "I do not want a wife with two men." I said that it was up to Gertel to make her choice. He agreed, and we returned together to his home. When we told Gertel of our agreement, she objected. "I love both of you," she said. When both of us insisted, she fell silent for a long time, looking from one to the other; finally she put her hand into mine. She later told me that looking into our eyes, she saw that Oscar's were cold and hard, and mine were warm and tender; that had decided her.

I had won Gertel; but what next? I could not take her to my small furnished room in Darmstadt; I could not ask her to leave her lovingly furnished nest for a cold hotel room. Gertel and Oscar retired to a neighboring room. After about an hour Gertel came back; she said, "I cannot leave him alone like that." I knew she was right; Oscar had nobody in the world but Gertel. He had no friends and his relations with his mother were cool. His love for Gertel was deep and genuine.

Oscar asked that I allow Gertel three months to think it over, during which time I would not see her. I readily agreed; I was sure that three months' separation would make no difference. I left and returned to Darmstadt late in the night.

What with Gertel occupying my heart; the political struggle, my mind; and the search for a farm, my body, my studies had gotten short shrift. Not surprisingly, I failed several subjects in my final exam; on a second try, some weeks later, I managed to squeeze through.

With this burden off my back, wanderlust took over again. I first went to Uhenfels, my uncle's estate in Swabia, where my mother was visiting, then set out to wander southward, visiting old towns, churches, and monasteries. I had mentioned my plans to a fellow student, Leonie P., one of the few Communists among the students. She had expressed interest in joining me, to which I responded ambiguously. I was aware that she was in love with me, but for me Gertel was the only woman on earth, and I wanted Leonie to remain just a friend and comrade; as usual, I got my way.

Leonie arrived at Uhenfels to find that I had just left, but caught up with me at my next stop. We hiked as good friends southward through the green meadows and forests of the sub-alpine hill country. I was enchanted by this landscape and quite satisfied with having the Alps just as a backdrop. But Leonie, who was from Vienna, wanted to hike in the mountains. To my surprise, we received permission to cross into Austria without trouble. After the war it had been difficult for Germans to leave the country, and I had felt very much cooped up. Once I found that the frontiers were no longer so tight, longing to be in Italy once more took over, and I decided to make a trip to Verona and Venice which I had planned almost ten years earlier, in Munich in 1912, but had deferred at that time. We hiked a few days in the Vorarlberg Alps. Then, on a Friday at dawn, I set out for a 60-kilometer hike, including a 1000-meter climb, to Innsbruck; but the Italian Consulate had closed an hour before my arrival.

Prison once again. Rather than wait for Monday for a visa which probably would be refused anyway, I decided to take a chance and enter Italy illegally. I figured that, if I was caught, the penalty probably would be a fine or an arrest of no more than a week. The penalty was indeed a week of arrest, but it took four weeks for the decision to arrive from Rome.

I had crossed the border unnoticed, hiking over the mountains in drizzling rain; but on the railroad platform an Italian soldier asked for my identification papers and took me into custody. Accompanied by this rather pleasant young fellow, I boarded my train as scheduled and left it, as scheduled, at Brixen, which the Italians had renamed Bressanone, where I landed in the county jail.

Including the few hours during which I was locked up in the

Schwerin barracks, the four weeks at Brixen were my fourth prison experience, and it turned out to be the most unpleasant one. This was in no way due to ill will. The guards, all inherited from the Austrian regime, were as friendly as could be; we were allowed long hours to play or talk in the large, sunny prison yard. My fellow inmates were pleasant; most of them were young German or Austrian workers who, like myself, had tried to cross the frontier illegally. The man whom I liked best, however, was in for second-degree murder; he was a farm hand who had slain his boss during a dispute.

But the beds crawled with vermin and the food left one hungry. We were two in a fair-sized room. My first partner, a young Austrian, was a devout Catholic. I was taken aback by the violence of his hatred of the rich; I had never encountered such intense hostility among Socialist or Communist workers. Because they understood the class structure of society, they realized that their class enemies acted as they did because of their role in the structure rather than from personal viciousness. It is not the least of the merits of Marxism that it can immunize the oppressed and exploited against the corroding venom of personal hatred.

After a week my first cell-mate was released, and his place was taken by a young German worker. I had some money, and every day I bought a small loaf of bread which I, of course, shared with him. One day he threw his piece down, saying, "I do not want your bread if you watch every bite I take." I of course denied his accusation, but I knew it was true and felt and feel ashamed of it. He was a proud and moody man, and there was deep sadness in his eyes when I was released and took leave of him.

Compared to what many of my friends and comrades went through and, in particular, were to go through in the following four decades, my prison experiences were of course minor jokes. But they made me realize what prison can do to men; and abolition of prisons is even more important to me than abolition of the death sentence. I do not dare propose it, because I know of no substitute for the purpose of general deterrence; but we must make every effort to find one and should certainly reduce the number of persons sent to jail.

Returning home. After my release I took a look at Innsbruck and at the old monastery of Stams in Tirol. While I was sketching the building, a boy of about seventeen, the monastery's cowherd, asked me if I would be willing to make a drawing of his favorite cow. I was; he liked the portrait and gave me a few shillings. It is the only money I ever earned by my artistic talents.

I returned to Darmstadt and soon after to Brunstorf to complete my master's thesis, which I mailed to the university. It was accepted and I received my degree.

I had toyed with the idea of proceeding to doctoral studies. I knew what my thesis would be: the form of cities as determined by their function. The theme has stayed with me, though I have learned that it is not the one-to-one relation I had assumed. My first article on city planning, published in America in 1943, was entitled "Form and Function in Urban Communities," and I have returned to it time and again. I consider the interaction between form and function to be the central problem of city planning and building.

But by the fall of 1921 I was approaching the age of thirty, and it was time to finally start practical work and to learn to stand on my own feet. I was hired by a small architect's office in Hamburg. At the end of the week I received a letter from my boss saying that he had no time to train apprentices; no check was enclosed. It was not an auspicious beginning.

I took the hint and started to work with another architect as an apprentice, with only pocket money as remuneration. He introduced me to all aspects of architectural practice, very thoroughly and conscientiously.

When I had returned from Darmstadt and told my mother of my intention to live with Gertel, she was not happy. She had met Gertel immediately after our first night in Munich and liked her very much, and Gertel adored my mother. But my mother was opposed to my marrying her. I was, indeed, neither economically nor emotionally ready for marriage. My prospects for employment were poor. I would not starve; my mother would see to that. My mother in turn, recalling that her father had left her an equal share of the family fortune which was invested in the Warburg bank, felt entitled to a share of its earnings, and her banker brother would not refuse her the money she needed. But I could not accept the situation that I, a Communist, should live on the charity of a millionaire capitalist.

There were several additional difficulties. Gertel wanted to have a child by me; because of a hip broken in her childhood by a fall from a horse, this would require a Caesarean section. Gertel was repelled by the thought of having to appear in court, and she refused a formal divorce. With her unlimited courage and total contempt for convention she wanted just to live with me. I knew what this would mean in the Germany of the 1920s; nor was I willing to have a child which would legally be that of another man. Finally, I feared that a being living as intensely as Gertel could not live long. I had noticed that many living at a high pitch of intensity, both painters and musicians, had died between the ages of 33 and 37: Giorgione, Raphael, Watteau, Géricault, Van Gogh, Mozart, Bizet — and Gertel was 31. Actually, Gertel lived to be 49, when she was felled by a brain hemorrhage, without any previous warning.

With all these thoughts on my mind, it was no wonder I was depressed. My mother went to see Gertel for a week and told her that I was not happy, as one would expect a bridegroom to be. In the end Gertel stayed with Oscar, and my relation to her remained as before. But instead of being separated by the one-hour train ride from Darmstadt to Karlsruhe we were now parted by almost 1000 kilometers, and I was tied down by a five-and-one-half-day working week. So our meetings became few and far between.

Gertel came to visit us. My mother had come to like Brunstorf, and I loved it. So did Gertel; she called it "a unique combination of greatest simplicity and highest culture." In September we had a week of perfect happiness at Kampen on the island of Sylt. It was after the holiday season; a strong west wind was blowing, and we both loved the stormy North Sea.

CHAPTER V

Journeyman Architect

1921 – 1930

HAMBURG

After four months of apprenticeship, I finally got my first regular job, with the architects Hans and Oscar Gerson. I did not obtain it on my merits; the Gerson brothers had a big commission to renovate and enlarge the Warburg bank.

I soon came to like and respect Hans and Oscar Gerson, both as architects and as human beings. By German standards of the time, it was a medium-sized firm with about a dozen people employed. With the exception of the typist, all were called "architects" and were on an equal footing. Specialization had not yet taken over; all of us dealt with all aspects of architectural practice: designing, drafting, writing specifications, dealing with clients, contractors, and building inspectors, and supervising on the site. Most of us were younger men, university-trained. But there were also three slightly older men who had been trained at the very good local building-trade school. We academics often asked them for advice; they never needed ours.

Generally, I liked my work. Most of my time was taken up with supervising a cooperative apartment containing ten six-room apartments and servants' quarters in the attic.

Inflation was accelerating; materials were in short and erratic supply at wildly fluctuating prices. The contractor, a man with a reputation for solid work, resorted to shortcuts and used an inferior brand of cement. When I noticed it, I ordered work stopped. The contractor and his assistant invited me to a nearby tavern "to talk things over." They plied me with beer and "schnapps" with the obvious intention of getting me stone drunk. I left, gulped down several cups of black coffee, and returned to the site, where, as I had suspected, work was going on. I stopped it again and called the building inspector to back me up, which he did. For several days the site lay idle, while wages, of course, had to be paid.

In proletarian solidarity, I also leaked to the carpenters knowledge of extra pay which the contractor had granted to the bricklayers. The carpenters demanded and got the same. Soon after the building was completed, the contractor stated that it was I who had driven him to bankruptcy. Maybe I did, and I felt sorry for him. But I would not have acted differently even if I had foreseen the consequences.

Each one of the future occupants, or their wives, wanted changes in the plan of their apartment. For each change I had to make a drawing, get a cost estimate, and see to it that the changes were carried out correctly. When the building was completed, there was a mountain of bills to be paid to the cooperative by each individual member. I was charged with sorting out the mountain and adding up every cooperator's debt. It was an absurd task, because during the construction period inflation had reduced the value of the mark by about nine-tenths. It just did not make sense to me to spend weeks on end adding up apples and oranges, and I threw up my job.

I had a commission in mind. I had become friends with Fritz Saxl, an art historian from Vienna who was the director of the Warburg Library — it was not yet called an Institute. Saxl's father-in-law, who lived in London, had sent him £400 to build himself a house; Saxl had acquired an option on a site and commissioned me to be his architect.

I designed the house, found a reliable contractor, went over the drawings with him, and drew up a contract. The contractor was willing to undertake the job at the stipulated price but wanted to be paid in dollars rather than in pounds, so Saxl exchanged his pounds against dollars. My contract was signed by both parties. Also, to forestall inflation, I bought a sufficient quantity of cement from a fellow worker in the Gerson office.

The house was never built; fortunately, I would say. It would have been quite comfortable to live in, but the architecture was mediocre, to put it mildly.

Saxl got frightened by the unanticipated complexities of building a house and decided that it would be wiser for him to buy one. By mutual agreement the contract was cancelled, and Saxl relinquished his option, at some cost. He lost much more when he reconverted his dollars into pounds to repay his father-in-law. Churchill had chosen just that week to raise the price of the pound versus the dollar. At the same time the invisible hand of the market, in its inscrutable way, had dropped the price of cement. I got rid of my hoard only after much trouble and at a sizable loss. So the result of my first commission was: house not built; client loses money; architect loses money.

This was the end of my career as an independent architect.

I continued to be an active member of the KPD. In my trade union, the League of Technical Employees and Civil Servants ("Butab"), I led the small leftist opposition. We had sharp discussions, but they did not weaken our solidarity. I looked on the Social Democrats, who were in the majority, as erring brothers whom we had to lead back to the true revolutionary path which their leaders had deserted at the beginning of the war.

In the Party I met Rudolf and Edith Hommes. He was a high-school teacher, unemployed for years, and the vice-chairman of the party in Hamburg; she taught in a business school; both became lifelong friends. Through Hommes I met Ernst Thälmann, who was to become the national leader of the KPD three years later. At that time he still worked in a shipyard and was the chairman of the Hamburg KPD. I liked Ernst Thälmann, and the feeling was mutual — surprisingly, considering his mistrust of intellectuals. I lived at the edge of a workers' district where he also lived. After he returned from his first trip to the Soviet Union an attempt had been made on his life, and at a meeting of the district organization we decided that three of us should stand guard at his apartment. When Thälmann returned, he said, "Boys, go home. I can take care of myself." We chatted; he had been greatly impressed by Lenin. He also said of the Soviet Union, "I do not know if I would like to live there." Later, in early 1924, when I told him that I was going to the USA, he said, "You will like it; it is a good country." I asked with surprise, "Have you been there?" He explained that, while working as a seaman, he had jumped ship and had worked for a few months as a longshoreman on the Brooklyn waterfront. He also told me of the tricks the Hamburg longshoremen used to break up boxes with desirable contents and to smuggle the loot through the guards. I knew him as a warm, sensitive human being, full of humor, not the red plaster-saint of his official biography. In every respect, including his amusements, he was a workers' worker, and he had an almost uncanny ability to anticipate workers' reactions; he had a very quick intelligence. Above all, he was a man of unflinching courage. The Nazis arrested him in the first weeks of their rule. They tortured him for twelve years in the hope of forcing him to make a statement in their favor. He never caved in, and they murdered him shortly before their fall.

In 1922, Joseph Wirth was chancellor. He had succeeded Erzberger as leader of the left wing of the Catholic Center party and had become leader of his party. The Center was the only party which participated in all governments of the Weimar Republic. Later it preferred coalitions with the right, largely under the influence of the clever and powerful papal nuncio, Cardinal Pacelli, later Pope Pius xii.

The minister of foreign affairs in Wirth's cabinet was the Democrat Walther Rathenau, a remarkable and controversial figure. My friend, the art historian Erwin Panofsky, who had a sharp tongue, called him "Jesus in coattails." He was the multi-millionaire head of the AEG, which, with its rival Siemens, dominated Germany's electrical industry. He had been the main proponent and organizer of Germany's war economy. He believed in state capitalism and wrote about it. In one of his books he wrote, "Nobody will own much; only one will be immeasurably rich, the state." It was not a view to endear him to the property-owning right. But his greatest crime in their eyes was the Treaty of Rapallo, concluded by Rathenau, who was Jewish, with the presumably Jewish-dominated Soviet Union. He was shot dead by a fanatic in June 1922.

The murder of Rathenau touched off a huge wave of protest and demands that government clamp down on the right-wing terror groups. Millions of SPD, USPD, and KPD followers marched through the streets of all German cities in united demonstrations, joined by non-socialist democrats. The movement was entirely nonviolent but so powerful that it could not be disregarded. Wirth attempted to include the USPD in his government, but the negotiations collapsed.

Wirth remained true to his left-democratic convictions. After

World War II, which he survived by several years, he supported the (East) German Democratic Republic as a member of the Christian Democratic party.

The protest movement against the murder of Rathenau was the last of the three great waves of the German antimilitarist movement, following the overthrow of the Kaiser in November 1918 and the defeat of the Kapp Putsch in March 1920. This wave ebbed even faster than the two previous ones.

In November 1922 the center-right Cuno government took over. It repudiated Germany's obligation to pay the reparations stipulated by the Versailles treaty and asked for renegotiation. The French, in retaliation, occupied the Ruhr; the mark collapsed completely. Unrest grew; for the first time Hitler's party became important. The cynicism of Nazi demagoguery is still not completely understood. Racism certainly is a constituent of Nazi ideology. But at that time I saw with my own eyes, on the streets of Hamburg, Nazi posters which called on the workers of the Ruhr to fraternize with the black and white French proletarians in common struggle against French imperialism!

Western, in particular American, corporations had invested heavily in Germany after the war. They felt that it was time to bring Germany back into the family and to help it get back onto its feet; a compromise on reparations payments was worked out in the form of the Dawes Plan. In August 1923 Cuno was replaced as chancellor by Stresemann. The French agreed to evacuate the Ruhr area.

I viewed this as the end of the postwar period and the beginning of a long period of capitalist stabilization in Germany and Europe. My estimate was correct; what I overlooked was that between the agreement to put Germany back on its feet and its implementation several months would pass, during which inflation and tension would reach their peak.

For almost five years I had felt myself obliged to be available if some revolutionary event required my participation. Work for socialism continued to be as necessary as ever, I felt, but for years on end it would be the dogged work of political education and organization, which could be interrupted for lengthy periods of life experience and reflection. I was no longer tied down to what I considered to be my duties as a citizen.

I was even less tied by professional work. I was unemployed, with no job anywhere on the horizon, idling my days away in

Brunstorf. It was a pleasant enough life; I had plenty of time for hiking and reading. But was it a life for a man of thirty, in the prime of his strength? I got more restless from day to day. I now strongly suspect that sexual frustration had a lot to do with my restlessness. Anyway, whatever the hidden motives, delayed adolescence took over, and I decided to go on the road. My mother was worried, of course, but broadminded as always, she put no obstacles in my path.

INTERMEZZO: ON THE ROAD

There were two conscious motivations — or rationalizations — for my wanderlust, really conflicting quite strongly. I wanted to go to Italy; and I wanted to live as a proletarian, by the work of my hands rather than on inherited money or on the fruits of the education that money had bought.

The first motive needs no explanation; the second may warrant some discussion.

Following a train of thought more Tolstoyan than Marxist, I wanted to share the life of the working class with which I identified. I had hurt my mother's feelings when I declined invitations by my wealthy relatives in Hamburg; not that I disliked them, for they were nice people. But I felt it was inappropriate for a Communist to indulge in bourgeois luxury.

I have, of course, long ago discarded that particular kind of foolishness as superfluous; there are plenty of others left. But I still take a dim view of Socialists and Communists who spend large amounts of money on their personal satisfactions, even if they have earned that money by their own work, e.g. Pablo Picasso. Spending money means buying slaves or, to put it more precisely, ordering others to perform work which they would be happier not to do. Other men and women sweat it out to provide me with food, housing, etc.; how much work am I doing for them? I do not insist on exact equality; but if I buy ten or a hundred times more work than I do, I certainly am exploiting a lot of people. I am always surprised that other people, and in particular Marxists, do not see things that way.

Germany. On a beautiful August morning I set out, clad in corduroy trousers and jacket, sandals on my feet and a very light rucksack on my back, containing not much more than a toothbrush and a safety razor, to hike to Lauenburg, a charming little town on the Elbe River. I felt a profound sense of liberation.

From Lauenburg I took the train first to Lüneburg and then to Celle, two other medieval towns, where I visited architectural monuments, occasionally making sketches. Drinking in the beauty of the world, man-made or natural, has of course always motivated my lifelong love of travel.

Taking to the road has a long and honorable tradition in Germany, dating back to the journeymen of the Middle Ages. Every municipality, big or small, was bound by law to provide wandering men with free shelter; there was no such provision for women. In Celle, as was usual in towns, the "herberge" was a solid building with large sleeping quarters. The beds were narrow and the mattresses were thin, but the sheets were clean and there were showers. I slept soundly and felt happy. In the small village where I spent the following night, the shelter was a small barn with a layer of hay, and I washed in the neighboring creek; I much preferred the outdoors to a washroom.

My mother had insisted on sending me some money to a scheduled stop, which was Paderborn, a town in Westphalia known for its Romanesque churches; but by the time it arrived, its value had shrunk. I discovered that there were no porters to meet the last train of the day, so I earned some money by carrying the luggage of late arrivals. It was enough to pay for a room in the attic of a little inn and for enough food, bread, and potatoes to keep body and soul together.

I went to the labor exchange and was directed to a farm, where I was served a huge ham sandwich and coffee. I really would have liked to work on that farm. But when I inquired about wages, I felt it would be scabbing to work for that nominal amount, and left.

As I wandered on, there formed in my head the only serious poem I ever created in my life, praising the beauty of the Earth.

I knocked on the doors of farmhouses, asking for work. The answer was always the same: "No work, but I guess you are hungry"; and they gave me some bread, soup, or milk. Soon I discarded the "looking-for-work" spiel and just asked for food and for shelter at night. I was never refused. Once a farmer came out, saying, "I put butter on your bread, because you asked so nicely." Another time a young fellow, lounging in the corner of the farm kitchen, pulled a Hungarian five-forint bill out of his pocket and gave it to me; like any solid currency, it went quite far at that time.

When I went to a cobbler or tailor to ask for needle and thread to fix my sandals or clothes, they soon took them to do the work properly. When I started to wash my laundry at a stream, expert female hands took the work from me. Whenever I needed help, there was always somebody ready to give it, often without my asking for it.

This experience profoundly and forever strengthened my confidence in the human race. It removed the last remnants of the bourgeois superstition that one cannot live without money. Gertel had often said, when I worried about my future as an architect, "Tomorrow will take care of itself." I now completely adopted her philosophy.

I have to admit, of course, that money *is* important — but only if you do *not* have it. If you have enough to keep the wolf from the door, raising the figures in a bank account means chasing a pure abstraction. Erwin Panofsky once said that he liked bankers, because they were the last faithful to uphold the philosophy of the Medieval Schoolmen who, following Plato, believed in the superior reality of ideas and of symbols, such as words, which incorporated them. Strangely, these Schoolmen called themselves "realists"; even more strangely, so do their contemporary successors who believe that money is more real and important than life.

From other men on the road I learned that work was available on the construction site of a power dam and station on the river Lenne, at the town of Plettenberg. I was taken on and applied for a little room that was for rent in a workers' house. The landlady asked, "Are you Catholic or Protestant?" I replied, "I am Jewish." "But Jews don't work!" she exclaimed. I laughed, saying, "But I do." I got the room.

The work consisted of carrying cement sacks, mixing concrete, and removing the scaffolding from structures after they had hardened. The work was not difficult. Once a fellow showed off by carrying two sacks of cement, to general admiring hilarity. I noticed then, as I often noticed later, that many people — certainly not all — enjoy their work more than they care to admit to themselves, let alone to the boss.

By now inflation had completely galloped out of control. Wages were paid each evening, and everyone rushed to the stores. I also paid my rent every evening.

After ten days wanderlust took over again; I wanted to get to Italy before winter set in. I took a train to Frankfurt to see my sister. Train fares could not keep up with inflation and had become nominal. Margaret was doing research work for the National Association of Welfare Agencies. She had become engaged in Hamburg to Alfred Plaut, a pathologist. Alfred had gone to America with the understanding that she would join him. She did so shortly after my visit and they married in New York.

I took a train to Nürnberg, where I met Gertel for three days. I accompanied her on her train back to Karlsruhe but got off at the town of Eschenbach, still in Bavaria. From there on it was all hiking to Merano in Italy, about 300 kilometers as the crow flies. I put my sandals into my rucksack and marched barefoot. Soon my soles were hardened so well that I had no trouble walking on any rough ground — except on the stubble of a cornfield, as I soon found out. I took in old towns, churches, and monasteries, all the way being fed and sheltered by farmers. I stayed two days with Gertel's parents, who lived in retirement in a suburb of Munich. I was warmly received; her father played Beethoven and Schubert on his violin, and her mother and I talked about the subject closest to both our hearts: Gertel.

I wandered on southward through the rolling foothills of the Alps, famous dairy country. The milk, fresh from the evening milking, tasted incomparably better than any milk I have ever drunk before or after. I crossed the Austrian border into the mountains of North Tirol. One evening, when it started to rain, I got work on a farm. I worked about an hour, got a clean bed and a copious supper and breakfast. In the morning the sun was shining brightly, and I told the farmer I would move on. He laughed heartily, saying, "I knew at once that you would not stay."

Italy. I crossed the watershed between the Inn and the Adige ("Etsch" in German) and descended the valley. Italy had extended its boundaries to the watershed, and the German-speaking people of South Tirol, who had always looked down on the Italians, did not like it. The South Tiroleans were very proud of their history; they were the only Germans who had spontaneously risen against Napoleon, in a long-drawn-out guerilla war in 1809. The leader of the uprising, a peasant by the name of Andreas Hofer, was a popular national hero comparable only to Wilhelm Tell in Switzerland. The people were also proud of the fact that the Tirolean riflemen had been by far the best soldiers in the Austrian Army.

They welcomed every Austrian or German with open arms. I was received by a well-to-do farm family. They had read about the German inflation, were curious about it, invited me to their dinner table, and besieged me with questions; then they put me up for the night in their guest room.

The next day I followed the Adige down to Merano and went up the hill to visit the well-preserved medieval castle of the Counts of Tirol which gave the country its name. In the village, also named Tirol, I found employment in the wine harvest. Culling grapes under the mild October sun was fun. The owner of the vineyard kept an inn; his wife was a professional cook who had worked in Paris. The combination of French and Austrian cuisine which she served, washed down by as much of their home-grown wine as one could swallow, would have done honor to any first-class restaurant. I shared a spotlessly clean, large sunny room, with a wide view of the beautiful valley, with the other farmhand, a pleasant, fun-loving young chap. In the evening we danced with the village girls. I could not think of a better life.

The harvest was finished in a week, but they kept me on for a few more days to do odd jobs around the yard. Then I took my leave and the train to Verona, with money in my pocket. The amount was very modest, but it was real money, not the evanescent paper-millions I had known in Germany.

At long last I was in Italy; Italy once again! Beautiful Verona became, and has remained, one of my favorite cities.

I again set out on the road for a 120-kilometer hike to Venice. The peasants in Italy were as hospitable as were those in Germany and Austria, but they were much poorer. Instead of soft hay it was hard corn stover, and instead of bread, milk, or soup, it was dry polenta, which I found hard to get down despite my healthy appetite. But I did not mind; I was in Italy.

I admired Palladio's palaces and unique "basilica" in Vicenza and the masterworks of architecture, sculpture, and painting in Padua. Then I followed the river Brenta, lined with the Renaissance palaces of Venetian patricians. At the mouth of the Brenta I found a little boat that was to carry vegetables to Venice. I helped them carry the baskets on board, and they took me across the lagoon to Venice. The boat went through the Giudecca, turned the point of the Dogana, and suddenly the view of the Riva dei Sciavoni opened up, with the Doge's Palace, the columns of the Piazzetta, and the Libreria, with the Campanile and the golden domes of San Marco. It was *the* way to enter Venice, through its glorious front door, rather than sneaking in at the back, as do all those who arrive by rail or road.

I immediately fell under the spell of the island city of canals and wandered for hours through its streets. At one point it suddenly occured to me that I had not seen any water for quite a while; but the spell had not been broken. I realized that it was due not just to the water and the buildings, but primarily to the fact that the streets of Venice have been designed and built exclusively for pedestrian movement. Vehicular movement, by gondola, "vaporetti," and a strictly limited number of water-taxis, went on at a lower level, on the canals.

From that hour I knew that grade separation is the secret of building good cities. Leonardo da Vinci had discovered it five centuries ago, but his prophetic vision has been ignored by generation after generation of city builders. The Venetians have not invented grade separation; they inherited it from the Lake Dwellers. In fact, Venice is the last, greatest, and most glorious of the Lake Dweller towns. That has made it the most beautiful of all cities.

The pedestrian streets of Venice are free from all the restrictions which govern the design of vehicular traffic streets. They widen and narrow; they curve and go around corners. Movement changes not only horizontally but also vertically: steps lead up and down the vaulted bridges which cross the canals. The picture changes from step to step and draws you on to never-ending discoveries.

In recent years "pedestrianizing" streets has become very fashionable. But with few exceptions these streets are much too wide, too long, and too straight to be attractive pedestrian streets; there is no variation, nothing to discover.

I am, of course, aware that cars are not gondolas, that a depressed freeway is not the Grand Canal, and that cars and delivery wagons want to be able to stop at every door. But if a dense net of arteries at a level below that of the general street system were provided, trips on the nonarterial street system would be few and short, and their speed could be limited to fifteen kilometers per hour or less, by design, as has been done in the Dutch "woonerfs." Residential streets would once more be outdoor communal living rooms, with neighbors chatting and children playing as they do in Venice. Venetian children hardly ever fall into canals; and if their ball does, the next passing gondolier throws it back.

If a big city were built from scratch, it would not be too difficult to establish such a two-level system; but Brasilia and Chandigarh have missed their opportunities.

Venice was heaven to my eyes, but not to the rest of my body. Obtaining food and shelter was more difficult in the city than in the country. The first night I still slept in a bed in a little *albergo,* the second in a gondola, the third on a bench, and the two following ones in the municipal asylum. It was not as comfortable as a German "herberge." There were no mattresses, blankets, pillows, or showers, and naked 100-watt bulbs shone into my eyes all night.

My mother had asked Giovanni to send me some money from Rome, but mail was slow. I stood in line with hundreds of miserably poor people to pawn my watch at the municipal "Monte di Pieta," but the loan increased my purchasing power only slightly. I had to go back to the mainland. I instructed the post office to forward mail to Treviso and proceeded to walk back over the causeway. But I found that the causeway accommodated only railroad tracks, no walkway. I had to buy a railroad ticket, and my pockets were empty. Once more I exploited my Jewishness. I went into the ghetto, politely explaining my plight to anyone who would listen, and begging for money. The response was not enthusiastic; it took me over an hour to accumulate enough *soldi* to pay for the few kilometers' train ride to Mestre. I set out on the road to Treviso and found shelter and polenta on the approaches to that city. The next morning there was a cold drizzle; I walked in sandals. A boy of 14 or 15 stopped me, asking, "Are you looking for work?" — "Yes, of course." We walked together toward the city; he looked down at my feet and said with a frown, "Don't you have socks?" I made myself look respectable by putting them on.

The work consisted of unloading machinery from flatcars to a truck and lasted little more than an hour. I was pleasantly surprised by the more than generous wage, which paid for bed and food for more than a day. Only years later, when I saw a similar scene in a movie, did it dawn on me that I had been paid for participating in a risky, if nonviolent, train robbery.

Several times a day I inquired at the Treviso post office. Finally the girl at the counter asked what I was expecting. I explained my situation. She took pity on me and gave me some money. On my third day in Treviso my money arrived.

The sun was shining again when I visited the Villa of Maser, built by Palladio and decorated by Paolo Veronese. I had never before connected these two great artists. Seeing them inspired by the same vision deepened my understanding of the Italian High Renaissance.

I hiked across the Dolomites to Trento; the November rains had set in and I saw nothing of the Dolomites. From Trento, train and boat brought me to Konstanz, where my friend Walter Koessler lived.

The day after I arrived at Konstanz, the German inflation stopped: one billion old marks could be exchanged against one new *rentenmark*. Nobody believed that the new currency would maintain its value, but it did. This "miracle" was credited to the "wizardry" of Hjalmar Schacht, the head of the Reichsbank; it was, of course, due to the solid support of the American and British banks.

I borrowed money from Walter and traveled to Karlsruhe to see Gertel, then proceeded to Hamburg.

I was back home in Brunstorf; my three months on the road were over. I would not have missed them for anything in the world; they had broadened my view of life. Among the people I had met on the road was an inveterate wanderer who complained about increasing harassment, worst of all in "free" Switzerland. In his opinion the only free countries left in Europe were Turkey and Greece. Premodern "despotic" governments look at homeless poor people as one looks at the beasts of the forest; they do not care how or if they live or die, and they do not interfere. It was a new notion of "freedom" to me, radically different from the liberal-democratic one with which I had grown up, and probably just as valid.

WAITING

When I had arrived at Verona, I read in the papers that a Communist uprising had occurred in Hamburg but had ended the same day. I was surprised and disturbed.

What had happened was the following: in the states of Saxony and Thuringia, in the "Red Heart" of Germany, Socialist-Communist coalition governments had come to power. They were perfectly legitimate, based on majorities in freely elected parliaments. They enacted some mild minor reforms. But they felt threatened by the government in Berlin, and there was much talk of organizing workers' defense forces; the national government, stating that this was a violation of the constitution, now openly threatened intervention. They had never threatened to intervene in Bavaria, where the right-wing government had organized their "Heimwehr" (home defense) and tolerated the organization of the Nazi storm troops. Demands for armed defense of Saxony and Thuringia increased, and the Communists promised to support it by a concerted action of armed uprisings throughout Germany.

On the eve of the occupation of Saxony and Thuringia by the Reichswehr a meeting was called in Dresden. The Social-Democratic leaders of the two states, very sensibly, decided not to resist. Couriers were dispatched all over Germany to notify everybody that the action was off. For reasons still obscure, the courier from Hamburg, returning late at night, informed the Communist party only the next morning. By that time the uprising had started and had occupied all key points in the city. The authorities were taken completely by surprise; not one of the 4000 men involved had leaked a word, a tribute to Ernst Thälmann's uncanny ability to judge people. As soon as the Dresden decision was known, orders were given to wind down the rebellion. But fighting occurred, with victims on both sides.

By the time I returned to Hamburg, most local leaders were under arrest or in hiding, but the Party still operated legally. I was charged by the provisional leadership with rebuilding the secret military organization. I was to get instructions from a man whom I was to meet at a designated spot in a park. Nobody showed up within one-and-a-half hours from the appointed time, and I left, relieved. I felt that, in view of the impending stabilization, the whole plan was absurd, would fail, and would do much harm to the Party. The KPD leadership had enough common sense to arrive at the same conclusion; nothing more was ever heard of the plan.

While I was on the road, my mother had, unbeknownst to me, found a job for me in America, with an architect in Little Rock, in the southern state of Arkansas. He was a relative of the Solmitz family. Ernst Solmitz, a banker, had been my father's closest friend since long before his marriage. The two older Solmitz children, Olga and Robert, were of our age, and the five children of the two families grew up together much like brothers and sisters. Our homes were only a few minutes apart, and we played together in each other's houses and gardens, and in the meadow and hayloft of the common property at Borstel, where we also worked together growing vegetables and strawberries.

For me, Olga was and remained a sister; I long refused to see that her feeling for me was different. Hers was a deep and abiding love, which never wavered from childhood to death. For her I was the only man on earth — and for me Gertel was the only woman.

This made her life a tragedy of frustration. There were men, one in particular, who wooed her and could have made her life happy. I tried to persuade her to marry him, but she would not listen. It was as impossible for her to renounce her dream of marrying me as it was for me to fulfill it.

My mother very much wanted me to marry Olga and never gave up that hope. She loved Olga, and Olga loved my mother. Olga spent more time living with her at Brunstorf than she did at her parents' home.

It was through the Solmitz connection that I had got that job in Little Rock; or, rather, a firm promise of it, because hiring someone from abroad was illegal under American law. I was not much attracted by America and even less by Little Rock. But it was my only chance to get back into architectural work. I recognized that I could learn much from working in the world's technically most advanced country. I also felt that I needed a time of reflection on my political views. I had known capitalism in Germany in a very distorted form; it was only fair to study it in the country of its greatest achievement. I resolved to refrain from political work and contacts during my stay in America, which I never thought of as permanent.

It was, however, not enough for me to accept the us; the us had to accept me. The German quota was full. I knew that engineers were exempt from the quota. I asked an acquaintance who worked at the American consulate if that exemption extended to architects; she said it did not. So I had to find another way.

Ernst Fuhrmann, the man through whom I had met the revolutionaries of Schwerin, was now heading the prestigious Folkwang publishing house in Darmstadt, which published art books on exotic regions, such as Africa and Java. Fuhrmann gave me a letter making me the Folkwang representative in America, and the addresses of some leading booksellers in New York with whom he had been in contact. I got my visa.

In March 1924 I left Hamburg. My ticket went via London and

Liverpool, where I was to board a ship of the White Star Line. I spent a few days in London. I was surprised that the world's largest city was composed almost exclusively of small buildings and by the informal efficiency of the English. I was impressed by the beauty of Raymond Unwin's work at Hampstead Garden City. I met Ogden and a few other of Franz's Cambridge friends. One of them recommended Sinclair Lewis' *Main Street* as a good introduction to America, which I found it to be.

I enjoyed the ocean passage because of, rather than in spite of, stormy weather. I consider ships to be the only civilized mode of travel. It is a crying shame that you can now cross the Atlantic only by submitting to imprisonment in an airplane seat.

In Cork about 300 men came on board, IRA fighters from the six northern counties. I had long talks with them; I had never known the depth of feeling of Irish nationalism and hatred of the British. They disembarked at Halifax, but all intended to somehow get into the United States.

The ship entered New York Harbor in the morning mist. I peered through the mist to see the Manhattan skyscrapers. Suddenly I discovered them, sunlit above the mist. It was a magnificent sight.

AMERICA

Ellis Island. We disembarked at Ellis Island. I sat on a bench for hours, with hundreds of other arrivals, in a large bare room; from time to time someone was called out. I wondered what it was all about; I had a valid visa — what was I waiting for? I did not yet know that the favorite sport of departments of the United States government consists of fighting each other about their respective jurisdictional boundaries. The Department of Labor, in charge of immigration, was not going to be told by the State Department whom to admit into the Land of the Free; a visa issued by *them* was of no importance to *us*. Nobody was ever told why or even that he or she was not admitted. The guards regarded us as cattle; they barked at us and shoved us around. In none of the prisons in which I had been had the inmates been treated with such utter contempt for human dignity.

As dusk fell, the men were herded into one big room with hundreds of two-tier cots, the women into another. The sheets were clean and there were showers, but the water was either scaldingly hot or icily cold. The food which we were served was adequate, but we were rushed through the meals and seated on stools so tightly that one could not move one's elbows.

Most of the day we spent in another big hall. Not surprisingly, tension was high and quarrels and shouting matches were frequent, sometimes ending in fistfights. I noticed that the best behaved of the many nationalities — called "races" by the US authorities — assembled in the hall were the English; until I discovered a small group of Chinese quietly sitting in a corner. One of them, a student, spoke English. I asked if the others also were students. No, they were seamen whose ships were loading or unloading in New York. While their shipmates reveled in the customary joys of shore leave, they were cooped up in this dismal hall — because their skins were yellow.

There was also a high-caste highly educated East Indian. He had studied at Oxford and been admitted to Columbia University. We had long and interesting talks; he was a man of outstanding intelligence. Probably he later rose to an important position in the Indian government. He was so indignant over the American treatment of foreigners that he had decided that, if allowed to land, he would forego Columbia and return to Oxford. "How to make friends and influence people."

Thanks to the fact that I spoke good English, I found a decent man among the guards who took me to my luggage so that I could take out my toothbrush and other necessaries. None of my fellow inmates enjoyed this privilege.

There was worse. An epidemic of scarlet fever had broken out among the children who were interned with their mothers; many children died. Fathers did not see their children before they died, nor their bereaved wives thereafter.

One evening we were led out into a large hall, decked out with the Stars and Stripes. "Daughters of the American Revolution" welcomed us to the Land of the Free and led us in singing "Oh Say, Can You See."

We were not allowed into the yard, but we got fresh air on large terraces enclosed by ten-foot fences. From there we watched our guards in the yard engaged in a strange tribal ceremony involving a ball. To anyone with a knowledge of ethnology it was evident that the mysterious movements of the ceremony were derived from some secret cult. The high value ascribed by Americans to this ceremony was confirmed after the Second World War, when the American educators deemed it to be the most effective means of converting their German pupils to democracy.

It turned out that, as an architect, I was exempt from the quota. On that basis my sister obtained my release after seventeen days.

NEW YORK

My sister Margaret lived with her husband Alfred in a two-room apartment on Broadway, in the eighties. When I emerged there from the subway which I had boarded at the "battery," I was taken aback: there was no street! There were just lots of sky-scrapers scattered around between one- and two-story buildings and vacant lots, but there was no defined street space as I had known it in Europe. Should we build street spaces in contemporary cities? Or should we, as Le Corbusier advocated, discard the "corridor street" and strive for a new and different kind of urban beauty? The question is still moot.

I liked much of the architecture of New York. It was eclectic, as was most recent architecture in Europe, but of a far higher standard. The profiles and details of buildings, derived from the Italian Renaissance, were much more refined; the beautiful New York light may have something to do with that. I admired some of the work of McKim, Mead, and White: Pennsylvania Station and the Morgan Library. (The Bank of Montreal building in Montreal, which in my opinion is the masterpiece of that famous firm, I discovered only thirty years later.)

There were other surprises in New York. Scanning the "help wanted" columns of *The New York Times,* I found one that looked promising and showed it to Alfred. He said, "You cannot go there." — "Why not?" — "It says 'gentiles only.' " — "What does that mean?" — "They will not hire Jews." In Hamburg a few architects were known for not hiring Jews, but they would never have thought of advertising their bigotry. In this respect at least, anti-Semitism was stronger in America than it was in Germany.

I had expected that in the world's technically most advanced country everything would be more modern than in Europe. I found garbage being burnt on the sidewalks and freight cars being shunted through city streets — phenomena which had long disappeared from German cities. The piers of Manhattan were obsolete by Hamburg standards, too narrow and not equipped with gantry cranes. Soon I found that good pencils had to be imported from Germany or Bohemia, and that American industry had not yet discovered the secrets of making usable erasers or even thumbtacks. I learned that technical progress is uneven, industry by industry, and that it may be quite misleading to judge the technical level of a country on the basis of a few products.

I found that I could not hold a draftsman's job without being familiar with nonmetric measurements and American drafting techniques, which differed substantially from those I knew. So I practiced drafting in my furnished room during free hours, while working at odd jobs to make a living. I had several jobs as a carpenter's helper, but each lasted only a few days. I worked a day as a longshoreman and was surprised that I could handle the job with ease. I worked a week for Western Union but threw up the job because I felt cheated by their mysterious system of piece-work pay. I delivered telegrams at night in the Times Square area; my clientele was sharply divided into two groups: rich whites in luxury establishments, and poor blacks in run-down tenements. The poor blacks always gave me a tip; no rich white ever did.

My longest-lasting job was wrapping parcels in Gimbel's basement in the evening. My workmates were high-school and college kids, and we chatted and joked all the time. I kept that job until after I had found regular work as a draftsman in an architect's office which specialized in movie palaces, a field new to me. It was followed by an office specializing in apartment houses. I had worked on apartments in Germany, but the approach here was quite different; while some standards were higher, others, relating to air, light, and sunshine, were much lower. I learned not to be dogmatic. By this time I had also given up any idea of going to Little Rock.

I remember my surprise when one of my fellow workers said, "My hometown." It had never occurred to me that an American city could be a hometown. I had looked at them just as places to make money — "money-mining camps," as I later put it.

TRAVELING

When my second draftsman's job came to an end, I decided to extend my search for the next one beyond New York. I hitchhiked to Philadelphia; I had no luck there and felt depressed by the monotony of the streets of row houses. "This is a city where I never want to live," I said to myself; I later lived there for fourteen years and came to like it.

I continued to Baltimore, where I found a draftsman's job. On the weekend I went to see Washington and Annapolis and found them, both in their very different ways, more beautiful than I had expected.

I liked the leisurely Southern lifestyle of Baltimore, and I spent much time in the public library. The job lasted four months, after which I returned to New York. I longed for Gertel, wanted to see my mother, and hoped there might be a chance to work at home. As I could only afford the transatlantic fare with difficulty, I decided to work my way to Hamburg. It was an unlikely prospect, but once more my luck held. While I was hanging around the piers of the Hamburg-America Line, a man greeted me. He was Alfred Plaut's laboratory assistant. When he learned of my intention, he said, "I think I can help you; I used to work on the *Thuringia,* which is tied up here, and am just going to visit my old shipmates." He introduced me to the second engineer, who took me on at the usual fictitious hire of one dollar for the trip.

My work consisted of odd jobs: washing paint, polishing brass, hoisting garbage on deck and into the ocean. It was early January 1925 and stormy, but I enjoyed the ten-day trip.

When I asked my friend Richard Tüngel, who was employed at the Hamburg City Planning Office, about chances for work in architecture or planning, he said there were none whatever. I might still have tried to find a job in Germany, but my friend Walter Koessler had moved from Konstanz to Los Angeles and wrote enthusiastic letters urging me to join him. So I decided to try California.

Gertel came to Brunstorf for a week; we met again for the last week before my departure in Paris. It was my first visit to that great city. On our last day, when we went to take leave of our favorite stained-glass window in Notre Dame, she suddenly broke into tears. I did not quite understand the depth of her despair; she could not bear the prospect of a second separation for many months.

The *Aquitania* took me to New York in five days. While I had been sailing on the *Thuringia,* Olga Solmitz had crossed the ocean in the opposite direction to visit my sister, but primarily to see me. It was a bitter disappointment for her to learn that I had left, but she waited for my return. I stayed about ten days, then went west. Riding the train by day, I spent the nights in Chicago and St. Louis in flophouses, an environment that somewhat shocked me. My heart jumped for joy when I saw Santa Fe and nearby Pueblos on the high, sunlit plateau. I stood silent a long time at the edge of the Colorado Grand Canyon; there are things in the world that have to be seen to be *not* believed. I had the same sensation later on two more occasions: at the Registan in Samarkand, and at the pyramids of Gizeh. All three sites I knew quite well from photos; it took a long time to sink in that this was real.

Los Angeles

In Los Angeles I got a chance at last to work as a designer rather than as a draftsman, in small offices. For almost a year I worked for a man named Munro, who was not an architect and left the design work entirely to me. I designed Andalusian-style houses. The office was in Beverly Hills and I rented a room in a cottage on the beach in Santa Monica. Each morning I plunged right from my bed into the Pacific for a long swim.

Munro was subject to periodic drinking bouts. He did not pay me for eight weeks, saying he was waiting for payment from a lawyer for whom I had designed a big house built around a patio which he had immediately sold at a $10,000 profit. I finally went to the lawyer, who told me he had paid his bill long ago. I confronted Munro, who said he could not pay. I appealed to the Labor Relations Board, which summoned Munro. He said all he could pay right now was $100 and promised to pay the rest later. He never did, and I was over $400 in the hole.

I had commuted from Santa Monica to Beverly Hills by the Southern Pacific Electric Railroad. I disliked the long waits but liked the fact that I always got a window seat. Both phenomena were, of course, the result of heavy underuse. The Southern Pacific can hardly be blamed for selling the concession, nor General Motors for buying it with the obligation to provide bus service for five years. GM could make money during those five years by selling buses to its subsidiary and by selling the off-street rights of way which formed parts of the Southern Pacific network. After their five-year obligation period ended, they let the concession go back to the city, which continues to this day to operate the buses.

To this day, the story is being told in many books and articles how a deep-seated conspiracy by GM wrecked the excellent public-transport system of Los Angeles in order to force reluctant Angelinos to buy their cars. That is a myth; for GM it was a straightforward business deal. The blame for letting the most desirable electric service go should be put on the City of Los

Angeles. I do not feel much at home as an apologist for Big Business, but *Magnus amicus Platon, magis amica Veritas* (Plato is a great friend, truth a greater one).

It is sad, but true, that door-to-door travel practically always takes less time by car than by public transit. I found this out when, having left Munro, I was again job hunting; the job had always gone to somebody who had called a few minutes earlier. I decided that I needed a car to be competitive. For one hundred dollars I bought a Model-T Ford; I later sold it for fifty. I enjoyed driving and took pride in being able to reach the exhilarating speed of thirty-five miles per hour. But expenses for repairs and tires made a second hole in my savings.

My last and best job in California was with a builder in Pasadena who built one-story Spanish-style houses, not with a wooden frame, but out of light nonreinforced concrete, a material much closer to the adobe of the original models. I enjoyed designing these houses.

Shortly before Christmas of 1926 this job also ran out. I was excited by the "Modern" architecture that was developing in Europe and decided to go home.

I had stuck to my intention to keep out of politics in America. Only twice did I go to a Communist meeting, one addressed by William Z. Foster and the other by "Mother" Ella Reeve Bloor. I was very favorably impressed by both.

America had not converted me to capitalism; in a roundabout way it had strengthened my Communist faith. What Marx calls the second, highest state of communism — when the individual's consumption has no longer to be restricted by property rights, but merely by mores and morals — had been a distant "ideal" for me toward which one marches without ever hoping to attain it. The enormous productivity of modern industry, together with the ever-increasing waste of human labor on distribution — the "sales effort" — made this ideal look less distant.

Life in America was easier than in Europe, and I always got along well with my fellow workers. I was surprised that I, the foreigner, was always the one whom they asked, "How do you spell that?" There must be something wrong with a system of education that in twelve or sixteen years can teach its products neither to read a foreign language, nor to write their own.

I concluded that Americans and Germans have the same bad characteristics — they are both schoolmasters obsessed with telling others how they should live — but their good attributes are opposed: the good thing about Americans is that they take it easy, and the good thing about Germans that they do not take it easy.

I had not fallen in love with America. Something very essential seemed to be missing; life was not quite real. I was reminded of Ulysses's visit to that island far out west in the Atlantic, the Isle of the Dead. The people there looked like humans, moved like humans, talked like humans; but they really were shadows.

There is hardly anything from those three years in America that is deeply engraved on my memory. Emotional depth decreases with age. But from my following twelve years in Europe there are many moving memories.

My feeling of a lack of depth in America is of course subjective, but it may not be entirely individual. In the 1970s one of my colleagues in Toronto, who had emigrated from Hungary in 1956, told me that, comfortable and successful as his life was in Canada, he felt something was missing. When I replied with my Ulysses story, his face lit up. "That's it, that's it," he said.

Back to Europe

A Long Voyage Home. I took a boat from Los Angeles to San Francisco and, after a few days in that most attractive of all American cities, I embarked on a Swedish freighter which carried some twenty passengers. I was in no great hurry to get back to work; I have always made the best of periods of unemployment, of which there have been many in my life.

Five weeks at sea were a dream come true. Sailing along the coasts of Mexico and Central America, one saw the mountains during the day and the fire of the volcanos at night. The ocean was full of life; there were whales and giant turtles, and flying fish sometimes landed on deck. I got acquainted with the sailors and learnt enough Swedish to read a collection of short stories that one of them lent me. I also started to translate into German a book that had impressed me: *Dollar Diplomacy* by Joseph Freeman and Scott Nearing. I later found that the German rights to the book had been previously acquired by someone else.

Mostly I slept on deck on the hatches; the tropical sunrises were an incomparable spectacle.

The ship loaded coffee at four little ports in Guatemala and El Salvador. I watched the longshoremen carrying the sacks from their bobbing boats up the ship's ladder. The work required far more skill and effort than had my work at the Staten Island dock. I enquired about wages: eighty cents for a ten-hour day. I learned that this was a high wage; the men harvesting the coffee got only 40 cents a day. I had been paid forty-two cents an hour for longshoring. I recalled the five-cent cup of coffee I had drunk at lunch. Only a small part of that ever got to the harvest workers; but as far as that part was concerned, I had exchanged one hour of my labor against ten hours of theirs. This was blatant exploitation; how did it come about?

The question about the origin of the unequal exchange of labor remained in the back of my mind. "Neoclassical" economists referred to "unfavorable terms of trade"; Marxists talked about "monopoly capital." Years later, while waiting for dinner in the library of a friend in Vienna, I took down the second volume of Marx's *Capital* and hit upon the section dealing with the transformation of values into commodity prices by differences in the "organic composition" of capital: if the composition is low, with wages accounting for most of capital, prices are below value; if it is high, they are above value.

Without denying the importance of the power of multinational corporations and of the states associated with them, I believe the different organic composition of capital to be basic to the unequal exchange of values between the "First" and the "Third" Worlds.

I regard the term "Third World" as an apologetic misnomer. It is really just the backside of the "First," capitalist world on which the upper body and head press with all their weight. Of course the ass does not look as pretty as the face, though the latter also needs increasing amounts of grease paint to keep looking attractive.

We went through the Panama Canal to Plymouth; from Southampton I crossed the Channel to Le Havre and, with a stop in Rouen, went to Paris. In the train it struck me how similar the workers' conversations were to those of their German counterparts, quite different from talk among American and even British workers. In Charlemagne's empire the Germans and French were one nation; from then on everything went right with the French and wrong with the Germans. The Germans are really just misshapen Frenchmen. I had previously been puzzled by the discovery that the Alsatians were both very German and very French. If only all Germans had become Alsatians!

In Paris I met Otto Freundlich. He told me about Chartres, and on leaving Paris he accompanied me there. Chartres is not just a cathedral, or the most beautiful cathedral; it is *the* cathedral. If all other medieval art were lost, but Chartres remained, one would know what that great art was; if all others remained but Chartres were lost, one would never know it.

Miraculously spared by the dangers of war and revolution and the greater dangers of "restoration," its architecture, sculpture, and stained glass is an inexhaustible world of beauty. I stayed a second day; then, with several other stops in France and Italy, I joined my mother in Nervi, where Gertel visited us somewhat later.

I had not foreseen what two years of separation would do to both of us. My pent-up sexuality had found irregular channels, involving much promiscuity. Gertel, still sharing an apartment with Oscar, was living with Walter Waffenschmidt. Waffenschmidt, already a doctor of engineering, had gone back to university at Freiburg to add a doctorate in economics. He had become a friend of my brother's, and Gertel had met him through me. He was a high official in the Labor Ministry of the state of Baden and also taught economics at Heidelberg. He had lived exclusively for his work and his science; Gertel rekindled the flame of life in him, as she had done in others, both men and women.

Waffenschmidt had the courage later to give Gertel the child she so badly wanted. At the time she did not know how to tell me; she hesitated, but came to see me at Nervi. She later told me how relieved she was when I talked first about my sex life; then she could tell me of her life with Waffenschmidt. I was not jealous, as I never had been jealous of Oscar; I was sure that Gertel's heart was big enough for deep love of more than one man.

Some weeks after Gertel had left, Olga came to Nervi. We stayed there for a while, then went together with my mother to Rome, and Olga and I continued to Palermo. Olga returned to Rome, and I went on a tour around Sicily, partly on foot. My deepest impressions were of the Greek temples of Selinus, the magnificent stonework of the fourth century BC of the great fortifications of Syracuse, and the Norman cathedral and cloisters of Monreale. One evening, lying on a hillside in Agrigento, I contemplated the so-called Temple of Concordia, a well-preserved Doric temple. It seemed to me that the *naos,* or *cella,* the house of the god, was floating within the *peripteros,* the rows of columns which surrounded it on all four sides. It occured to me that these two elements must at one time have been two different buildings, married at a high point in history to form the most perfect work of architectural sculpture ever created by man. The notion became an obsession, which I took up thirteen years later, in another period of happy unemployment. I have now, in 1985, written it up.

HAMBURG

I returned to Hamburg at the end of April 1927. Prosperity had returned to Germany and building was booming. I soon found a job with a good, fairly conservative firm, and then with Karl Schneider, the leader of the Modern Movement among Hamburg architects. Schneider had assembled in his office a crew of talented young architects, all younger than I was. Two of them had successful careers later in America, where I met them in the forties and fifties. Schneider also went to America after Hitler came to power, but he died before his great talents had the opportunity to unfold.

The work in Schneider's office was stimulating; discussions were lively. Our biggest and most interesting job was a competition for a very large housing project, including design both of the site plan and of the houses and community facilities. We won second prize but not the commission. The volume of work dropped, and I was laid off. For some weeks I stood in line three days a week to collect unemployment insurance; then the Labor Office sent me to see Hanns Henny Jahn.

Jahn was a man of many talents. He was well known as a writer, had received the prestigious Kleist Prize, and his tragedy *Medea* was being successfully performed in Hamburg. But he was also interested in music. He had formed a religious community named "Ugrino" in order to be able to publish sixteenth-century music without having to pay a business tax. He was a renowned expert on organs. He had been commissioned to restore to its original sound the organ of St. James Church, built by the famous seventeenth-century organ builder Snitger, on which Buxtehude, Bach, and Telemann had played. The restored organ sounded marvelous, but after a few weeks it went out of tune. Jahn found that the tower, to which the organ was attached, had inclined; and I, as an architect, was called in to investigate.

I crawled around in the old fourteenth-century tower and

found cracks wide enough to put my arm through. By all the rules of statics it should have collapsed. We called in the head of Building Inspection, who was so alarmed that he thought of closing the adjacent streets, two of the city's main thoroughfares. Subsequently the church architect took over; nothing much was ever done. In World War II the whole area was destroyed by bombing, including the vaults of the church. The tower still stands. So much for statics.

Jahn employed me to make detailed drawings of the mechanism of the old organ, and of acoustic ceilings for other buildings in which he installed organs. We parted as friends.

I was again unemployed. My mother had met, at a spa, the Viennesse architect Wlach, who was associated with Joseph Frank, one of the leaders of the Modern Movement in Austria. He had expressed interest in me, and I traveled to Vienna to present myself.

On my way back I stopped at St. Wolfgang, where Margaret and Alfred were visiting with friends. Noting my torn sweatshirt under my transparent shirt, they said indignantly, "You will never get a job if you run around in such sloppy attire." The next day a letter arrived from Vienna, offering me the job. "Now all is lost," exclaimed Margaret. Once more my education had failed.

In the mid-twenties Germany had moved to the right. In 1924 old Field Marshal von Hindenburg was elected president. It is curious that people believe that defeated generals make good presidents. After their defeat in 1870 the French elected MacMahon; after their defeat in 1918 the Germans elected Hindenburg. After their defeat in 1940 the French made Pétain their president. After having lost the Philippines to the Japanese and almost losing Korea to the Chinese, MacArthur had a serious chance of being elected president of the United States.

Immediately after I had returned to Hamburg, I joined the Communist march on May Day. I found the quality of the membership much improved; the lunatic fringe had dropped out. The men and women with whom I marched were the type of solid workers who, with stubborn patience, had built the prewar Social Democratic party and the trade unions. There is a myth propagated both by Communists and by their adversaries that the skilled workers were Social Democrats, and the lower layers of the "Proletariat" were Communists. Almost all the workers whom I met in the Party were pretty good workers. They had to be; otherwise, as Communists, they would be the first to be fired. It was a process of natural selection.

I resumed my work in my trade union, the Butab. I found that the little left-opposition group had painted itself into a corner; they had assumed the role of the elect preaching to the heathen who were too blind to see the light. I resumed my fraternal approach to erring brothers. We had two ultraleftists in our group. When I had prepared a resolution which I felt had a chance to be accepted, I always let one of the wild men speak first; after their rantings, my proposal sounded moderate and reasonable, and usually was passed. I recommend this tactic to anyone who wants a proposal to be accepted by a group, political or other: always have an extremist speak first; then your proposal will be seen as a sensible middle-of-the-road compromise. Our opposition gained respect and sympathy; at the next leadership election we got forty percent of the vote.

Thirty years later the Social-Democratic head of our Butab local came to Canada with a delegation. The other members of the delegation wondered how we had come to know each other. My ex-opponent said, "We once worked together in the Butab." I added, with a laugh, "Yes, together and against each other." He said, "Oh, that was not so bad."

The motion picture industry in Germany was almost completely dominated by militarist reaction. The Berlin propaganda center of the KPD initiated a move to form a "People's Film League" to counteract this influence by showing progressive films: Chaplin, Lang, Eisenstein, etc. The move was welcomed by a broad spectrum of public opinion, pacifist, liberal, and nonpartisan. I went to see Theodor Haubach, who was then the editor in chief of the Social-Democratic paper in Hamburg. He promised his support; but when I visited him again, he informed me that the national leadership of the SPD had decided to oppose the League as a "Communist Front." Some SPD members and practically all liberal and non-Party members continued their support, and the League did some good work.

The KPD center also decided to launch a second paper in Hamburg, less doctrinaire and appealing primarily to white-collar workers, to be read during their lunch hour. Albert Norden, its editor, became a lifelong friend. I wrote a few reviews of movies and other public events for this paper.

As the trip to Brunstorf took too long for daily commuting, I had rented a room on the waterfront, with a magnificent view down the Elbe River. I was a member of the KPD local organization; it was in a working-class district which included one of the city's oldest slums. The KPD had copied the organizational scheme of the Russian party: members were organized primarily at their place of work; only those working in small enterprises, pensioners, and housewives were organized on a neighborhood basis. I saw this as a serious mistake. It had made sense in Czarist Russia, where most workers had left their families in the village, lived in barracks near the factory, and worked a porous eleven-hour shift. In Germany the workers had less opportunity to talk during work and rushed home at the end of their shift; their life centered around home and neighborhood. Without minimizing the vital importance of organization at the workplace, I advocated making the residential district the primary basis of Party organization. The question was often discussed, but nothing was changed.

The organizational secretary of my district was a worker in a small factory, a very capable, warm-hearted woman. I was made political secretary; we worked well as a team. My main task was political education. We struggled against the SPD for the hearts and minds of the workers. In order to train our members, I assumed the role of an SPD spokesman. Sometimes, when my arguments put my comrades on the spot, they got mad at me, and I had to switch roles.

During my year of tenure there were four elections. We climbed up tenement stairs to talk to people and to distribute literature. I learned how proletarians, and also how lumpen-proletarians, live and think. We also, of course, put up posters.

The first election was to the parents' council of the local school. As Communists practiced family planning extensively, we had difficulty finding candidates but finally put up a respectable slate. The next two elections were for the parliament of the City-State of Hamburg, the first of which was ruled unconstitutional by the courts. The last and most important election was for the Reichstag, in 1928. We made headway in all four elections; in the elections to the Reichstag both the SPD and the KPD made substantial gains. Another myth was exploded: the notion that the KPD thrived only by exploiting the misery of the masses, and that it would fade away with prosperity.

While Germans are not "born soldiers," in the twenties they

still liked to play at soldiering, marching in uniformed ranks to the sound of drums and fifes — a music very different from that of the battlefield. The right had organized the "Stahlhelm" (steel helmet) under the protectorate of President Hindenburg. The SPD followed suit with the "Reichsbanner," and the KPD with the "Red Front." The Front was entirely separate from the secret military organization that had fought in Hamburg in October 1923; it was purely an instrument of propaganda.

The Stahlhelm held its big annual rally in "Red" Hamburg. Most Social Democrats as well as Communists considered this a provocation, but the SPD government of the city-state gave it full police protection. This was part and parcel of the SPD policy of appeasing the enemies of the Weimar Republic which paved the way to its downfall.

We posted groups along the route of the Stahlhelm parade, shouting "Down with the Fascists!" The police interfered immediately. I organized a laughing choir, which annoyed the potbellied bemedaled marchers much more than did the shouting. The police stopped that also. "Is one no longer allowed to laugh?" I asked. "Not here and now," they replied. The route of the march went through a cut in the escarpment which borders the Elbe, and was crossed by a street bridge. We posted ourselves on the bridge and laughed down from there until the police caught up with us. In the afternoon there was another big parade. The police were on trucks and jumped off, swinging their rubber truncheons, as soon as we started shouting. I did not run, but walked straight toward them, and they went around me. In the evening, groups of Stahlhelm men were walking down the Reeperbahn, the heart of Hamburg's famous amusement district, which was lined by hostile crowds. I planted myself right next to a tall, husky policeman and shouted, "Down with the Fascists!" In utter surprise he looked down at the runt at his side and finally said, quite politely, "You have to stop that; you are disturbing the peace." "If you say so, officer," I replied, and walked away amid general hilarity.

These were harmless little skirmishes in the guerilla war which was spreading in Germany and soon grew into deadly street fights. The clashes were between KPD and SPD on one side, and Stahlhelm and Nazis on the other. I never heard of clashes between Communists and Social Democrats. The hostility between SPD and KPD was sharp at the top, but it never really destroyed the solidarity of the working class at the base.

Another minor event during that period illustrates the fatal blindness of the Social Democrats. A friend took me to an SPD meeting where the speaker was the Belgian Socialist Henrik De Man. De Man advocated replacing class struggle by "People's Socialism." I attacked him sharply; nobody else had a word of criticism. When the Nazis occupied Belgium, De Man became their collaborator.

The Nazis had fared poorly in the 1928 Reichstag elections. But I noted that their vote in Hamburg had been increasing in the three successive elections held there, and I also noticed an increasing number of visitors, including workers, at their office which I passed daily on my way to work. I said to the comrades in my district that we should no longer concentrate our fire on the SPD, but should also tackle Nazi propaganda. Nobody agreed; they all said contemptuously, "Them — everybody knows that they are enemies of the workers."

The skill and flexibility of Nazi demagoguery has been greatly underrated. Many misguided idealists sincerely believed in their proclaimed goal of "National and Social Liberation." Anti-Semitism played only a minor role in their propaganda, at least in Hamburg, and its proclaimed goal coincided with that of the Zionists: "Send the Jews to Palestine!" There was only one industrial plant in Hamburg where the majority of workers were Nazis, a small ship-wrecking yard. A strike broke out there over wages. The SPD and trade unions gloated, "Serves them right, will teach them a lesson." The Communists proclaimed their solidarity with the strikers but did nothing effective to support them. The Nazis kicked the owner of the shipyard out of their party and sided with the workers.

The Nazis had stolen its name, "Socialist Workers' party," its holiday, the first of May, and its red flag, which they disfigured with the swastika, from the traditional labor movement. Now many workers began to take their "Social Liberation" seriously.

In the first week of May 1928 I visited the Bauhaus in Dessau, under the pretext of applying for a job teaching statics. Hannes Meier, who had succeeded Gropius as head of the Bauhaus, asked me, "How much statics do you know?" — "As much as the average architect." — "That means: nothing." We both laughed, and then ensued a lengthy discussion on my real interest, housing policy. We parted friends.

On my way back from Dessau to Hamburg, I stopped in Berlin

to participate in a big national demonstration of the Red Front (I was not a member). As I heard the miners from Central Germany sing the beautiful revolutionary song, "Brothers, to Sun and to Freedom, Brothers, Upward to Light," tears came to my eyes. I felt in my bones that the future for them held not light, but utter darkness.

I saw and still see the history of Germany in the fourteen years following World War I as a race between revolution and war. In December 1918 I had run into Max Warburg at the door of the family bank which he headed. He told me my political ideas were wishful thinking. The term was new to me and hit home. But what was Max thinking? He believed in the full restoration of prewar Germany in a prewar world. But the war was no accident, and identical causes are bound to have identical effects. Powerful states compete with each other for a "place in the sun" for their national capital, their rivalry sharpening until they resort to the "ultimate reason of kings." If German imperialist capitalism is restored, it will restart the war for its "place in the sun." Only a revolutionary transformation could prevent it, so I believed.

Revolution lost, and German imperialism resumed its aggression after a twenty-year pause. My expectation has come true, but was this unavoidable? If the prosperity of the 1920s had not been ended by the economic crisis, World War II might not have happened. But then, was the crisis avoidable in a capitalist world economy?

Throughout this period the SPD, having accepted restoration of the prewar social structure, had to appease militarism. The KPD was the only party consistently fighting it. I am proud of having participated in that fight.

VIENNA

On October 1, 1928 I started work with the firm of Frank and Wlach. Joseph Frank had a fine, subtle, and skeptical mind, typical of the best of the Viennese intelligentsia of the period. I learned much from him. Once, when I asked him what was really the common characteristic of the wide range of different approaches that made architecture "modern," his answer was, "Modern architecture is light." When we discussed Le Corbusier, he said, "He is a great lyric poet." I was surprised; but Ronchamp has proven him right.

Our most interesting project was a competition for a large

housing development near Berlin. At that time the received wisdom was that rows of houses must always be oriented to have eastern and western exposure. Frank convinced me that southern exposure was the most desirable one, admitting full sunshine in winter and providing protection against the midday sun in summer, especially if faced with a balcony; the north side could, depending on the size of the dwelling unit, be used primarily for stairs, halls, kitchens and bathrooms. An eastern and in particular a western exposure admits far too much sunshine in summer and, dependent on many factors, rarely all favorable, scant sunshine in winter. Most of the two-story row houses and three- or four-story apartments of our project faced south; those facing east and west had different floor plans. We learned later that a sizable minority of the jury had preferred our plan; the majority, committed to the east-west doctrine, rejected it for that reason. Gropius won the first prize and the commission.

In the last days of May 1929 my mother, then in a clinic at Wiesbaden, suffered a stroke. I rushed to Wiesbaden; her mind was still clear. She knew she was dying; I did not. She wanted to go back to Hamburg; the journey was difficult, but she felt more at ease in a private clinic there. I wanted to be closer to her than I was in Vienna. Not having found a job in Hamburg, I tried Berlin. I saw some of the leading Berlin architects: Mendelsohn, Luckhardt, Gutkind; they were interested but had no opening at the time. When I returned to Hamburg after two days her condition had worsened; her mind was clear only intermittently. She passed away in her sleep during the shortest night of the year; I left her bedside and walked in the dawn the long way to the suburban home of Robert Solmitz where I was staying.

After visiting Gertel in Karlsruhe, I went back to Vienna. At the end of 1929 there was not much work at the office, and I was unemployed once again. I decided to carry out my long-delayed plan to see Greece, and also Egypt, and had stepped out of my door to go to the Lloyd Triestino Line to arrange for the passage, when the mailman handed me a postcard: the architect Kulka asked me to present myself for an interview for a temporary job. I discovered that Kulka was an associate of the famous architect Adolf Loos. I did not go to the Lloyd Triestino; the pyramids would have to wait a few weeks more for me.

I had encountered Loos once before. On my first visit to Vienna, in 1912, Jacques Rosenberg, the youngest brother of my

Russian grandmother, had taken me to a talk by Loos about his struggles for his building on Michaelerplatz, a work of modern architecture facing the Imperial Palace — *lèse-majesté* in the eyes of all good burghers of Vienna.

Jacques Rosenberg was quite a character: a *grandseigneur-bohémien.* When I met him in Berlin late in 1918, he said, "You know, Hans, those Bolsheviks are right, they are quite right — but I am glad that I lived before this time."

Loos had been commissioned to design a group of row houses for exhibition of the "Werkbund" in Vienna, and I was hired to carry out the work on the basis of his sketches; Loos came to Kulka's office several times a week for one or two hours. He talked not only about the work in hand. When he learned that I had worked in America, he told me that, as a young man, he had worked in Sullivan's office with Frank Lloyd Wright. He called my attention to the craftsmanship of the chairs in his office, repeated his favorite story of the arts-and-crafts professor who had designed a saddle,* and talked of his struggles for Arnold Schönberg's music. After work on the row houses was finished, I was kept on to work on two large "villas," one in stone and one of log construction. Loos thought and designed in three dimensions, even more than Joseph Frank. Once, when I had designed a long room with windows at both ends, he rejected it, saying it would have the effect of disturbing twilight. I had studied the lighting of interior spaces for years, in particular of stairwells; Loos' remark added a new dimension.

I liked Kulka and admired Loos, but my work in their office lasted only six weeks.

I greatly enjoyed living in Vienna. I loved the old streets and squares of the city, its baroque palaces, churches, and gardens. There was hiking and swimming in summer, skiing in winter, and first-rate music. My monthly salary was exactly the same as my weekly check in Los Angeles, but I enjoyed life more. Commodity prices were pretty much the same, but rent and services were much cheaper, and I needed no car. We worked a divided shift,

---

* "An arts-and-crafts professor designed a saddle and showed it to a master craftsman. The master: 'Herr professor, if I knew as little as you do about work, about leather, about horses, and about riding — I could also design such a saddle.' "

with a break from 12:00 to 2:00 p.m., and I spent many hours in the Art Museum which was next door to Frank's office.

I had good friends in Vienna, Valentin and Franya Sobotka, who had studied with Margaret in Heidelberg. They had lived in Hamburg in the early twenties, where I had remodeled their apartment. Valentin was the youngest of four brothers who owned a factory making baking powders. He once told me, "My brothers are very proud that we never had a strike and pay wages above union rates. But it is really very easy; wages account only for about three to four percent of the sales price of our products." In such conditions high wages are much less costly than loss of production by a strike, or damage to machinery or material by negligent work. High organic composition of capital is, of course, characteristic of "developed" countries and determines their general level of wages. This is the "secret" of the substantial rise in real wages and the level of living of the working class in "developed" countries, which Marx could hardly have foreseen when he wrote *Capital.*

Leonie P., whom I had known at Darmstadt, had returned to Vienna and lived with her aunt, Dr. Friederike Lubinger, a medical doctor. Lubinger was a remarkable woman, a militant old socialist; before the war Trotsky had been a frequent visitor in her home. I spent much time there.

Despite my generally happy life in Vienna, I could not get rid of the feeling which had plagued me for years that I was performing below my capacity. I had read a bit about psychoanalysis and had met, through Gertel, the analyst Dr. Groddeck, who admired Gertel and her work. I was greatly impressed by Groddeck. I suspected that my poor performance might be connected with my unsatisfactory and irregular sex life, and that an analysis might help. On the recommendation of my brother-in-law I went to see Alfred Adler, the founder and head of the school of "Individual Psychology."

I was not impressed by Adler. I felt that his face was vulgar, and his questions and remarks utterly primitive. He had invited me to visit him at his country house on a Sunday afternoon. When I arrived there after a two-hour hike, I found the company, other patients of Adler, utterly repugnant. Adler showered me with praise for my prowess in hiking for two hours. This ridiculous praise of a most ordinary performance was obviously intended to help cure my presumed "inferiority complex," his pet theory.

There was not a shred of evidence that I really fitted into that particular box.

I know, of course, that at a certain stage of an analysis the patient develops "resistance," aversion against the analyst. But at that stage Adler ended his "treatment" and went to America. I had periodically paid his fees, which were stiff and absorbed the better part of my salary, with a few weeks' delay. Ten days after he left, I received a threatening letter from his lawyer, demanding that I pay the bill for the last three or four sessions, with a hefty lawyer's fee to boot. I showed the letter to Lubinger, who indignantly called it a gross violation of medical ethics. This parting shot may have distorted my judgment of Alfred Adler. Be that as it may, there was probably nothing wrong with my psyche; my underperforming was simply due to my being a square peg in a round hole. As Ludwig Klages had correctly concluded almost twenty years earlier from analyzing my handwriting, I was not made to be an architect. I lack the essential of the creative artist: to be *innerlich voller figur* — internally full of shape, or form, as Albrecht Dürer had put it. In five centuries nobody has been able to improve on this formulation of the great German artist of the Renaissance.

City planning is a different calling. The three main interests which I had developed since childhood converged in it: art and architecture, geography, and socioeconomic problems. Also, vitally important for a city planner is the ability to express himself clearly in speech and writing. I knew that I could write (You, dear reader, may disagree). Composition had been my strong suit in high school, and my occasional contributions to newspapers had been well received. But I laid no store on verbal skills; I wanted to *do* things, not talk or write about them.

If something comes easy to one, one thinks everyone can do it, if he only tried. Gertel, to whom drawing was as natural as breathing, never would believe that I could not draw.

Good writing has something to do with clear thinking. Many years later, in 1955, when I told Dorothy Schoell, who was a leader of the Housing Movement in Philadelphia and for a while had been my boss, that I was leaving to go to Toronto, she exclaimed, "That is a great loss for Philadelphia." I objected that others could do just as well what I had been doing. She countered, "No, there are very few people who can take a problem, analyze it, and come up with an answer."

At the time I regarded her flattering statement as a gross exaggeration. I now believe it may be true. Time and again I have seen colleagues, including some whose work I highly respect, flounder, unable to come to a conclusion because they could not see the forest for the trees.

The ability to see the forest is probably identical with what Patrick Geddes, the great pioneer of urban and regional planning, called "synopsis," seeing things in relation to each other. The horrible jargon word is "holistic."

Geddes' synopsis has meaning on two levels. It means seeing the physical environment as a unit. But it also means seeing the life of human beings in society as a unit.

Why do so few people take a synoptic view? Noticing the many stupid things that people say, write, and do, I had concluded that they had no brains. That conclusion was wrong; they do have brains, as is evidenced by the many clever little things they do. They do have brains; they just don't have the guts to use them. They do not dare to use them where it really matters, on the basic questions of human life in society and nature. There they rely on received wisdom or, worse, on public opinion, which is increasingly manufactured by hired public-relations men.

When I went to Vienna in 1928, I was not sure whether I would join the Social-Democratic or the Communist party. The Austrian Socialist party, unlike its German counterpart, took Marxism seriously and prepared for the defense of the republic by organizing the workers in the "Schutzbund," a genuine workers' army. I admired and still admire the constructive achievements of the social-democratic City-State (called Province) of Vienna. The tiny Austrian Communist party I suspected of being just a bunch of "coffeehouse intellectuals."

Shortly after my arrival in Vienna, I met Franz Koritschoner, one of the founders of the Austrian Communisty party, at Lubinger's place, and we became friends. I found that the Austrian Communist party, small as it was, was a genuine workers' party, and I joined. In the following year I heard a public speech by Otto Bauer, the leader of the Socialists, defending the shortlived Streruwitz government, a coalition of social democrats and the party of industrial capital, a small party which called itself "Liberal" under the Monarchy and "Grossdeutsch" (Great German) under the Republic. Before and after this period Austria was governed by the "Blacks," the Catholic party, with the support of the "Grossdeutsch." Bauer justified the Streruwitz government as a coalition of the forces of the city (industrialists and workers) against those of the country (landlords and peasants). I was shocked at this betrayal of the solidarity of the working people of city and country against their exploiters. It confirmed my conviction that I had made the right choice in sticking to the Communists.

At that time Yugoslavia was ruled, behind a "democratic" facade, by the brutal terror of King Alexander. Communist refugees came to Lubinger's apartment. I arranged an interview for them with Cahen, the correspondent of the prestigious *Frankfurter Zeitung,* whom I had met in Paris through Gertel.

One of these refugees had become Leonie's lover and lived at the Lubinger apartment. He was regarded as a hero because he had managed to escape from prison three times. The Party found out that he actually had broken down under torture and betrayed others to the police, who had arranged his escapes. The Party decided to send him to Berlin and thence to Moscow, and asked me to accompany him to the railroad station to increase his confidence. The following year, in Moscow, I tried to find out what had happened to him, but I met a stone wall. Probably, I collaborated in sending him to his death.

The "Red Aid" sent money, in dollar bills, to Yugoslavia to aid the families of the victims. As Austrians needed a visa to enter Yugoslavia and Germans did not, I served as a courier. My instructions were to act like a wealthy tourist and to bring back nothing on paper to avoid suspicion. I got a *losung,* a word to be dropped in conversation to identify myself, the address of a contact, and a second address to be used if the first one failed. I used the weekends for my trips.

On my first trip my contacts were an intellectual couple in Zagreb, capital of Croatia. They were tense and nervous; they insisted that I take back a long written report. On my suggestion, I waited for the wife one afternoon in the lobby of a movie theater, followed her in line to the counter, and sat down beside her in the darkened theater, where she passed the manuscript to me.

My second trip was more difficult. At the house of my contact a young man came out of the door and told me that my contact had been arrested during the night. There was clearly a danger that I would be followed. For hours I crisscrossed the city and the crowded open-air market to shake off any follower; then I went to the house of my second contact, which was adjacent to the market. A very pleasant young man opened the door and invited me in. I said I had been told in the market that in this house they sold *opanki,* the embroidered shoes of the Croatian peasants. He could not understand who could have given me this misinformation, nor why. When I finally dropped my *losung* in the course of our conversation, he countered with the prearranged key word. The ice was broken and I gave him the package of dollars. He told me that he expected three comrades for lunch and asked me to stay. Soon his guests, who impressed me favorably, appeared. They insisted on giving me a written receipt for the money, on a small scrap of paper. After lunch I left. At the railroad station, where I had checked my tourist-style bag, I hid the scrap in the hollow for soap in my shaving brush. Years later I saw a movie in which the first thing done by a detective searching an apartment was to unscrew a similar shaving brush; I had not been as smart as I had thought.

A few days later, in Vienna, I learned that within an hour of my leaving the house the police had come in. My comrades had fought back with firearms and had all been killed. Had I unconsciously put the police on their trail? Am I responsible for the death of four good men? I will never know.

My only other political work in Vienna was with the Communist opposition group in my trade union, the Austrian Building Workers' Union. As I was the only white-collar worker in the group, they made me its secretary. When the First Soviet Five-Year Plan got under way, the group, all skilled workers, decided to offer their services to help build socialism; they sent a letter with their proposal to the Soviet Building Workers' Union and asked me if I wanted to go. I said that, as far as I knew, the Soviets needed engineers but had plenty of architects, but that they could include my name anyway. After several weeks the Soviet trade union replied, requesting details about "the architect who had worked in America." I sent them the relevant information.

Over a month passed. I thought the matter was a dead issue. My work with Adolf Loos was finished, and I again prepared to go to Egypt and Greece when I got a letter from the Soviet Trade Representative in Vienna offering me a job with the "Second Building Trust" in Moscow.

I had somewhat ambivalent feelings about going to Moscow. I

wanted to build socialism. But I preferred a sunny climate. I had read a lot about hardships and shortages in the Soviet Union, which struck me as worse than they had been in Germany in the immediate postwar period, and I was not quite masochistic enough to relish the prospect. At Lubinger's I met Sebald Ruetgers, a splendid man. Ruetgers was a Dutch engineer and economist. He had been one of the founding members of a small left-wing party which had split off from the Dutch Social Democrats because of the colonial question. During the war he had worked in America. After the October Revolution he organized a group of engineers and workers to help the Soviet Union to develop a new industrial base in the "Kusbass," the rich coal fields of Western Siberia. Ruetgers really was the inventor of "foreign aid." Unfortunately, few of the later practitioners of that art have matched the selfless dedication of Ruetgers and his group.

Ruetgers assured me that I could live quite comfortably in Moscow — he proved to be right — and strongly encouraged me to go. I had not the faintest notion what the Second Building Trust did, but I accepted the job. I intended to go first to Egypt and Greece, and thence through the Black Sea to the Soviet Union. But the Trade Representative's office insisted that I was needed immediately, so I once more deferred that trip. When I came to Moscow I found, of course, that the Soviet Union would not have collapsed if I had arrived six weeks later.

CHAPTER VI

In the
Soviet Union

1930 – 1937

EXPECTATIONS

What did I expect to find in the Soviet
Union? Certainly not paradise. I had not yet read Engels's blunt
statement, in his introduction to Marx's *Theses on Feuerbach,* that
"there never will be a perfect society," but I saw the goal of a
"classless and stateless society" as a very distant one, many generations in the future. I accepted — and still accept — the dialectical
notion that only a strong state can abolish the class division of society,
and that only a classless society can hope to live
without a "state," meaning a monopoly of violence on a given
territory. I agreed that during a civil war there can be no freedom
of speech for those fighting you, and not too much in a belea-
guered fortress such as the Soviet Union clearly was. I was willing
to accept the discipline necessary for unified collective action.

I was aware of the poverty and backwardness of old Russia and
of the utter devastation and starvation which foreign invasions
and civil war had inflicted on the country, and which it had barely
overcome by a heroic effort. I expected that people, as everywhere, would work primarily for their own and their family's
welfare. I did not think of the Communist party as a community
of saints, but I expected its members to seek happiness primarily
in the satisfaction of building a better society in the Soviet Union,
as an example for the whole world to follow. I was looking forward to participating in that great task. I would no longer have to
choose between professional and political work; both would be

the same. I now could pursue my ideal by working for, rather than fighting against. When I was greeted at the frontier by the banner reading "Workers of the World, Unite!" I felt I was entering a country that shared my aspirations.

Moscow

The Second Building Trust was not an architectural office; it was a construction enterprise that produced buildings designed by outside architects. During the many years when building in Russia had been almost at a standstill, the rift between designing office and building site had widened to an abyss. The task of the architects employed by my Building Trust was to translate the beautiful architects' designs into working drawings which were much less beautiful, but which could be carried out with the limited materials and skills available at the time. It was a very necessary task but hardly an inspiring one.

I had started to learn Russian at various times but had not progressed much beyond being able to read the Cyrillic alphabet. To help me communicate, a young architect by the name of Lutsky was assigned to me. He spoke excellent, very refined, upper-class German. When I asked him where he had learned it, he said from his German governess. I knew — and it had disturbed me — that the Soviets had barred children of the bourgeoisie from university study, so I asked, "If your father was a bourgeois, how come you were allowed to study?" He answered indignantly, "My father is a proletarian; he is employed as legal counsel by a Soviet trust." It was a different concept of the proletariat than the one I was used to.

This was not my only surprise. A few weeks after I had started work, I was told that there would be a staff meeting after work to discuss overtime payment. We worked nine-to-five, with a luncheon break and two tea breaks, tea being served in the office; I had regarded this as a perfectly normal working day. It turned out that the legal working day for white-collar workers was six-and-a-half hours, that the luncheon break was supposed to last only half an hour — it rarely took less than one — and that the tea breaks did not count; so we had been working two hours of overtime. By law the pay was 150 percent for the first and 200 percent for the second hour; the administration wanted to pay only 150 percent for the second hour. After a long and heated discussion the senior engineer got up and said, "There isn't really that much work to do; we can handle it quite well with one hour of over-time." Everyone agreed; the question was settled.

The main speakers on both sides had been Party members. Where was the "monolithic character," "the leading role," and the "collective wisdom" of the Party about which I had read so much? Through Lutsky, I asked our Party secretary, a nice young engineer. He was surprised. "I represent the workers, and he (his main antagonist) represents management; that we are both Party members has nothing to do with it."

I knew that Lenin, following the example of the Paris Commune, had introduced "Part-Max": workers elected to office were to be paid no more than their normal wage. I had understood this as a strict limit on the earnings of any Party member. So, when Lutsky asked if I wanted to share some evening work with him for another office, I felt obliged to hand over my pay to the Party organization, which only accepted it with great reluctance. I found out that "Part-Max," as I had understood it, did not exist and had never existed.

The trust had put me up in a little hotel, since demolished, on the lower part of the Red Square. From my third-floor window I could look into the Kremlin. Repairs of the Kremlin walls were under way. I noticed that many of the workers took naps during working hours — right under the eyes of the Soviet leaders. In capitalist countries labor discipline is maintained by the worker's fear of losing his job; but in the Soviet Union it is almost impossible to fire anyone. Freedom from the fear of being fired and from the consequent labor discipline may be more important to most workers than freedom of the press.

My group of Communist building workers from Vienna arrived in Moscow shortly after I did, as did a similar group from Berlin. One of the Viennese workers, a certain Gassner, was a specialist in scaffolding. He was horrified by the forest of timbers which the Russians used for scaffolding, and wanted to introduce "scaffold-ladders," an efficient technique of light scaffolding. He came to me and asked me to make drawings of it. With Gassner indicating every detail to me, I made the drawings, wrote the specifications, and went to several building organizations trying to persuade them to adopt them. They had committed all their forces to ful-filling their plan, and declined to take on any new task. I went to the "Workers' and Peasants' Inspection," which was at the time a very powerful commissariat, able and willing to cut through red tape. With their aid the Moscow City Building Administration was persuaded to create a section to manufacture, erect, and take down scaffold-ladders. I was offered the job of heading that new section but declined; I felt unqualified for the job and preferred to work as an architect. Gassner, who evidently had hoped to obtain some higher position than that of carpenter, was furious when he got none, returned to Vienna, joined the Social Democrats, and gave speeches about the horrors of life in the Soviet Union.

In that period, when the First Five-Year Plan of super-rapid industrializaton got under way, the Soviet Union hired specialists from all over the world, with Germany and the USA supplying the biggest contingents. At that time most Russians still had a very primitive notion of what makes a good specialist; they regarded him as the owner of a number of secret recipes. When the foreign specialists failed to produce recipes, they were suspected of holding back secrets.

As my old friend from Darmstadt, Fritz Löw, whom I met again in Moscow, remarked, the greatest contribution of the foreign specialists was their effect on the "old" Soviet specialists. These were always afraid of being accused of sabotage if anything went wrong, as may happen with any innovation. Therefore most of them had taken the safe way out by sticking to established obsolete routines. When they were challenged by the competition of the foreign specialists, they began to apply their very considerable theoretical knowledge to the practical tasks of the day.

The Workers' and Peasants' Inspection established a committee consisting of some foreign specialists, who were also members of the Communist party, to advise the government. I was appointed to this committee. We were asked to report on the question of building a subway in Moscow. I said yes; the majority were inclined to say no at first, based on the following reasoning: Moscow had a population of two million — that was the figure found by the census of 1926-7; in 1930 it was probably closer to three — a city of two million people could be adequately served by an improved streetcar system; Marx and Engels had said that big cities are bad and would gradually disappear under socialism; the Soviet government, at an early date, had established a commission for the "unburdening" of the capitals, Leningrad and Moscow. "We have a planned economy; if the government decides to limit the population of Moscow to two million, it will be two million."

I did not believe in the omnipotence of the state. One day, after a meeting of the committee, I discussed the question with Sebald Ruetgers. I said, "How do you want to stop the growth of Moscow? There are only three ways. First, fascist methods: have policemen take people by the scruff of their necks and throw them out." — "We can't do that." — "Second, use good democratic capitalist methods: create a lot of unemployment." — "We can't have unemployment in a socialist country." — "Well," I said, "There remains only the third method: make living conditions in Moscow much less attractive than they are in other places." Ruetgers laughed and said, "We can't do that; important people such as you and I live in Moscow." In the end, the committee recommended building the subway.

I am still puzzled that so many people, in the West as well as in the East, refuse to recognize the simple truth that you cannot have an attractive city without attracting people.

The administration of the trust drove me to see the apartment they had found for me. I wondered why they drove a Rolls Royce. They explained that, because of the lack of repair facilities in the Soviet Union, it was the most economical car for them.

The apartment complex in which I was to live for the following seven years was owned by the Commissariat of Heavy Industry, which used it to house its specialists, both foreign and Soviet. It consisted of two five-story walk-up apartment slabs, each containing about fifty or sixty apartments, built to German standards of the 1920s. My apartment was on the fourth floor of the second block, facing the court between the two slabs on one side and the large garden of a neighboring hospital on the other. It contained, in addition to a kitchen with a covered balcony, and a bathroom, three rooms of 23, 15, and 11 square meters respectively. I was given the choice of one of the rooms. I knew that the average bedroom space per person (there were few, if any, rooms in Moscow which were not used for sleeping) was only five square meters, and I felt rather like a greedy bourgeois in choosing the biggest one. But it faced the crowns of the big old trees of the hospital garden, while the two other rooms faced the barren court, and I could not resist. It was furnished with a bed, table, and chairs, which I supplemented by some pieces of my own, sent from Hamburg, and a folding cot which I bought for guests. I had many of them, male and female, often unknowns who had been recommended to me by friends. I shared the apartment with the Russian engineer who, with his wife and little daughter, occupied the other two rooms.

Food rationing had been introduced, with special privileges for foreign specialists. I did not want privileges and refused to accept a foreign-specialist ration card, and they refused to give me a Soviet one. For the first few months I got along quite easily on unrationed food, but in the fall rationing was tightened and I accepted a privileged card, swearing to myself to buy only what could be bought on ordinary cards.

In the summer I heard that the newly organized State Institute for Projecting Cities ("Giprogor") was looking for staff. I had always been interested in city planning. I had read quite widely in the field, starting in 1913 with Raymond Unwin's classic *City Planning in Practice*. When I had returned from America in 1927, the head of the Hamburg City Planning Office, Maetzel, had invited me to his home. "I want you to tell me what we can learn from America," he said. I had replied, "The most important thing I have learned from America is to do everything you can to promote public transit and to restrain the private automobile." He was surprised, but after a lengthy discussion he agreed. He wanted to take me on his staff but there was no suitable opening at the time. Now at long last I had my chance. I applied to Giprogor and was immediately accepted.

Giprogor did not deal with new towns. These were the responsibility of a different organization under the Commissariat of Heavy Industry. It was in that organization that Ernst May with his group from Frankfurt worked. Giprogor worked on contract with municipalities and other organizations on the reconstruction and enlargement of existing cities. All Soviet cities of a certain size were obliged by law to have a general plan, but only very few had planning offices; of the constituent republics only the Ukraine had established its own "Giprograd," a year prior to Giprogor. Cities in the other republics relied on Giprogor.

In the eighteenth and early nineteenth century Russian city planning had outstanding achievements to its credit. But with the rapid development of capitalism after the middle of the nineteenth century, public control of urban development was abandoned to a much greater degree than in any other European country. In that respect, as in many others, Russia was more akin to the United States — both great continental nations marching from the Atlantic to the Pacific. But the driving energy which had created the skyscrapers, great parks, and civic centers of America had been held down by the oppressive czarist regime. It exploded with the revolution.

For Russians — liberals as well as socialists — the concept of "Revolution" was suffused with quasi-religious notions of rebirth and resurrection. Hence slogans like "Not art for art, but art for revolution," which I could not accept. I saw revolutions — as Marx did — as a way to liberate artistic creativity as the most important part of the full potential of human nature: "Revolution for art" rather than "Art for revolution."

Both the "City Beautiful" and the "Garden City" movements had their adherents in Russia. Interesting plans were developed by architects, but for an entire decade, from 1915 to 1925, building was almost at a standstill. As was the case everywhere, the plans were "Ideal-End-State" plans, with little attention paid to the time span and even less to the financial means required for their implementation.

When the Soviet party and government turned their attention to city planning at the beginning of the First Five-Year Plan, they wanted it to be closely coordinated with socioeconomic planning. This was a sound approach, but it overlooked the great difference in the time horizons of socioeconomic and physical planning. The elements of the latter, buildings and trees, last for generations, even centuries; streets, railroad rights of way, and waterways last even longer. The elements of economic planning are subject to frequent unpredictable changes resulting from scientific and technological developments, discovery of new sources of raw materials and of energy, and changes in foreign trade.

The longest time span used by the economic planners was the fifteen-year "perspective" plan. It determined the population size and the industrial profile of the city; for physical planners these were "givens." Of course, the physical planners frequently proposed substantial modifications of these "givens," which usually were accepted by the economic planners. But the fifteen-year time span to the "target year" was laid down by law. By and large, cooperation between the two types of planning worked well.

Very few foreigners ever worked at Giprogor. At the time I joined the staff there was only one, Rosenberg. He was born in Russia, and had emigrated with his parents to America at the age of thirteen, where he had become a landscape architect in Los Angeles. He was not a Communist but, like most of the foreign "bourgeois" specialists, was attracted to work in the Soviet Union by the much greater scope for creative work than was available in the West during those years of depression.

The Soviet professional staff consisted mostly of architects; the balance were economists. Very few of them were Party members, but they were enthusiastic about the future of the Soviet Union and wholeheartedly devoted to their work. However, they had an aristocratic contempt for money and were unwilling to consider the cost of their often grandiose schemes. Many of them were, in fact, descendants of the nobility. Rosenberg, referring to the title of one of Turgenev's great novels, called Giprogor "A Nobleman's Nest."

The staff was divided into working groups called "brigades." Along with Rosenberg, I was attached to a brigade headed by Alexander Mukhin, a talented and hard-working architect. He respected his staff, left us full freedom, and backed us to the hilt. In addition, there was an economists' section, members of which were attached to projects as the need arose; it was headed by a very able man, a former leader of the Jewish "Bund," a socialist party which had strongly opposed the Bolsheviks. Moreover, we had staff consultants, leading specialists in the many disciplines which contribute to city planning. Our architectural consultants were the three famous Vesnin brothers, leaders of the "Modern Movement" in the Soviet Union. Our transportation consultant was the railroad engineer Obrastsov, a brilliant mind and an enthusiastic supporter of Milyutin's proposal for a "Ribbon City."

The director of Giprogor was not a specialist but an old Bolshevik, a very kind, well-educated, modest man. The technical head was Organov; he had been the city engineer of Moscow under the czars. He was as wise and knowledgeable a planner as I have met anywhere. I learned much from him.

Because of the acute shortage of workers of all categories, Soviet enterprises at that time "hoarded" workers well before they needed them — which of course made the shortage even more acute. Giprogor also had no idea just what I was to do when they hired me. I suggested, and they concurred, that I work on a pet project of mine, a "city without streets." It consisted of huge multistoried apartments, several hundred meters long, located at right angles to a railroad station. Persons were to reach their elevators by walking along an endless corridor; freight was to be carried by electric carts — nonexistent at the time in the Soviet

Union — in the basement. I got stuck when I thought of fire trucks; they would need roads, as in fact would most other goods vehicles. My freight-delivery system was completely unworkable, as was indeed the whole scheme, in addition to being abhorrent and unlivable in its inhuman scale.

In recent decades I have often been reminded of this childish scheme when faced with similar proposals. North Americans, having transformed their fallen god, the car, into the devil, in the time-honored manner of new religions, want to ban him completely and forever from the sacred precincts of the true believers. It seems to be a law of nature than every generation must reinvent the follies of its fathers.

I was asked to work on the general plan for Dzujambe, the capital of Tadjikistan. I studied the documents, but my departure was delayed from week to week, and finally the job was given to another man. Only later did I learn the reason. In those turbulent years of forced-draft industrialization and collectivization, there was great unrest in Soviet Central Asia. Counterrevolutionary bands invaded the country from Afghanistan. While their main purpose was loot, they were also fanatical Moslems. The principal target of their wrath were women who had dared to throw off the *chadar,* the head-to-boot heavy black veil; they cruelly mutilated and murdered them. But they also murdered any Soviet employee on whom they could lay hands. Giprogor did not want to expose its foreign specialists to that risk.

Instead, Rosenberg and I were charged with developing the site plan for a branch of the Soviet Academy of Agriculture in the countryside near Moscow. On a sunny spring morning, when we were driving in a horse and buggy through the landscape, I said to Rosenberg, "We really have picked a nice profession." "Yes," he said, "You know, back in the States people always asked me, 'What is this town planning you are doing; is there a lot of money in it?' — 'No, barely enough to hold body and soul together.' — 'Is it a steady job?' — 'No, you never know if and when you may get your next commission!' — 'Does it give you standing in the community?' — 'No, nobody respects a town planner.' — 'Then, why the hell are you doing it?' — 'I'll tell you why: you can do what you darn please and call it work!' " I do not know of a better recipe for a happy life. I consider myself highly privileged to be one of the fortunate few able to follow it.

Finally, I got a real and important city planning job, the

"sketch" general plan for the town of Vladimir, about 200 kilometers east of Moscow, on the river Klyazma. In the early Middle Ages the princes of Vladimir had been the most powerful rulers in Central Russia. Two churches and a city gate dating from that period are national monuments. But the Tartar invasion had put an end to its role, and it had become a sleepy provincial market town. Now, a plastics factory with over 2000 workers had started operations, and site preparation for an aviation-instrument factory with over 4000 workers was under way. It was my task to provide for the transformation of Vladimir into a modern industrial city, several times the size of the old one.

When I arrived in Vladimir late one evening in November 1931 I saw, by the light of the full moon, towering above the river and the railroad station, a beautiful white city crowning a long ridge, with the steep southern slope of the hill covered by cherry trees. That beautiful image had to be preserved in the transformation of the city. It was a far more interesting and challenging task than planning a new town from scratch.

The local paper had carried a notice announcing my arrival and asking everyone to cooperate with me. So I was well received, and the heads of industrial plants and institutions were willing to give me all the information they had. But they had no notions or plans beyond the current five-year plan. The outfit responsible for power supply aside, they were not concerned with the long-term future. The only exception to willing cooperation was the railroad administration; its personnel even flatly refused to give me exact data on the horizontal and vertical location of their tracks.

I later found that the same attitudes prevail in the West: the public utilities do long-range planning, and the railroads, publicly or privately owned, refuse to talk to city planners. These attitudes are rooted in the character of their work. The specific "forces of production" determine the "ideological superstructure" of those who operate them and are part of them. This should not surprise Marxists, but they seem as unwilling as are anti-Marxists to admit that the similarities between "East" and "West" are more extensive than the differences.

The most interesting interview was at the jail. When I entered the gate, I saw prisoners in the yard joking with their guards. I was escorted to the director's office; I found a young woman in charge of this men's prison. She said, "We are the only outfit in town which needs no space; we are going out of business." I said, surprised, "I know, of course, that crime is supposed to disappear under socialism, but do you really expect it to happen so soon?" She laughed and said, "No, but it is the policy of the government to close all prisons and to transfer the inmates to camps where they can do truly productive work." One knows how terribly this sound approach has been distorted; and the Vladimir jail still stands and is reputed to be the worst in the Soviet Union.

I saw two principal planning problems: first, to develop new residential areas to the east and northeast of the existing city, close to the two new factories; and second, to provide land for future industry, for which the flat valley lands to the east of the city should be reserved. I proposed to develop the heights as residential neighborhoods and the valleys as parks. Then, I proposed to develop the ridge road, the only continuous east-west street in the city, clearly destined to remain its main street. In order to prevent it from being overloaded by traffic, I proposed a by-pass road, which also would improve access to the railroad station and to a new freight yard. The western, upper section of the ridge road was already largely devoted to "main-street" uses, public or commercial; with the great expansion of the city to the east, the eastern section, which gradually descended to the plastics factory, would be required for similar uses. This section was at the time occupied by miscellaneous low-intensity uses, in particular the college of agriculture, which occupied the large area of a former monastery. I suggested to them that they should relocate at their experimental farm on the outskirts of the city. They replied that they could not obtain the funds for construction. This touched off a train of thought to which I will return shortly.

I had never heard the term "ecology," but I was interested in recycling. I devised a triangular scheme: humans would utilize their excrement to fertilize vegetable fields, and the offal of their food to feed pigs; the pig meat would nourish the humans, and their excrement, the vegetables; in turn, the vegetables would feed both the humans and the pigs. This part of my plan was not carried out.

I proposed another innovation, two plans for different "target dates," one for twenty-five years, and a more detailed one for fifteen years in the future; because of the legal fifteen-year limitation I called them fifteen- and ten-year plans respectively. "City plans" are really cross sections through a stream of anticipated and/or planned urban development. There should be several of them, the number being limited only by the availability of time and manpower.

No previous estimates of future population, predicted or planned, had been made. I made them for points fifteen and twenty-five years in the future. I based them on the assumption that Vladimir, because of the resources of the region in manpower skilled in cottage industries, its accessibility by existing and planned transportation lines — rail, road, and possibly water — and its proximity to Moscow, would be an attractive location for industry. This went against the grain of the accepted "functional" method of population prediction. This method started from the number of workers to be employed by "basic" industries, meaning those producing for users outside the city, and then used "multipliers" to add the number of "service" workers and of nonworking dependents. My colleagues questioned me about the type of basic industry I assumed for Vladimir. I replied that there were many potential candidates, including industries not yet in existence, and that some of this potential was likely to be realized. My estimates were deemed to be too high: a growth from not quite 40,000 to 110,000 in fifteen years, and to 140,000 in twenty-five years. Recently I have traced the curve of actual population growth of Vladimir, as given by the census counts of 1927, 1939, and 1959, and found that my estimates were pretty much on line.

Before a project was submitted to the client, it was carefully vetted by the professional staff of Giprogor. A critic was appointed to evaluate the proposal. My critic was particularly well qualified, because he had developed a plan for Vladimir before the big new factories had been planned. His report raised many questions and objections. The staff meeting, which also dealt with a project for another city, also raised many objections. In particular, they found that my plan lacked "structure," meaning a geometrically definable system of streets. My plan was derived from the natural and man-made topography of the site, the other project from a strict geometric scheme. In the end old Organov said, "One of these projects has a bit too much structure, and the other not quite enough"; both projects were approved with minor modifications.

I returned to Vladimir to present my proposal to the city council. Meanwhile, there had been a municipal election, and the new council and mayor were very economy minded. So the mayor, after thanking me for my efforts and praising the plan, said they had no money to proceed to the next step: the elaboration of a final general plan which, after approval by the provincial authorities, would be legally binding. It was not a very far-sighted decision; they were obliged by law to have a general plan, and they would have to pay for it sooner or later.

As mentioned earlier, I had failed to get the agricultural college of Vladimir to relocate. I realized that under conditions of a free market economy the college probably would have agreed, because they could have recovered much, possibly all, of their construction cost by selling their large holding of urban real estate for its "highest and best use": public and commercial buildings for which its central location on the main street was greatly preferable to any other.

All urban land, though not all buildings, had been nationalized. (Small houses remained and still remain the property of their occupants.) The land is administered by municipal land offices which allocate parcels at a purely nominal rent to applicants: factories, institutions, or houses built by any level of government, cooperatives, or individuals. I proposed a differential rent, to be established by competitive bidding.

There were two other aspects of the economy which seemed to me to call for some reform. There was no way to bring operating costs and capital costs to a common denominator. The State Bank charged interest for short-term loans but not for long-term investments. I proposed that the same rate of interest be charged for long- and short-term loans, and that the rate be based on the rate of average annual increase in productivity.

I was also concerned with finding a rational base for the pricing of goods and services. I proposed that prices be proportional to the amount of labor required to produce a unit.

I wrote a memo entitled "Three questions of a city planner to the economists," which I submitted to the economists' section of Giprogor; later, an Austrian official of the State Bank, to whom I had given a copy of my memo, invited me to present it to the club of senior officials of the bank. In both places there ensued a serious and lively discussion which dealt, however, almost exclusively with the first question, differential rent. There was agreement that the then-current system encouraged wasteful underuse of urban land and that charging a differential rent for it would be desirable. But it was pointed out that it was politically very touchy.

Trotsky had proposed a differential rent for agricultural land. The Party — rightly, I think — had rejected his proposal because it violated the sacrosanct principle, "The land belongs to him who works it," which was the basis of the alliance of workers and peasants. It was the cancellation of all rents and mortgage payments which had won over the majority of the peasants and of the nation to the side of the October Revolution.

In recent decades the question of urban differential rent has become the subject of lively discussion and experimentation in the Soviet Union. Competitive bidding has not been adopted, but some ingenious methods have been developed to determine the "value" and rent of different pieces of urban land.

As to the second question, I found that its first part had largely been solved in practice. Long-term projects were required to pay the capital investment within fifteen years. Translated into cumulative interest payments, this resulted in an interest rate practically identical with that paid for short-term loans. The second part, the establishment of a rational base for the level of the interest, seems to be neglected in the Soviet Union, as it is in the West.

The third question, pricing, is of course a constant subject of discussion in the Soviet Union, but I have not been able to follow it.

After the work on Vladimir came to an end, Giprogor proposed to send me to their newly established branch office in Gorki, then still named Nizhni-Novgorod. I had strongly advocated decentralization of city planning and readily agreed. I was to go there in February 1932, but shortly before my departure I broke an ankle, which delayed my voyage.

In the years since my arrival a number of foreign architects had come to work in Moscow, and I had met most of them. Among the group around Ernst May I had established a lasting friendship with Hans Schmidt from Basel and with Grete Schütte-Lihotsky and Wilhelm Schütte, a couple of architects. Hannes Meier, who had been dismissed from the Bauhaus because he was a Communist, also came, with three of his most gifted assistants. Jecky Perfanoff, a German architect born in Bulgaria whom I had met at Gutkind's office in Berlin, had come to Moscow with his wife and two little daughters; during their first week I had put the family up in my room, while I slept in a temporarily unoccupied room in a neighbor's apartment. I also met the Danish construction engineer Bent Gregersen, who became and remains a very close friend.

At that time a German-language weekly newspaper called *Moskauer Rundschau* was published in Moscow. It was the only newspaper in the Soviet Union published by a Social Democrat, Otto Pohl. He had been the Austrian ambassador in Moscow, and when he retired, Litvinov, the head of the Soviet Foreign Office, invited him to stay in Moscow to publish this paper, as a kind of unofficial spokesman for Soviet foreign policy. When the numerous German-speaking foreign specialists arrived, the *Rundschau* assumed a different function: it became a platform for them to express their views, questions, criticisms, and proposals on their Soviet experience. The editor was Lotte Schwarz, the stepdaughter of Otto Pohl. I met her when, in 1930, I submitted an article to her paper. We found that we had much in common and became good friends; Lotte is now the person closest to me.

A few months after my arrival I had been admitted into the Communist party, an honor conferred only on a minority of the members of other communist parties. For ordinary members, membership meant no privileges, only some duties. Party members, in addition to being expected to be models both in their work and in their private life, had to assume a *nagruska* (load), voluntary work assigned to them by the Party with their consent. I was picked to be the chairman of the German Workers' Club, presented as a candidate to the membership, and elected. I had the assistance of the secretary of the club, a worker from Berlin who had already lived several years in Moscow, and of a board elected by the members.

The club had previously consisted mainly of Party members and had devoted most of its time to political discussions. These continued but now played a secondary role. The main function of the club was to serve the educational, cultural, and recreational needs of the workers and specialists who had come to work in Moscow, very few of whom were Party members. During my year of tenure an English-speaking and a Hungarian section were added, and we became the "Foreign Workers' Club."

The club had been housed in a few rooms of an old building; now we needed a bigger and better home. The club secretary, who spoke fluent Russian, presented our demand to the Moscow City Council. Kaganovich, at the time head of the Moscow Party Committee, said, "We need these people; give them anything they ask for." I inspected premises all over Moscow and settled on a building in Ulitza Gertsena (Herzen Street), close to the center of town.

It had been built in the nineteenth century as the palace of the Counts Sheremetiev. The low-ceilinged ground floor was occupied by other users. A magnificent broad staircase led to the high-ceilinged "piano nobile," the floor which the Sheremetievs had inhabited (the ground floor had housed their servants), and which now was ours. There was a long, broad reception hall, with a large hall, the former ballroom, on one side and a suite of smaller, but still spacious rooms on the other. I was struck by the exceptionally harmonious proportions of all these spaces. I was equally struck by their beauty when I revisited the building in 1959.

We had to move our furniture and other equipment from the old to the new building. A horse-drawn cart was hired from the municipal administration to help me and a woman member of our board load and unload the goods. The carter was a tall, handsome young fellow; when we loaded our scenic equipment, the other two teased him, asking him to play the kulak. He had in fact been a kulak, one of the well-to-do peasants who had been expropriated in the process of collectivization. He was very cheerful and obviously well satisfied with his new role as an urban worker. As we walked along, he explained to me why "we," the Russians, had lost the war: there was a Jew on each end of a secret telephone, and the one on the Russian side had betrayed all Russian military secrets to the one on the German side. When our moving job was finished, I asked my woman comrade, "I suppose we have to give them a tip; how much should I give them?" She answered, "Ten rubles, but don't give all of it right away, because they will ask for more, whatever you give them." So I gave my kulak friend five rubles. He looked at it in his outstretched flat hand and said, "malo" (small). I gave him another five rubles. He patted me on the shoulder, saying, "Germans are good people; if it had been Jews, I would have got nothing." I said, "But I am a Jew." He looked at me quizzically. "No, you ain't a Jew." Then, after a while, wagging his index finger at me, he added, "Maybe you are a bit of a Jew; otherwise you would have given me my ten rubles right away."

It was my only experience with anti-Semitism in my seven years in the Soviet Union. It did not scare me into becoming a Zionist.

There were concerts, dances, theatrical performances, games, courses in Russian and many other subjects at the club, and a lot of socializing over a glass of tea or beer, or a meal. There were also some meetings on political questions. Once the speaker was Stassova, head of the International Aid and at the time Stalin's first secretary. She arrived ten minutes before the appointed time; when most of our members arrived late, she shook her head sadly and said, "Comrades, this is not good; we had hoped that the German workers would set an example of punctuality for our Russians." There was not an iota of wounded prima donna vanity in her statement — just sincere regret about the failure of an educational experiment. She was very much the type of an American schoolmarm: honest, straightforward, and straight-laced. It threw a favorable light on Stalin that he had picked such a person as his secretary.

On the eve of May Day our speaker was Lozovski, the head of the "Red" International of Trade Unions. He asked me what he should say; what would be of interest to his audience. The modesty and sense of responsibility of these two top Bolsheviks impressed me greatly.

Other events disturbed me because I could not reconcile them with my concept of inner-party democracy. The first meeting at which I presided was devoted to the First Five-Year Plan. After the success of its first year, Stalin had warned his comrades against letting these successes go to their heads. But soon after, the targets of the plan were raised substantially. Some Party members, led by Bukharin, objected. They feared — rightly, as it turned out — that the result would be serious disproportions and bottlenecks. At our meeting Platten presented this viewpoint. He had been the Swiss Social Democrat who had devised the scheme of bringing Lenin and his associates back to Russia from Zürich in a sealed train through wartime Germany; he lived in Moscow as a highly respected member of the Comintern. As chairman of the meeting I tried, with little success, to protect his right to speak against unfair attacks of his opponents. After the meeting I said to one of them, "These questions must be seriously discussed." His reply was, "We do not discuss; the Central Committee has decided; the discussion is closed." This statement shocked me.

Later, early in 1937, I met Platten on the street. He told me that he had great difficulties. To my question whether Georgi Dimitrov, the hero of the Reichstags Fire trial who now was head of the Comintern, could not help him, he answered that he had talked repeatedly to both Dimitrov and his deputy, Manuilsky, the Soviet representative, but that the only man who really tried hard to help was Ercoli, who represented Italy on the Presidium of the Comintern. Ercoli was the pen name of Palmiro Togliatti, who after the last war built the Italian party into the strongest as well as the most broad-minded Communist party in the West. If I were an Italian, I would be a member.

Our library contained some writings by Trotsky, published when he was still one of the leaders of the Party. Orders came down to lock them up; I objected but was overruled by my board.

Not all of my work as chairman was on this level. Fuel was in very short supply in the winter of 1930-31. As soon as I learned that a supply of coal had arrived at the distribution point I rushed there with a handcart and pulled our ration through the streets of Moscow to the club.

GORKI

In April 1932 I moved to Gorki. There was a problem of keeping my room in Moscow. Legally I was no longer entitled to live there after I had left the Second Building Trust and hence the Commissariat of Heavy Industry which owned the house. In fact, shortly after I had joined Giprogor, the director had called me and showed me a letter from another organization saying, "As your specialist Blumenfeld is occupying our living space, we have had to rent a hotel room for *our* specialist. Vacate the room or pay the hotel bill." The director, who seemed inclined to pay the hotel bill — which was almost three times my salary — asked my opinion. I had by then lived long enough in the Soviet Union to know that all offices were understaffed and most letters remained unanswered. So I said, "Don't answer the letter." The director took my advice, and nothing more was heard of the matter. I stayed in my room; but if one is absent for over three months without reserving the space for certain reasons specified by law, the administration of the house can allocate it to somebody else. I therefore invited a German friend, who worked for the Comintern and lived in their apartment hotel but wanted another place because of unbearable domestic conflicts, to live there with his second wife. Nobody disturbed him and he vacated the room when I returned to Moscow.

My broken ankle had healed, but it still hurt. Before leaving Moscow, I had gone to the medical center of the Commissariat of

Heavy Industry, which was the most prestigious one in Moscow. When the collective agreement of Giprogor had come up for renewal the year before, the trade union membership — practically the entire staff — had instructed the negotiating committee to obtain admission to that center. When the committee reported that it had not been granted, the membership refused to ratify the agreement and sent the committee back for further negotiations, which were successful.

This prestigious medical center had refused my request for an x-ray and for massage, stating, correctly, that the rupture had healed normally. In Gorki, I went to the ordinary district center which is open to anyone. They immediately granted both requests and added treatment with mud packs. This experience showed me that the widespread notion that Moscow is a "showcase" and that everything is worse in the provinces is a myth. I found this confirmed when I hunted in stores for some of the "little things" which are so often in short supply in the Soviet Union. Some things I had not been able to find in Moscow were easily available elsewhere.

Gorki is a beautiful city, its core located on a steep hill above the junction of two broad rivers, the Oka and the Volga, and surrounded by forests full of nightingales. There was swimming in the summer and skiing in the winter. When skiing, the homes of some staff members who were local people became our headquarters to warm up with a glass of tea. I found that these privately owned wooden houses were very comfortable. Most of the staff, myself included, lived in a group of former summer cottages of wealthy local merchants, located at the edge of the hill. The view was beautiful, but the accommodations were primitive. Heating was a problem; water supply was from a pump in the yard; the latrines, about which the less said the better, were located in an unheated shed in the yard.

But we lived there as a happy family. We built ourselves a volleyball court. We had a cook who prepared our meals. I gave her my privileged ration book to buy food for our little community. Two days later the good woman took me aside to tell me, "I baked a cake for you and me." My high-principled resolution never to make use of my privileges melted away.

My task was the replanning of Vyatka, now Kirov, which belonged to Gorki Province but could be reached only by a ten-hour train ride, after crossing the Volga on a ferry. The city is located on the river Vyatka and on the Trans-Siberian Railroad, on the sixtieth parallel, in a forest region. Its population at the time was about 80,000; it was a center of woodworking industry. Two large new factories were planned to supply the schools of the Russian Republic with blackboards, rulers, and other equipment. Vyatka had been the center of a province and therefore had a competent staff of economic planners.

I was also asked to look at the neighboring small town of Slobodskoye. There were many smaller industrial villages in the area, and I came to the conclusion that it required a regional plan to deal with the road system, including bridges across the Vyatka River, water supply, sewage disposal, and cultural and recreational services, and I wrote a memo on this proposal. Regional planning was instituted, though it started only after my departure.

Another problem was the economic base. Zhdanov, one of the most powerful Communist leaders, was at the time Party secretary of Gorki Province. He had the ambition to build "his" province into a powerful industrial empire with its own metallurgical base. The iron was to be extracted from the low-grade swamp ore of the region. I came to the conclusion that it would be far more economical to import iron ore from the Urals, or even finished steel from the Donets Basin. I also questioned the accepted view that woodworking industries should be located close to their source of raw materials. I argued that with the development of wood chemistry most of the material of tree trunks would be used, and that it was far more economical to float trunks down the Vyatka-Kama-Volga waterway than to ship packaged finished products to the arid southwest of European Russia which accounted for a large part of their users.

The economic planners in Vyatka were very interested in the memos which I wrote on these two questions but were obviously afraid that they might arouse the wrath of Zhdanov if they ever came to his attention, so they were duly buried in some files. The same fate befell a third memo. It argued that not only factories, but also regional services — for education, health, research, culture, and also for goods distribution — were the basis of urban growth, and that Vyatka would have to serve a huge area of about 300,000 square kilometers because of the absence of any other city. This implied, though I was politically smart enough not to say so, that Vyatka should be the center of a province — which, of course, would have to be carved in large part out of Gorki Province. Kirov, as Vyatka is now called, is in fact now a provincial capital.

Despite Vyatka's location close to the Arctic Circle, the summer was scorching hot. Two students, who worked with me during their summer vacation, preferred to walk barefoot. But when they went to the city hall cafeteria, the municipal officials complained to me, and I had to tell them to put shoes on. During the period of the midnight sun people stayed in the parks until early morning. One night I heard two young workers eagerly discuss the question of whether engineers should be paid better than workers. Stalin had recently emphasized this, and one fellow put forward the standard arguments of long years of study and greater responsibility, but the other insisted on the equality of effort. The principle *Roma locuta, causa finita* (Rome has spoken, the case is settled) never prevented private discussion.

Our small party organization also discussed political questions. At that time the Party leadership stated that the Soviet Union had become a classless society. I raised the question of the contradiction of this claim with the notion of the dictatorship of one class, the proletariat. Our secretary, an old Latvian printer, replied that remnants of the old ruling classes and of their ideology still had to be held down. Our discussion was frank, serious, and friendly.

The only *nagruska* I undertook at Gorki was teaching a course in city planning at a technical middle school to fifteen-year-olds. When, before leaving Gorki, I used the last session for probing, I found that they had understood practically nothing of what I had told them. This beginning of my teaching career was not very auspicious.

Shortly after my arrival in the Soviet Union the eight-hour day for workers and six-and-a-half hours for employees had been replaced by a uniform seven-hour workday, and the seven-day week had been replaced by a rotating six-day week, with everyone working five days, but every fifth worker having a different "Sunday." This meant that machinery and equipment were fully used every day, and recreational facilities also were equally used every day, without overloading. Coordination of free days for several members of a family was successfully arranged. But after a few months the experiment had to be abandoned. It worked perfectly well for the great majority of workers, but it broke down when it came to the top layer of managers and professionals. They all had obligations in more than one institution and consequently never had a free day. One after another suffered a nervous breakdown. The five-day workweek was continued, but with the same free day for everyone.

I was entitled to two days' vacation for every month worked, or practically one month of vacation. I had taken two days around the May first holiday of 1931 to go to Leningrad. I stayed at the Trade Union Guest House and participated in their demonstration and their dance in the great ballroom of the Czar's Winter Palace. I enjoyed the unique beauty of that magnificent city.

In early August of the same year I embarked on a five-week vacation in the Caucasus. I took a train to Vladikavkaz, in the northern foothills. During a walk in the woods I met two young fellows who warned me that it was dangerous to go further. I asked, "Are there wild animals?" — "No, but there are Ingushi." My new acquaintances were Ossetes, and the Ingush were their traditional enemies. "They steal our cattle," they explained. We then hiked and swam together, and they talked with great pride of the progress which Soviet power had brought to the Ossetes. Throughout the Caucasus I found considerable traditional tensions between different nationalities, but no hostility toward the Russians.

In Vladikavkaz I joined a group of people put together by the Soviet tourist organization from all over the Soviet Union who, like myself, had dropped in at their office. They provided a bus, hotel accommodation, and local guides for a trip across the Caucasus to Tbilisi, on the "Gruzinian Military Road"; we stopped at several places for one or two days for hikes in the mountains. At the highest point of the pass children threw flowers into our bus, shouting, "Asia greets you." The Soviet Union is more than just Russia. When I asked in Transcaucasian ports, "Where is this ship going?" the answer was, "To Russia." After three days in Tbilisi, the beautiful ancient capital of Georgia, I took a train to Batumi, where my childhood friend Olga Solmitz joined me. She had traveled by train to Odessa and from there by boat to Batumi.

Batumi is an oil port, but it is a clean, handsome city with a long, pebbled beach. There was a café built on stilts in the bay, with a view to the snow-covered peaks of the Caucasus, where excellent Viennese and Turkish coffee was served. Coffee was at that time not available in Moscow, but there was smuggling from

Turkey. Any coffee taken from smugglers by the coast guard was given to this café, which was run by the "Red Half Moon" (the Moslem equivalent of the Red Cross).

We found a room opening onto a large terrace on a hill above the sea in the house of the Danish Consul. It was located five kilometers from the city in Zelyonny Mys (Green Cape), famous for its rich botanical garden. It was a most enjoyable vacation.

On the last day I had gone to Batumi and went swimming, leaving my clothes on the beach, as I had done many times before. When I came back, my pants were gone — together with my passport, our steamship tickets, and money. As I had no bus fare, I had to walk back the five kilometers in my underwear. Fortunately, we still had enough money left at our lodgings to buy a pair of pants and new steamship tickets to Sevastopol on the following day. With money sent from Hamburg to Sevastopol, we continued to Moscow, whence Olga returned to Hamburg.

This was in 1931, and we had planned that Olga would come again to share my vacation in 1932. As the Vyatka project had reached a critical stage in the fall of 1932, I had to hand over responsibility to a colleague. Olga came to Gorki, and we took the boat down the Volga to Astrakhan, a week's journey with a number of stops. As it was already late in the season, our only companions in the first class were a military couple; he was the equivalent of a brigadier general, and she was an army doctor. They were both from peasant stock and on their way to visit their folks in their native village.

At that time, October 1932, the depression was shaking the established order everywhere in the West, but particularly in Germany. While I was aware of the rise of Nazism, I still hoped that all antifascists, Communists, Social Democrats, and Christian Democrats would join together to defeat Hitler and open the way to socialism. We talked about our hopes for a socialist world, and I said to the general, "There will be no need for an army; what are you going to do then?" He answered, very seriously, "I will say to the people, 'I have served you faithfully, now you feed me.' " I said, "Sure, you will not starve; but you are still a young man. What are you going to do with your life?" — "I will study." It was a very characteristic answer. Everyone in the Soviet Union was learning. This already struck me in my first week in Moscow when, wandering through the streets in the evening, I noticed everywhere groups of adults sitting in rooms listening to a teacher.

From Astrakhan an old steamer carried us across a very choppy Caspian Sea to Makhatchkala, from where we took a train to Baku. To my surprise I found this center of the oil industry to be a white, pleasant Mediterranean city. We stayed a few days in Baku, then in Tbilisi and in Batumi, and finally a week in Sochi, the most famous resort on the Caucasian Black Sea shore. We returned by sea to Sevastopol and by train to Moscow.

I stayed for a while in Gorki, but felt I was no longer needed and returned to Moscow early in 1933. Giprogor had continued to decentralize and could not offer me a project for another city. I proposed to work on the rationalization and standardization of graphic presentation and symbols. At that time the economist Dr. Otto Neurath and his group had come to Moscow from Vienna. They had developed a system of graphic symbols for the presentation of socioeconomic data. I worked with Neurath and his group and also corresponded with Van Eesteren, the City Planner of Amsterdam, who was working on similar standardization for CIAM, the International Congress of Modern Architecture. I found the work more complex and challenging than I had expected, but very few of my proposals were accepted by Giprogor. Russian architects are extremely individualistic; each one insists on doing everything in his own way. They just would not accept any standardization.

The year of 1932 saw the growing threat of Hitler coming to power. The Communists, both in Germany and in the Soviet Union, were aware of the danger. Ernst Thälmann had warned the German workers, "Brüning has punished you with whips, but Hitler will punish you with scorpions." When Hindenburg's first term as president expired, the Communists proposed to the Social Democrats to put up a nonparty antimilitarist such as the writer Heinrich Mann, warning that Hindenburg could not be relied on to keep Hitler out of power. However, the SPD, like the other parties of the Weimar coalition, preferred Hindenburg. When the Communists put up their own candidate, as they had done in 1924, they were again accused of helping reaction: in 1924 because they refused to vote for Hindenburg's opponent, and in 1932 because they refused to vote for Hindenburg. Hindenburg won the election over Hitler — and made him chancellor a few months later.

Soon after the reelection of Hindenburg the "Harzburg coalition" of Nazis and Conservatives initiated a plebiscite against the

Prussian Government, which was still in the hands of the Weimar coalition. This posed a dilemma for the Communists which was passionately debated in Moscow. The immediate reaction was to fight the Nazis and to oppose the plebiscite side by side with the Social-Democratic and Catholic workers. On the opposite side were tactical considerations: there was a very real danger that the plebiscite would win, and then it would have been impossible to deny power to the Harzburg coalition. If the Communists also supported the plebiscite — as they finally did — a majority against the government would not mean a majority for a right-wing alternative. As it happened, the plebiscite was defeated; but the Prussian Government was nevertheless taken out of the hands of the Weimar coalition and handed over to the Harzburg coalition — by Chancellor Franz von Papen acting in the name of President Hindenburg.

With hindsight, it is evident that the Communist support of the plebiscite was a serious mistake because it widened the tragic rift between Communists and Social Democrats. But it certainly was not motivated by any speculation that a Nazi victory would pave the way for communism; in all my years in the Communist party none of my comrades ever advanced that crazy notion. "Hitler is riding Germany into catastrophe," was Thälmann's reaction on the day Hindenburg appointed Hitler.

Nobody can know whether the strategy of the United Anti-fascist Front, advocated by the Communists, could have prevented Hitler from coming to power. We only know that the alternative policy of the Weimar coalition, relying on Hindenburg, has tragically failed. Many of the Social-Democratic leaders actually believed that Hitler would discredit himself by economic failure and that Hindenburg would be forced to call them back within a few months.

No less blind were the leaders of the Western democracies who refused, despite clear evidence, to see that Hitler meant war. When Hitler released his terror after the burning of the Reichstag, he singled out three groups: Communists, pacifists, and Jehovah's Witnesses. These three had only one thing in common: firm opposition to war. But all too many in the West welcomed Hitler, as they had welcomed Mussolini, as a "bulwark against communism."

MAKEYEVKA

While these tragic events were going on in my homeland, I was involved in trying to rationalize graphic presentations. At the same time, construction was going on all around me. I got fed up with paper work; I wanted to participate in real building. An opportunity soon arose: through Lotte I met a man by the name of Anders, a German-speaking Communist economist from Czechoslovakia who was in charge of constructon for a large steelwork in Makeyevka, in the Ukraine. Makeyevka, at the time a city of about 200,000, is located in the Donets Basin, the main coal-steel area of the Soviet Union. The Kirov Steelworks had got their start as a French-Belgian enterprise, but had been expanded tenfold under the Soviets to a capacity of almost two million tons annually.

The industrial structures were designed by a specialized project office for the steel industry, but all nonindustrial buildings, including their infrastructure, were designed by the project office of the steelworks. Anders had offered me the job of heading that office, but I considered it better to have a Soviet architect take care of the administrative aspects. I took charge of one "brigade," while the other one was headed by Weiss, a Hungarian architect who had practiced a number of years in Berlin. I also persuaded Bent Gregersen, the Danish building engineer, to come from Moscow to Makeyevka.

At the time of the First and Second Five-Year Plans heavy industry had absolute priority in claims for funds. As a result, practically everything which would normally be a municipal responsibility had to be built by the steelworks. Our office was responsible for designing and supervising the construction of houses, schools, children's institutions, clubs, sport facilities, etc.

The area of the steelworks was a strip about one kilometer wide extending five kilometers from south to north. To the east was what was called the "city," and on the west the "settlement," started by the steelworks before the revolution and since greatly extended to the north. A plan developed by the Dutch architect Mart Stam, of Ernst May's group, had been adopted the previous year. Based on the observation that winds were predominantly from the east, the plan proposed no further residential development west of the steelworks. A "new town" was to be built two kilometers east of the present one, but as it could not be started for some time because of lack of materials for the infrastructure, for the time being development was to occur in the "city." I soon realized that this recommendation was based on an oversimplified interpretation of the data; it had treated the entire area of the steelworks as a source of pollution, and it disregarded any characteristics of wind except frequency. In fact, the sources of pollution were concentrated in the southeastern quarter of the site of the steelworks, and the predominant eastern winds were dry, cold, and strong winter winds which carried the pollution high over the adjacent area. As a consequence, the newer part of the "settlement" suffered very little from pollution, which settled heavily on the "city," carried by slow-moving, warm, moist air currents from the southwest during the summer months. We therefore developed a plan to extend the "settlement" to the north, and to limit building in the "city" as far as possible.

Within the budget provided for nonindustrial construction we were free to develop our own program for each year. It had to be approved in the preceding November by the central administration of the "South-Steel" corporation in Kharkov. In 1932 and again in 1933 I spent several days going over our projects with their specialists; they were very interested in the innovations which we had proposed and approved them. We also required approval for each individual project from the municipal government and, of course, worked closely with them in developing our program.

The predominant housing type at the time was a five-story walk-up apartment house, with each dwelling containing three or four rooms — occupied by two or more families — in addition to kitchen and bath. We developed a number of alternatives: two-room apartments, two-story row houses, one-story detached and semidetached single-family houses, apartment houses with access from galleries. We also built schools, kindergarten and nursery schools, dining halls, a club, and a sport park containing a stadium as well as facilities for water sport on the lake which served to cool the water from the steel plant.

The slag from the blast furnaces was used for a variety of building materials. I was asked to build tennis courts. I figured that a mixture of two-thirds granulated slag with one-third clay should give a firm, elastic, and fast-drying surface; it worked. My colleague, Weiss, developed a more ambitious plan. He designed the machinery for a factory to make hollow blocks out of slag, which were both lighter and better insulators than the solid blocks which were made from the same slag. The steelworks built the factory and put him in charge of running it.

Our projects had to be approved by a municipal committee headed by the city engineer. In general we worked well together, but there were a few conflicts. At that time the Party line favored a "rich" wedding-cake architecture. I continued to design simple buildings which relied on good proportions. When I presented a particularly straightforward design for a dormitory, the city engineer said, "I know you can do better; evidently you just did not have the time," and insisted that I submit an alternative. I was annoyed, and that night, as soon as I got home, set out to design some god-awful, gaudy facade. I found it more difficult than I had expected; as I went along, it got better and better. Anyway, the city engineer accepted my design — after which I put it aside and built the dormitory according to my original design.

A second case proved more difficult. I had designed two three-story houses in an area zoned for two stories. Although they fitted in very well, the committee refused to approve them for the familiar reason of "not setting a precedent." But, because of a shortage of steel, at the time central heating was permitted only in houses of three or more stories, so I had to redesign for stove heating. Foundations had already been laid for buildings which provided access to the apartments from exterior galleries. I realized that these galleries would become messy if coal and ashes had to be carried over them; so I redesigned them overnight for access via staircases.

When Weiss left the project office, a young Russian architect succeeded him as head of the brigade. He agreed to take the job only under the condition that one of the members of the brigade, B., was taken off. B. was a psychopath who constantly got involved in shouting matches which disrupted work. The head of the projects office told me that I would have to take him into my brigade. This aroused a storm among the members of my group, who threatened to resign if I admitted B. I told the head — as I had done before — that he should fire B. A few days later, just before I left for my annual trip to Kharkov, he told me that he had done so. On my return, finding B. still in his place, I asked the head if he had lacked the guts to fire him. He said, "No, I did, but the trade union put him back." In principle, disagreements between management and trade union can be settled by the courts. But as the courts are always known to side with the unions, they have the last word and it is practically impossible to fire an employee.

In the absence of the fear of losing one's job — the mainstay of labor discipline in market economies — the Soviets have developed elaborate systems of incentive payments, based on "piecework," the volume of work performed. This generally worked out to about 150 percent of the salary. It inevitably meant a purely quantitative evaluation which I felt was inappropriate for architectural design. It was particularly wrong for the head of the brigade, who could charge only for a certain "share" of the drawings produced. This could easily be abused; in fact, this happened in one brigade of the engineering department. In that case, however, the draftsmen complained that they had actually done 100 percent of the work. The brigadier was called to account in a public assembly, and he had to repay his undeserved earnings by deductions during the following months. Shortly before I left Makeyevka, the system of paying brigadiers was reformed, in conformity with my proposals, by paying them in proportion to the quantity and quality of the work performed by their brigade.

On the level of the workplace democracy did function during my years in the Soviet Union. There were genuine elections with several competing candidates for trade union representatives, and also for delegates to the local borough council.

Before I had gone to Makeyevka, I had asked a German architect who had worked there how he had found conditions. He said, "It is difficult; they will not talk to you." It turned out that some of the people with whom he had to deal had refused to talk Russian, insisting on Ukrainian. This did not happen to me, because meanwhile a party resolution had stated that the fight against "Great Russian chauvinism" had gone too far and that it was necessary to fight the opposite extreme of "bourgeois nationalism." However, there was still some discrimination in favor of Ukrainian. I obtained the right to subscribe to *Pravda* — a privilege at the time — but only on condition that I also subscribe to an Ukrainian-language paper. When I told the head of the city school department that we were going to build a school in the "settlement," he said, "That is fine, but we need one even more urgently in the city." I replied in surprise, "But we just built a big school for you there." His answer was, "Yes, but that is an Ukrainian school; we are terribly short of schools for Russian children." When I suggested that they might convert a school from Ukrainian to Russian, he rejected that as quite unthinkable.

Under these conditions there was little reason for anti-Russian or separatist tendencies among Ukrainians, and I never encountered them. I was therefore rather surprised to read recently in the respected French paper *Le Monde,* on the occasion of the fiftieth anniversary of the starvation of 1933, that it was due to a planned "genocide" of the Ukrainian nation. Given the dire shortage of labor in the Soviet Union at the time, this hypothesis is rather absurd. It is equally absurd to assume that any government could be so stupid as to believe that starvation could be an effective means to break national resistance — in the face of the experience of the Irish famine of the 1840s and many others.

There was indeed a famine in 1933, not just in the Ukraine, but also in other semiarid regions of the USSR, the Lower Volga and the North Caucasus; and Makeyevka, located near the junction of these three regions, felt the full impact of it. Many peasants from there came to the city; the steelworks tried to employ some of them, but most left, finding the work too hard. Some were already too far gone, with swollen limbs. There were also many lost children, which were either taken into children's institutions or, very frequently, adopted by urban families; two of my old friends, building workers from Vienna who at the time worked in Makeyevka, each adopted one such child. Only once did I see a child with spindly legs and a swollen belly; it was in the garden of a nursery school at the hand of a nurse waiting for the doctor. Nor did I ever see a corpse lying in a street. I did, however, find a boy of about 15 years of age, lying on the sidewalk one evening, obviously near death. With the help of a passer-by I carried him to the other side of the street, where an awning sheltered him from the drizzling rain, and went to the police station. On my insistence a policeman went with me to confirm that the boy was actually in their precinct, and he promised to take care of him. When I returned half an hour later, the boy was still lying there, so I again went to the police station. They claimed that the hospital would not accept him before the next morning. I went to complain to the GPU, who, however, confirmed the information concerning the hospital. When I went to look the next evening, the boy was no longer lying there. But if his body was removed alive or dead, I will never know.

There is no doubt that the famine claimed many victims. I have no basis on which to estimate their number, and I doubt if anybody has. What were the reasons and what could have been done to avoid this terrible calamity?

There was a conjunction of a number of factors. First, the hot dry summer of 1932, which I had experienced in northern Vyatka, had resulted in crop failure in the semiarid regions of the south. Second, the struggle for collectivization had disrupted agriculture. Collectivization was not an orderly process following bureaucratic rules. It consisted of actions by the poor peasants, encouraged by the Party. The poor peasants were eager to expropriate the "kulaks," but less eager to organize a cooperative economy. By 1930 the Party had already sent out cadres to stem and correct excesses. One of the cadres engaged in this work later reported his experience: the local Communists had told him, "We are building socialism in the village, and you and your Stalin are stabbing us in the back." After having exercised restraint in 1930, the Party put on a drive again in 1932. As a result, in that year the kulak economy ceased to produce, and the new collective economy did not yet produce fully. First claim on the inadequate product went to urban industry and to the armed forces; as the future of the entire nation, including the peasants, depended on them, it could hardly be otherwise. In addition, the depression in the West destroyed the market for oil and timber, with which the Soviets had hoped to pay the debts incurred during the First Five-Year Plan. So, instead of being able to import grain, the Soviet Union actually exported some. What alternatives did they have? I can see only two: use their gold reserve, or get a loan in the West. They tried to do the latter, but obtained it only in 1934 when they no longer needed it. If blame for the terrible suffering of 1932 has to be assigned, it falls in equal parts on the Soviet government for refusing to part with their gold reserve, and on the West for refusing a loan when it was needed.

Probably most deaths in 1933 were due to epidemics of typhus, typhoid fever, and dysentery. Waterborne diseases were frequent in Makeyevka; I narrowly survived an attack of typhus fever. The workers, through their trade union, demanded that the steelworks install a sewage system. The management replied that they would supply the pipes and the disposal plant, but workers were needed to dig the ditches. The union mobilized its members to do the work in their spare time, at the union rate per cubic meter.

Everybody pitched in; like everybody else, I also worked an hour in the early morning on a number of days.

In 1933 rainfall was adequate. The Party sent its best cadres to help organize work in the kolkhozes. They succeeded; after the harvest of 1933 the situation improved radically and with amazing speed. I had the feeling that we had been pulling a heavy cart uphill, uncertain if we would succeed; but in the fall of 1933 we had gone over the top and from then on we could move forward at an accelerating pace. Certainly, stupidity and callousness inflicted much avoidable suffering during the process of collectivization, and many Soviet kolkhozes continue to suffer from the fact that they started on the wrong foot — in contrast to those in other countries such as East Germany and Hungary, which have learned from the mistakes made in the Soviet Union. But Soviet agriculture is not the monumental failure which it is often regarded as in the West. Despite the invasion of close to half of the cropland by Hitler's army, lack of food did not lead to military collapse as it had in World War I. Nor is it entirely irrational for the Soviet Union to export minerals and industrial products in order to pay for the import of grain.

The year and a half which I spent in Makeyevka were very satisfying because I could see useful results of my work, both in improving the living environment and in developing the qualifications of the members of my brigade. But by the beginning of 1935 we had caught up with the most urgent needs and had developed a staff competent to carry on. So I decided to take some time off for study and travel, and I returned to Moscow. My room had been reserved for me because the owner, the Commissariat of Heavy Industry, used reservation of living quarters in Moscow as an incentive for workers to go to less attractive places such as the Donets Basin. During my absence it had been occupied by a young German architect.

Meanwhile, the engineer Shabadin, which whom I had shared the apartment, had been arrested, and the smaller of the two rooms which the Shabadins had occupied had been reclaimed by the management of the house and let to my friend Gregersen. Shabadin had been arrested because the floor of a warehouse which he had designed had collapsed, resulting in loss of life. However, he was able to prove that he had insisted on providing a stronger construction and had signed the drawing providing for the weaker one only on a direct order from his supervisor; he was soon released. While he was under arrest, he had worked as an engineer on the Moscow-Volga Canal. The GPU had been well satisfied with his work and offered him a job on a site near Moscow after his release. He accepted and came to Moscow frequently, in GPU uniform, to stay with his wife and daughter. However, as he was provided with housing at the construction site, the lost room was not returned to him.

CENTRAL ASIA

I planned a trip to Soviet Central Asia and asked advice from acquaintances who had been there. About half of them said foreigners needed special permission, and half said none was needed. So I went to the GPU office responsible for issuing residence permits to foreigners, where I received mine every year. The officer in charge first thought no permit was required, but then found that I should get one from the commissariat where I worked. Although I no longer worked for Heavy Industry, I went to see them. The man in charge asked, "Where do you want to go?" I said, "Tashkent, Samarkand, the Ferghana Valley." His answer was, "Well, buy yourself a railroad ticket and bon voyage." I did, and nobody questioned my right to travel, not even when I once strayed into a military establishment.

After having traveled two days and nights under gray skies, I woke the third morning in the railway station at Turkestan, under a cloudless blue sky, in the midst of a sunlit green carpet dotted with thousands of red and yellow poppies as far as the eye could see. The sight reminded me of a verse in the first book of Goethe's *Western-Eastern Divan,* "Liebliches." There was another sign that I now was in the world of Islam: in the corridor of my sleeping car a bearded Kazakh spread out his prayer rug and knelt down to perform his morning prayers, facing in the direction of Mecca. Throughout my journey I observed that Islam had a much stronger hold than had Christianity in the Soviet Union. While I had seen very few young men in churches — mostly old women, some old men, some young women — there were many young men in mosques. Not all of them were engaged in worship or prayer; many just sat around, chatting or resting. There was no indication that they felt their religion to be in conflict with their being Soviet citizens.

Indeed, the old and the new were interwoven in curious ways. Most of the men wore their handsome striped caftans, white cotton trousers, and colorful skullcaps. The wearing of the *chador* by the women varied from place to place: in a few towns almost all wore it; in some none; in most, including Tashkent, a varying proportion. It was only worn by the sedentary peoples, Uzbeks and Tadzhiks, not by the traditionally nomadic Kazakhs, Kirghiz, and Turkmen.

There were everywhere the traditional teahouses, often built on stilts over the canals which irrigate the plains. Men sat on the carpeted floor, drinking tea and nibbling sugar, as they had done for centuries. There was a radio blaring, a modern contraption; but then again, what came out of it was mostly traditional music, played on native instruments. I visited an Uzbek opera, with the music largely based on native tunes, quite beautiful in sound, sight, and performance. Live opera and theater are of course innovations. I saw a good performance of Hamlet in Uzbek. I noticed some women who were emancipated enough to go to this newfangled thing in pairs, without male accompaniment; but some of them still wore the veil.

I was surprised to discover that the part of Tashkent which had been built by the Russians in the nineteenth century was very pleasant. Its center was a park; from it some very broad streets radiated, supplemented by somewhat narrower semicircular streets. All streets were planted with two rows of native shade trees; but the radial streets had, in addition, two rows of poplars. I also visited the geophysical institute in Tashkent, which was doing very interesting work on the impact of buildings on microclimates; they also produced electricity from solar energy.

I traveled through the Ferghana Valley, stopping at several smaller towns. Islamic towns have developed and preserved an original urban culture and way of life more distinct from the "Western" one than have those of other civilizations. I was fascinated by the craftsmen working in specialized sections of the bazaar; there were also acrobats and storytellers. I admired the traditional architecture based on a highly developed technique of brick vaulting as well as of carpentry, and the incredibly rich and beautiful ornament of cut pieces of ceramics of many colors which cover the walls and vaults, particularly of religious buildings, both inside and out.

But I also wanted to hike in the mountains, which rise to over 5000 meters in that part of the world. When I inquired at the offices of "Proletarian Tourism," I was always very cordially received by pleasant young people, but the answer was always, "You can't go there before the 15th of May." Finally, on a train trip in the Ferghana Valley, I met a couple of Russians who had lived in Central Asia since czarist days. They were the most reactionary people I ever met in the Soviet Union; the woman expressed admiration for Hitler! But she told me of a place called Arslan Bab — Persian for the Lion's Gate — located north of Djalalabad in Kirghizia, in a western extension of China's Tien Shan Mountains. She said there was a teahouse where one could stay.

I arrived by train in Djalalabad, the terminal of the rail line, on the first of May, and went for a hike in the lush grass of the foothills. Suddenly I saw a familiar sight to the north: the silhouette of the Three Sisters and the Piz Langard which I had known in St. Moritz thirty years before! I decided that was where I wanted to go. I asked about a dozen people how to get to Arslan Bab; none had ever heard of it. Finally a fellow said, "Oh yes, that is way up in the mountains. Halfway up there is a mine; a truck goes there every morning; it may take you along." It did, over dirt roads and through rivers. In the dining hall of the mine, where the workers were at breakfast, Arslan Bab was not known either. Finally, I found a young fellow who told me I could get there by going back a few kilometers on the road on which I had come and then taking a trail to the north. I did not take the trail, but hiked across the grassy hills. Toward dusk, clouds gathered, so when I met a peasant, I asked for a *kishlak,* a village or hamlet. Most of the languages of Central Asia are close to Turkish, and with the remnants of the Turkish I had learned during the First World War and a Russian-Uzbek pocket dictionary I could get along in the countryside where hardly anyone knew Russian.

In the hamlet I entered a house which had a hammer-and-sickle sign and turned out to be the office of the kolkhoz administration. I was met with some mistrust until I produced my trade union membership book. Then I was warmly welcomed and accompanied to the house of the chairman of the kolkhoz, who treated me as his guest. The house was a fairly sizable one-room, flat-roofed structure with thick adobe walls which contained niches for various belongings. There was a fireplace with a chimney. I was invited to share the meal, which consisted of pieces of mutton and vegetables served on a large brass plate from which everyone picked his or her share with fingers, and pieces of the very tasty unleavened wheat bread which is the staff of life of that area. The women slept in the house, while the man, his younger brother, and I slept on berths on a covered porch. As it turned out, it gave me a view of the thunderstorm over the mountains.

The next morning after breakfast I set out on a dirt road, where I soon met a camel caravan going to Kashgar in China. A Russian with the caravan knew Arslan Bab. He said there was no teahouse, but that I could stay at the state farm which managed a walnut forest. I climbed up the trail which led from the caravan road to Arslan Bab, did not stop at the state farm, but continued to the hamlet. When I asked a man about the teahouse, "Chai-Khana" in Uzbek, he took me to a ruin. When I indicated that I was look-ing for a place to sleep, he beckoned to a young fellow who took me quite a way out of the hamlet. But we arrived safely at the hut where he lived with his gray-bearded father. It was much more primitive than my abode of the previous night. There were nei-ther windows nor a chimney; the smoke from the fire that was lit on the dirt floor escaped slowly through the thatched roof. When the fire was not burning and the door was closed, it was pitch dark. So I never found out what was in the soup which they served me; but it was tasty and, together with bread and a few eggs, nourished me adequately. I also slept well in my sleeping bag on goatskins spread out on the dirt floor.

For two days I explored the hills and valleys, forests and water-falls of the area, enjoying the ever-changing views of the sur-rounding snow-capped mountains. When I descended on the third morning, I met a crowd welcoming the first truck to drive up since the last fall. Down in the valley I met a young man on horse-back who pointed to my rucksack. I first thought that he offered to carry it for me, but soon realized that he wanted to rob it. For a while we pulled on it; then he gave up and galloped off, cursing me as a "son of a kulak." I stayed the night at an empty teahouse, in the company of a merchant who was carrying tea from China by mule.

I went by train to Samarkand, which I found to be one of the world's most beautiful cities: a city garden rather than a garden city, with fruit and mulberry trees hanging over the often orna-mented clay walls which separate the compounds from the wind-ing lanes. In the center of town is the Registan, the great square, surrounded by the tiled facades of three mosques with their deep niches and slender minarets. Not far from there is Gur Emir,

Timur's burial place. The great conqueror rests in a crypt in which there are two sarcophagi; the smaller one contains Timur's body, the larger one that of his teacher — an unexpected expression of humility.

However, my greatest impression from Samarkand is of a group of burial chapels called "Shah Zinde" (the Living King) from the chapel crowning the hill where, according to legend, the leader who brought Islam to the region, and who fell in battle, still lives underground. The area covered by the entire group is smaller than a Manhattan city block, but it is a world of unending discovery of beauty: it expresses something which is "out of this world," or beyond man's world, in a quite different way from "monumental" architecture — a way which may be more profound and lasting than the grandeur which other cultures have used to express veneration.

From Samarkand I went to Bokhara. The old monuments are also beautiful but the total impression was, in contrast to the exhilarating atmosphere of Samarkand, rather oppressive, enclosed by heavy walls and with scarcely any green. It was the only Soviet city I ever saw which seemed decaying; in fact, as I later learned from the census of 1939, it was the only one which had lost population in the preceding decade.

I stopped at the ruins of Merv; I found the remnants of six successive cities, the oldest decayed to sand dunes, the youngest with an impressive sixteenth-century mosque still standing. In Ashkhabad, the pleasant modern capital of Turkmenistan, I was struck by the fact that the ruins of a temple from the Parthian empire looked no different from Roman ones of the same period in Britain or Morocco; that style was truly international. I returned to Moscow after crossing the Caspian Sea to Baku.

RETURN TO MOSCOW

My friend Gregersen told me that Konstant, the technical director of the Moscow Province Projects Trust, where he worked, wanted to see me. He was a German Communist, a worker who had come to the Soviet Union in the twenties and had been trained there as an engineer; I had met him casually before. He offered me the job of heading the architectural department, which had a staff of about 100 people. The trust also had a planning department; I felt that this separation between architecture and planning was not desirable, and told him so. But I accepted the job.

When I was shown my room, which was fairly large, I was surprised that one of the architects was also working there. It turned out to be a case parallel to the one which I had experienced in Makeyevka: he was a psychopath who disrupted work and whom my predecessor had therefore established, at his own inconvenience, in this isolated location. I knew that I could not fire him. I had, however, to approve his drawings before he got paid for them. As much of his work was faulty, this gave me a certain leverage; after a while he resigned.

The power of management, however, did not often work that way. Another architect had drawn a renaissance facade with a crowning cornice. There are two well-established ways to end a renaissance roof cornice, but he had shown neither, so that it would have been just cut off at both ends. I explained to him the two ways for ending a cornice and told him to show one. But he insisted that he had completed his work and would complain to the trade union if I asked him to do more work than he had contracted for. I gave in.

After a few weeks in my new position I fell sick and had to spend some time in hospital. When I reported back, Konstant told me that there had been a reorganization: I would no longer head the department, but he proposed that I head a brigade which would be charged with both planning and architecture for a new workers' settlement for a defense industry plant. It was clearly a demotion, but as it was the kind of work which I had proposed, I accepted.

Several weeks passed; finally I got my staff and started to work on the task. However, the formal contract between the trust and the brigade, which is required for work in Soviet enterprises, was not yet ready. My staff grew impatient; one of them threw his pencil on the table, exclaiming that he would not work until the contract was signed. I said, "That is a nice attitude for a Komsomolets" (a member of the Communist Youth). He countered, "The Party wants us to work well but also to earn well." The following day I was told that I could not work on this defense-related project because I was a foreigner. The director offered me some rather subaltern work; it would not affect my salary, which was protected by Soviet labor law. The director asked me, "Do you refuse the work?" It was obvious that he had orders to get rid of me. So I replied, "I do not refuse, but I protest."

A few days passed; then, one morning, I was told that I had been expelled from the Party by a meeting which I had not attended because I had the flu. It was against the statutes of the Party to exclude a member in his absence.

I concluded that I would have to deal with the problem on a different level and, after consultation with the central trade union adviser for foreign workers, resigned from the trust.

A Long Losing Fight

Without being fully aware of it, I had been caught by an eddy of what has become known as the "Great Purge." It was entirely unexpected. After the difficulties of 1932 and 1933 had been overcome and the level of living began improving rapidly, the victory of the revolution was no longer in doubt. We were looking forward to the blossoming of socialist society, including a gradual widening of diversity of opinion. Arthur Koestler has spoken of "darkness at noon." Darkness at dawn would be more appropriate.

When the accusations against Zinoviev and Kamenev were raised, they seemed to me improbable, and certainly isolated, cases. When the "revision of party membership books" was announced, I expected it to be just that, a technical operation. Membership books contained no identification, neither photo nor signature, and could easily be stolen or falsified. When arrests started of people who I felt sure were innocent, in particular among German Communists, I ascribed them to exaggerated fear of spies, possibly fed by infiltration of Gestapo agents, and I was confident that they would be corrected after due investigation.

It was true, after all, that while the Soviet Union was consolidated internally, she was increasingly threatened by the rise of aggressive fascism abroad, in Germany, Italy, and Japan. The Western powers rejected the Soviet proposals for collective security and condoned the invasions of Ethiopia and China. There was reason to batten down the hatches before a threatening storm. I could understand, though I deeply regretted it, that in this situation the generous internationalism inaugurated by the October Revolution was replaced by a certain distrust of foreigners. Under the laws still valid in 1935 anyone working in the Soviet economy had full citizenship rights. I could have been elected president of the Soviet Union; and, of course, many foreigners were members of the Soviet party.

Now, the question of Soviet citizenship was raised, and I had applied for it in the fall of 1935. Also, foreign specialists became less welcome, and some were ordered to leave. One of the first cases of which I heard was that of a Rumanian engineer. His wife, however, who taught at the German school, was told that she and her children were welcome to stay. After long consideration, she decided to leave with her daughter; the boy, who was in his last year in high school, insisted on staying. The authorities agreed under the condition that three adults assume responsibility for his support. One of the three was Gregersen, who accommodated him in his room. So, during my last years in Moscow, we established a common household of three men. Later, shortly after I had left, the boy was arrested and sent to a camp at Kolyma, the gold-mining region in the extreme northeast of Siberia. During the war he was released from the camp but was forced to stay in the area. He became the head of a truck brigade, and married. After full rehabilitation under Khrushchev, he decided to stay to take advantage of the right of early retirement which is granted to workers in remote areas. In the sixties he visited his sister in England.

In January 1936 I did not foresee such events. I was confident that my membership in the Party would soon be restored. After the secretary of the local organization at the trust refused to give me any explanation, I went to the next level, the rayon (borough). When the man who received me tried to brush me off by saying I was not a Party member, I got mad, banged the table, and shouted at him, "You are an irresponsible scoundrel," and, on his protest, "I repeat before all these people, you are an irresponsible scoundrel." That impressed him, and he reported to his superior, who told me to submit my case in writing.

Nothing happened. Some of my friends advised me to go slow. They may not have been entirely wrong; several months later the rayon secretary was removed because he had expelled Party members without due cause. However, I felt it my right and appealed to the next level, the Moscow Committee. I was received by a kind and conscientious older woman who expressed shock on learning that I had no work. When I answered her question about the reasons for my expulsion by saying that I did not know, she called for the file and read, "It says here that you broke Party discipline." On my question, "In which way," she found, after further search, that I had not paid my dues. In fact, after my return to Moscow, I had repeatedly offered to pay my dues, but had always been told by the secretary that he could not accept them because my transfer papers had not yet arrived from Makeyevka. The Moscow Party secretary said she would look into my case.

When I heard nothing for over a month, I took the final recourse. I appealed to the Central Committee of the Party. They appointed a member, a woman whose looks I did not like — and the feeling was mutual — to investigate, and then set up a committee of three. The chairman asked me what I had been doing in Central Asia. I could have truthfully answered that I had studied the architectural monuments and that I had explored the possibilites of working in the area — I had actually talked about this with the city planning office in Samarkand. But, taken by surprise, I rather stupidly said, "I traveled," at which he scoffed. The third member, obviously sympathetic, tried to save the situation by some additional questions; but, not unexpectedly, they did not restore my Party membership.

For the time being there was nothing that I could do. I had already written to Stalin and received the usual form-letter reply that my complaint would be looked into. But I was still confident that there would be an opportunity to reopen the matter once the atmosphere had cooled. I had procured letters of recommendation from two old and respected Party members: Anders, the man who had invited me to Makeyevka, and Koritschoner, one of the founders of the Austrian Party. As it turned out, soon after this, both of them were arrested. I do not know what happened to Anders. Koritschoner was, to the shame of the Soviets, handed over to the Germans on the occasion of the Molotov-Ribbentrop prisoner exchange; he perished in a Nazi concentration camp. It is to the credit of the Austrian Communist party that they always honored him as a hero and martyr of the antifascist struggle, disregarding the attitude of the Soviet authorities.

One morning in August 1936, when I dropped in at a neighbor's, a German architect, his wife received me wide-eyed, exclaiming, "Did you not see what the *Arkhitekturnaya Gazeta* says about you?" I had not yet seen the paper, which was the weekly published by the Soviet Architects' Union. It contained a report on the organization in which I had worked. It said that the chief engineer, Konstant, was not only a Trotskyite (which he had been at some remote time in Germany), but also an agent of Hitler's Gestapo; that he had organized a conspiracy to assassinate Voroshilov, the Commissar of National Defense; and that I, Gans Martinovich Blumenfeld, was his closest friend and "a venomous and irreconcilable enemy of the proletarian revolution."

My attempts to obtain a retraction of this statement turned out to be a classic example of the run-around. I went first to the editor of the *Gazeta,* who received me very politely. He said that their reporter had always been reliable, and he arranged an interview with him. The reporter said he had got the story from the Party secretary and asked me to put my version down in writing, which I did. I also talked to the secretary of the Architects' Union, Alabyan, whom I knew quite well. (I happened to run into Alabyan two years later in an elevator in a New York office building where he worked for the New York World's Fair on the Soviet pavilion which he had designed; he greeted me very cordially.)

As no retraction was published, I went to the district court to sue the paper for slander. I was told that only the district attorney could initiate such a suit. When I went to the attorney's office, I was told that this was not his business, and that I had to bring the suit to the court. So I went to the complaints office of the Commissariat of Justice. To my surprise, I was told that both refusals had been correct; I had no case for slander. I exclaimed, "But it is not true!" The answer was, "If the paper said that you had red hair, it would not be true, but you could not sue them; we have freedom of the press. The paper's statement is a political characterization, which may be true or false. As you are entitled to any political opinion, an erroneous characterization is not slander."

I went to *Pravda,* the party newspaper which practices very effective investigative journalism which often leads to correction of wrongs. After I had told my story to the two men who received me, I added, "Of course, you do not know me and cannot know whether the article is true." They answered, "Nonsense. If it were true, you would not be sitting here!" I have no doubt that they tried to investigate, but they evidently got nowhere.

I also went to the political police, the GPU (now the KGB). The jovial type who received me said, "We deal with guilty people and, as far as we are concerned, you are not one of them; why are you worried about a statement in that little sheet?" I answered, "It may be just a little sheet to you, but it is read by everyone to whom I apply for employment." He conceded the point but repeated that they were not in the business of issuing certificates of innocence.

My most rewarding experience was with the Bureau of Complaints of the Soviet government. It was headed by Marya Ilyitchnaya Ulyanova, Lenin's youngest sister. She was a wonderful person, transparently honest and radiating pure goodwill. She referred me to her assistant, who was also very understanding and friendly. They stated that my exclusion from the Party was a matter in which they could not interfere, but that the fact of my unemployment was within their jurisdiction. However, after several visits, the assistant said, "You have for several years worked in our system as a Party member; if someone came to you asking for a job under these circumstances, would you hire him?" I answered, "Of course not; that's why I came to you." He agreed, but stated that they were really powerless in my case.

After I had resigned from the Moscow Province Projects Trust, I had offered my services to several offices. All had been very interested and promised an answer within a few days, but none ever came. I soon realized that nobody would take the risk of being accused of lack of "vigilance" for having a "venomous and irreconcilable enemy of the proletarian revolution" on their staff. It was, however, quite possible to pay me for temporary help to some staff member. My first job of this type was with Kurt Liebknecht, an architect who was a nephew of Karl and a grandson of Wilhelm L. He had worked as an architect in Germany, had left when Hitler came to power, but had joined the Communist party only after his departure. Later, for a month, while he was on vacation, Wilhelm Schütte had me substitute in supervising the construction of a school; and I helped Grete Schütte-Lihotzky design standard nursery schools and kindergartens. My last job of this type was helping a young German architect design candy booths for subway stations.

During this period a census was taken in the Soviet Union. When the census taker asked my occupation and I answered, "Unemployed," he refused to write it down, saying, "There are no unemployed in the Soviet Union." It was and is true that unemployment for economic reasons does not exist there. However, there may be a few thousand who are unemployed for political reasons, as I was — at present, probably primarily "refusniks," people who have applied for emigration, but have been refused. Their economic situation may still be tolerable, as was mine.

I was not entirely without income. I also had some savings and sold some belongings; finally, I borrowed from friends. So I continued to live fairly comfortably. With time on my hands, I returned to my old love, the history of cities. After my return from Makeyevka, I had found, in a Moscow bookstore, an old French edition of Strabo, the great Greek geographer of the first century AD, a very rich source on my subject. I also read at this time the very excellent book on ancient Greek city building by Arnim von Gerkan, at the time head of the German Archeological Institute in Athens. I wrote an extensive review of this book, using it as a starting point to criticize the misinterpretation of Greek architecture and civic design then prevalent in the Soviet Union. As I told my Russian colleagues, "You say Phidias, you mean Palladio, and you build Charles Garnier," the architect of the Paris Opera (Hitler's favorite building).

I showed this review, written in German, to Macza, an Hungarian scholar in charge of History and Theory at the Soviet Academy of Architecture. He had it translated into Russian for publication in the academy's journal. However, soon after this, the journal was discontinued and the review has never been published. I had full access to the academy's library. Moreover, I obtained the privilege of a table in the Lenin Library. It is marvelously rich, second only to the Library of Congress and the British Museum. I found every book and journal I asked for, in German, French, English, or Italian. I regret now that I did not make more use of their Russian material, most of which is not available in the West.

So, while I was disturbed by the trials of old Bolsheviks and the growing numbers of arrests or other forms of persecution among many people I knew and trusted, I lived a peaceful contemplative life. I suspect that at heart I prefer to be a spectator of the Human Comedy, rather than an actor in it. Nobody interfered with my life. Only once was I called to the GPU and asked to explain how I made a living without a job. I did, first orally and then in writing, and nothing more was heard of the matter.

The attack in the *Arkhitekturnaya Gazeta* did not cause people to shun me. Two foreign Communists, both in fairly sensitive positions, asked me not to come to their apartments, but both offered at the same time to testify in my favor if I thought this could be of help to me. I heard from an acquaintance that the Hungarian architect Weiner had warned them against me. When I met Weiner at the architect's club, I confronted him. He said, "You have been publicly accused and have not replied." After I had informed him of my attempts to reply, he apologized. I later met Weiner again in Paris, and we became good friends.

The Architects Society and associated club were important institutions. Architects presented their projects to their colleagues, who always engaged in lively and often searching criticism. There were also cultural events: Prokofiev and Shostakovich played the piano, and Paul Robeson sang. The architects also owned a summer palace, built in the beginning of the nineteenth century, with a large park which served them as a resort.

As a foreigner I had a residence permit which was renewed every year. In 1935, when foreigners became less welcome, rules were tightened. Permits had to be renewed every six months, and foreigners were supposed to notify the police beforehand of any travel. This rule was, however, hardly enforced. I had forgotten about it when I had traveled to Dnepropetrovsk to see Anders. Somewhat later, when on a hot summer afternoon I found that my favorite swimming hole had been fenced off, I decided on the spur of the moment to take a train to Yaroslavl, an old city on the upper Volga, and to the monastery towns of Stary Rostov and Pereslavl, both of which are situated on beautiful lakes. Evidently the allegedly ubiquitous secret police never heard of my travels. In the Soviet Union, as everywhere, the old German saying still holds: "Nothing is eaten as hot as it is cooked."

My experience was not really one of a "police state." The GPU was as much respected and trusted as feared, in my time. The ordinary urban police was neither respected nor feared, but rather pitied. Twice I witnessed the same scene: a civilian knocked down a policeman; bystanders came to his aid and held the attacker until a second policeman showed up; the two law officers then took the culprit to the station, without twisting his arms. Another time, when a policeman admonished two young drunks, one of them, imitating the gestures of regulating traffic, shouted, "You, comrade regulator, just regulate your traffic, and don't hassle us!" The cop just replied, amid general laughter, "All right, boys, go home and sleep it off."

Subsequently, however, I was shocked on occasion to see large groups of men and women being roughly herded through the streets by soldiers. I found it hard to believe that they were all criminals. But I could not then, and for many years thereafter, believe that people were physically mistreated, beaten, or tortured in the Soviet Union. It was contrary to the profound and general condemnation of physical violence which I had found prevalent everywhere. Verbal quarrels were often harsh enough, but they never came to blows; this was considered "uncultured." In Makeyevka, where it cannot have been easy to maintain school discipline among tough kids, it was a great public scandal when a teacher ordered a boy to kneel in a corner of the classroom. When I lived and worked in the "East" I perceived a human face behind the mask.

On April 29, 1937, I went to the GPU office to get my residence permit renewed. While I was waiting, the woman in charge told several other foreigners that their permit would not be renewed and handed them their passports. I was kept waiting until everybody else had left. When she wanted to give me my passport, I refused to take it, saying, "I do not want a passport of Nazi Germany." I asked where I could appeal the decision, at the GPU or at the Commissariat of Justice. She said I could appeal to either, but that it would do me no good. I replied that that was my business, and left.

The thirtieth of April happened to be a free day, and the first and second of May were holidays, so I had three days to ponder my next step. An old Austrian Communist whom I consulted said, "In the end you will get your rights, but by that time you may have lost your sanity," and advised me to leave. Ever since the civil war in Spain had erupted, I had felt that my place was really there and had intended to join the Republicans as soon as my Party status was restored. I asked Ernst Fischer, one of the leaders of the Social-Democratic "Schutzbund" of Vienna, who had fought in defense of Austrian democracy and, after their defeat, had come to Moscow and become one of the leaders of the Austrian Communist party, if he thought I would be accepted by the "International Brigade" fighting in Spain. He replied that he would accept me but, of course, could not predict how others would react.

I decided to fight for my right to stay in the Soviet Union. I wrote a letter to the head of the GPU, requesting an interview. I stated that I regarded myself as a citizen of the Comintern, not of Nazi Germany. I added that if they considered me suspect, they might arrest me or send me to work on the Volga-Moscow Canal.

I was received by the head of the department of the GPU

responsible for foreigners, a man with the rank of general, flanked by his assistant for Moscow, whom I already knew. Referring to my letter, he said, "You are of course entitled to your — if I may say so — semianarchistic opinions, but for us, every person is the subject of a state; you are not a Soviet citizen, consequently you are still a German subject." He added, "You have committed no crime, so we cannot arrest you; for the same reason we cannot send you to work on the canal."

I asked whether my application for Soviet citizenship had been turned down. They said no, it was still under consideration, and I might write from abroad to inquire about it. (I did not care to engage in a correspondence from New York with the GPU in Moscow.)

When I pointed out that my passport had expired, they advised me to get it extended. I said, "I will not set foot in a Nazi embassy." After talking to each other in a low voice, they asked, "If *we* get the extension for you, will you accept your passport?" After a few moments of hesitation, I said yes. But then they said I might still have to go to the embassy to pick it up. I repeated that I would not set foot in that place.

Finally, I agreed to accept the passport and to leave the Soviet Union if I could gain admittance to a democratic country, but that I would need more time for that. They immediately agreed to extend my permission to stay from a week to a month.

I soon found out that no country would give me a visa. But I also found that Soviet ships would take me on without one. I felt that I could risk going to Sweden or Denmark without a visa; they would probably arrest me but treat me decently and not deliver me to the Germans. But there were no Soviet boats going there. I went to Leningrad to inquire at the Danish and Swedish consulates if any of theirs were scheduled, but there were none. There were Soviet ships sailing to London, but they went through the Kiel Canal, where the Germans could pick me up. The only other possibility was a Soviet ship which was scheduled to leave Odessa for Istanbul, Alexandria, and Haifa. I decided to take a chance on that. From a German acquaintance I got the special ink used by the German consulate for their passports and extended the validity of mine. My work was not professional and anyone using a magnifying glass could have detected the falsification.

LEAVING THE SOVIET UNION

While I was prepared to leave, I was not willing to do so without a fight. I went to the Central Committee of the Party to complain and to again demand an investigation of the slanderous article in the *Arkhitekturnaya Gazeta*. I was received politely and was assured that the refusal to extend my permit — which was not an expulsion — had nothing to do with the article, but was general policy. This was probably true.

I went to the complaint bureau in the office of Kalinin, the president of the Soviet Union. On being told that they could not interfere with the GPU, I asked how it was possible that the president of the country could not interfere with a government agency. The spokesman confirmed that this was the case. I asked, "Are you telling me that the GPU has extraterritorial status?" He answered, "You can put it that way."

Finally, I went once more to the Soviet Bureau of Complaints and asked to see Marya Ilyitchnaya. The people at the desk refused to call her, stating that she could do nothing in my case. I wrote a note to her: "I appeal to you, not as the head of this office, but as a human being, a Communist, and the sister of Lenin: help me." She came out of her office and, with an old woman's helpless gesture, said in a barely audible voice, "I cannot help you," and turned back. At that moment, I realized that it was over, definitely and irrevocably. For the first and only time in my adult life I broke into tears. After a while I regained control of myself, apologized to the staff, who had looked at me in silence and with obvious sympathy, and left.

I sat for a while in the little park under the Kremlin walls, then went to the Spanish embassy to inquire about volunteering and about ships leaving from the Soviet Union for Spain. They were friendly and cheerful, but referred me to their consulate at Odessa. I bought a boat ticket from Odessa to Istanbul and a flight to Odessa via Makeyevka, and decided to leave within a few days.

An additional problem had arisen during these last weeks. As mentioned earlier, my apartment belonged to the Commissariat of Heavy Industry. I had forfeited my right of occupancy when I had left them to work for Giprogor, but had regained it when I went to work for them in Makeyevka. Now the administration of the house tried to evict me. As I was no longer employed anywhere, I could not call on a trade union to back me up in court. I went to the lawyers cooperative which provides legal services for a very modest fee. Soviet law prohibits any eviction after five years of occupancy, and I had lived almost seven in my apartment. But the lawyers informed me that I could only claim continued occupancy from my second assignment for the Makeyevka period, and had therefore not a leg to stand on. They would take my case, if I requested it, but advised me that my only chance was to appeal to the court on compassionate grounds, which I could do just as effectively without the help of the lawyer. They also gave me information on procedure and timing of appeals.

Under Soviet law nobody can be evicted during the winter, so I had time until the end of April. I went to the court at the last possible date. I was favorably impressed by the informality of the proceedings, with the professional judge and his two lay assistants sitting at the head of the table and complainants, accused, witnesses, and lawyers at the sides; everybody was allowed to speak or question on an equal basis. However, I lost my case.

Again I waited as long as possible for my appeal to the District Court. I also asked the advice of an acquaintance who was a state attorney, and one of his lawyer friends agreed to represent me. But we lost the case again.

I had one more chance: the District Attorney could order review of the judgment, and pending review the order of eviction was halted. The District Attorney agreed to my request and assured me that my house administration would be notified immediately. However, on the evening of the following day, the administrator appeared with a policeman to evict me. I locked my room from the outside, put the key in my pocket, and told them of the suspension of eviction. They left, and the order from the District Attorney arrived the next day.

I did not notify the house administration that I would be leaving, or when, but told my neighbors, the Shabadins, so that they could immediately move into my room. They tried, but did not succeed.

I sold or gave away some of my belongings, shipped the balance to my sister in New York, and took with me only a small bag which I could carry easily. I took leave of my friend Gregersen and walked in the early morning to the bus which took me to the airport. A ten-seat propeller plane took me to Stalino. It was my first flight, and I enjoyed it greatly. From the Stalino airport, collective taxis took passengers to Makeyevka. I found myself seated next to the woman doctor who had saved me from typhoid fever. She talked with genuine enthusiasm about the great improvements in her hospital, as to staff, buildings, equipment, and supplies. Living conditions had apparently improved radically in Makeyevka in the two years since I left it.

I was eager to see the buildings which I had designed; but my main reason was to cash in the government bonds which I had subscribed to there, which were deposited at the factory office, and which could be redeemed only if and when one left the country. I wondered how my old colleagues would receive me. Of course they had read the accusation in the *Arkhitekturnaya Gazeta.* Moreover, Anders, who had brought me to Makeyevka, had been arrested, together with his close friends, the directors of the steelworks and the local building trust. As I learned, there had been a meeting at the project office where I had worked. A representative of the Party had reproached the staff for lack of vigilance because they had failed to discover that the "Germans," meaning me, Gregersen, and Weiss, were spies. But a young architect, a Party member, had stood up and said, "What do we know? These are just rumors; we have seen that these people did good honest work." While I wandered around, looking at row houses which I had designed, I met one of my former colleagues with whom I had had some conflicts. But he greeted me most cordially, showed me his house, and took me to meet other old friends over a beer.

Evidently the fear evoked by the "purges" among the Moscow intelligentsia had not reached the provinces. I had another surprising evidence of this the next day. On the plane from Stalino to Odessa I met two young Russian engineers who were going to Odessa on business. I told them that I was a foreigner forced by the government to leave the Soviet Union, but that did not deter them from inviting me to share a hotel suite with them, which I did. They, like all my Soviet friends and acquaintances, greatly pitied me for being thrown out into the cold, hostile, capitalist world where unemployment would await me. Their apprehension was not groundless; had not my sister and brother-in-law been able and willing to support me financially, my life might have been very difficult indeed.

I enjoyed my week in Odessa, with swims in the Black Sea. I went to see the Spanish consul. He was very cordial, but said no boat was scheduled for the rest of the month, and advised me to go to France and from there to join the International Brigade. This was indeed my intention, but so far I had no visa to go there. I went to the Turkish consulate and applied for a two-week transit visa. I waited for the reply, sitting in their pleasant garden-court. Time dragged on, and I was convinced that they had discovered my falsification of the date, when an employee appeared and handed me my passport with a two-week visa. I sailed on the evening of April 30, 1937, almost seven years to the day after I had arrived in the Soviet Union.

Looking Back

When I had left for the Soviet Union, a relative had expressed the hope that the experience would cure my revolutionary illusions. That did not happen. I left the Soviet Union more convinced of communism than when I had arrived. The Party had overcome one formidable obstacle after another and had succeeded in transforming the Soviet Union from a backward, semiliterate peasant country into a modern industrial state with a well-educated population, with equal opportunities for all, regardless of sex or ethnicity. While production was stagnating or receding in the capitalist world, with unprecedented mass unemployment, the Soviet economy was expanding rapidly, with employment and social security for everyone. While the utopian expectations of 1930 had been toned down by the difficulties of the three following years, there was confidence that progress would continue from year to year. You knew what you were working for: a better society.

Certainly there was not universal brotherhood, but there was much more warmth and openness in human relations than in the West; it is hard to know whether this trait was Russian or Communist. I recall an encounter in my last month in the Soviet Union. In my compartment in the train from Leningrad two GPU officers exchanged reminiscences. One of them, who was accompanied by his six-year-old daughter, talked with contempt of the behavior of his former wife. When he went out into the hallway, I followed him and said, "I would not talk this way of her mother in the presence of your child." He said, "Oh, she is too small to understand." I replied, "Children often understand more than adults think." He thought for a moment before saying slowly, "You may be right." How would an officer of the RCMP have reacted to a similar remark by an unknown Russian traveler?

But my strongest reason for identifying with communism and the Soviet Union was the fact that it was the only force defending mankind against fascism and war. The "West" praised Mussolini, favored Franco, and was at best ambivalent toward Hitler. In the Soviet Union there was never any doubt who the enemy was. There was instruction in sharpshooting available to everyone; I also took it. The target was a steel helmet with a swastika.

So I continued to consider myself a Bolshevik; I never thought of myself as a "Stalinist." I had been an active revolutionary for more than five years before I had ever heard the name of Stalin. When I saw photos, I did not like his face. But I found myself generally in agreement with his policies. I first doubted his statement in 1928 that the apparent capitalist stability of the 1920s was unstable and would be replaced by a period of wars and revolutions, but he turned out to be right. He also turned out to be right in other predictions and judgments; I concluded that it was foolish to evaluate a man by his looks, and that I could trust his leadership.

The "purges" disturbed me; evidently something had gone wrong, but what was it? It was hard to believe that old revolutionaries, who had proved their courage and devotion through a lifetime of work and struggle, could have become traitors. But it was even harder to believe that these same persons would not proclaim their innocence before all the world, given a chance to do so in a public trial. I read the verbatim transcripts of their trials; their confessions were very characteristic personal statements. Rykov, always dry and sober, when pressed by Vyshinsky to admit that he had committed treason, finally said, "As it failed, it was treason; had it succeeded, it would have been something else." Bukharin, sensitive and emotional, passionately rejected the statement that he had once, twenty years ago, considered killing Lenin — a statement quite irrelevant to the accusations in his trial, which he admitted, but vital to the honor of his name.

By a coincidence I had found independent evidence for the existence of a conspiracy. My friend Gregersen, on the eve of going on vacation to Copenhagen, was asked by an acquaintance by the name of Grasche to take a book to a friend of his in Denmark. When Gregersen asked why he did not send it by mail, which functioned quite normally, the answer was that it was a particularly valuable book, a luxury edition of *Arabian Nights* issued by the Academy of Art. Gregersen did not get around to picking up the book and did not see the intended recipient, a former Communist of Trotskyist bent who had turned against the Soviet Union. Soon after this, Grasche was arrested and sentenced as a spy in a public trial. No mention was made of a book; but in a different trial the very same edition was identified as having been used as a secret code. This cannot well be a coincidence.

After weighing all the available evidence, I have come to the conclusion that there had indeed been a conspiracy, but that the conspirators were justified in attempting to replace Stalin by a saner leadership. Different from the vast majority in the Soviet Union, including myself, the conspirators, being close to the center of power, had come to see that Stalin's driving energy had led to utter ruthlessness and that his cagey circumspection had degenerated into paranoia. When they failed to replace him, they realized that the Soviet Union would have to face the impending storm under Stalin's leadership and that they would weaken their country by discrediting him. In this respect they may well have been right: without the almost religious faith in Stalin, morale might well have collapsed in the Soviet Union under the terrible blows of the Nazi invasion, as it did in France.

Looking back on my personal fate, I now consider myself extremely lucky to have been able to leave the Soviet Union unscathed. There was no rhyme or reason in who became a victim and who was spared. Mine probably was a case of "Fools rush in where angels fear to tread."

CHAPTER VII

Intermezzo in Europe

1937 – 1938

Through the Mediterranean

It is not in my nature to look back asking, "What might have happened, if. . . ." As soon as I felt the ship's planks under my feet, I looked forward to my sea voyage. On board I met a British art historian who gave me valuable advice about Istanbul and Greece.

On a sunny spring morning the ship entered the Bosporus; it was an enchanting way to approach Istanbul, which I consider to be the most beautiful city I have ever seen. I had dreamed of seeing Istanbul since my high-school days; now, in my forty-fifth year, the dream came true.

Thanks to my rudimentary Turkish, I was not dependent on facilities for foreign tourists. Knowing a bit of the language means twice as much fun and half the expense to the traveler. I stayed in a small Turkish hotel right next to the bazaar, in the very heart of town. I found the Hagia Sophia the most wonderful interior space ever created by man. But I was also enchanted by the mosques, the treasures of the Old Museum, the old streets with their open wooden upper stories over closed stone walls, as well as the powerful Theodosian fortification. The weather was perfect, with clear skies every day, allowing a view of the snow-covered Bythinian Olympus across the deep-blue Sea of Marmara. As soon as the heat rose toward noon, a cool breeze started to blow from the sea, to die down only at sunset.

For three days I stayed in Brussa, on the other side of the Sea of

Marmara. I found it to be a charming town, with small houses and gardens on the slopes of Mount Olympus and beautiful mosques; the Green Mosque is a perfect jewel. I spent another day on the Princes' Islands, swimming in the sea. I also had an interesting talk with the German architect Bruno Taut, whom I visited at the university in Pera.

I had assumed that it would be easy to get a visa for a visit to France because of the Paris World's Fair. However, the people at the French consulate said, "No," very unpleasantly. I went to the British consulate, where I was received by a jovial John Bull type. He stated that as a German I did not need a visa; the decision to admit me would be made on landing. I bought a ticket to London, for travel by a French boat to Marseilles and by train to London via Dunkerque. With this ticket I returned to the French consulate asking for a 24-hour visa for *transit sans arret;* very grudgingly, they granted it.

The ship arrived at Piraeus, and passengers could visit Athens during the day. When I set foot on land, it suddenly struck me that, for the first time in my life, I was in a country where I did not speak a word of the language, nor of a related language. However, I managed to get around quite well. After taking an overview of the city from Lykabettos Hill, I wandered slowly through the streets up to the Acropolis.

I entered the precinct of the Acropolis. The sight of the Parthenon overwhelmed me. "I entered a completely strange world," wrote Goethe of his visit to the temple of Paestum. The Parthenon is only slightly less strange. It has absolutely nothing in common with the mild enlightened spirit of the so-called "Greek Revival." It is wild, exciting, indeed completely mad; a monument to Greek hubris, the insane pride which felt itself to be above all laws of God or man; it is the summit of the passionate going to the extremes which was the source of the greatness as well as of the downfall of Greece. The Greeks managed to be extremists in everything, even in their glorification of *sophrosyne* — moderation.

When I descended from the Acropolis into the city to look at the Byzantine churches, the contrast could not have been greater. They were small, dark, half sunk into the earth; after their magnificent spree of creativity and aggression the Greeks, dispirited and humiliated, had crept back into mother's womb.

In the evening the ship sailed out of the Saronic Gulf, around

Cape Matapan, through the Strait of Messina, and along the coast of Corsica to Marseilles. It was a beautiful trip in perfect weather. I talked with the French sailors; most of them were Communists who urged me to consult the Party's paper in Marseilles. At the paper I was received very cordially and advised to go to Paris to the *Humanité,* the Party's central organ.

PARIS

I took the night train to Paris, arriving in the early morning. As I walked through the streets and visited the cathedral, it struck me how dark, gray and black Paris looked after the white of Istanbul, Athens, and Marseilles.

Humanité referred me to the Paris organization of the German Communist party which organized the admission of volunteers to the German section of the International Brigade fighting for the Spanish Republic against the forces of Franco, Mussolini, and Hitler. Not surprisingly, they were suspicious of a man who had been excluded from the Soviet Party and from the country. I urged them to ask the Soviet Party for information on my person. I doubt that they did; but if so, they were not likely to receive an answer.

I soon learned not to bother about the fact that I lived illegally in France after my transit visa had expired. I learned that the written orders of expulsion came in the three colors of the French tricolor: red was harmless, white bothersome, but only blue really dangerous. My order was red.

I joined an anti-Hitler organization called the "German Popular Front." The leadership of the German Social Democratic party rejected it, but among its members were many Social Democrats, in addition to Communist, Liberal, Christian, and even some Monarchist opponents of Hitler's Third Reich; some were well-known writers and artists. We tried to inform the French public about the reality in their neighbor's land, and also to raise political and financial support for the Spanish Republic.

I rented a room in a somewhat dubious little hotel close to the office I had first visited on my arrival. My brother-in-law, Alfred Plaut, sent me one hundred dollars every month, enough to live quite comfortably. He sent the money through one of his relatives, Hugo Simon, who had been a successful banker in Berlin. In his house I encountered some Germans who opposed Hitler for reasons rather different from mine; they disliked his populist measures, such as the mass excursions organized by his "Strength through Joy" organization.

The French architect André Lurçat, whom I had met in Moscow and liked very much, had returned to Paris. I think it was through him that I met José Louis Sert, who had designed the Spanish pavilion, the best building at the Paris World's Fair. I later was to see Sert again in the US, first in New York, and later at Cambridge, where he became dean of architecture at Harvard. Then there was Otto Freundlich, the painter who had been a friend of my mother's, a wonderful human being and a good artist. While leading French artists admired his work, he was too unworldly to ever escape from poverty. He perished during the Nazi occupation. Through Freundlich I met the German art critic Max Raphael, a Communist. He had a remarkable mind and we had long and stimulating discussions. He also came to New York later.

After the German Communists refused me, I asked Raphael about other ways to go to Spain, and he mentioned the French Socialists and the group "New Beginning," formed by Max Seydewitz, a former Social-Democratic deputy in the Reichstag. It so happened that the Paris group of "New Beginning" was at that time dominated by Trotskyists (Seydewitz later expelled them). Several of them, who had fought with the Republicans in Catalonia, gave their interpretation of the Spanish Civil War as follows: it was a war between two imperialist groups, the "ins," Britain and France, and the "outs," Germany and Italy. As "true revolutionaries" they were opposed to both and had therefore fraternized with the Franco soldiers and played soccer with them. This was at the time when Franco was crushing the Basques and the only way to relieve them was to attack Franco's rear in Catalonia. Evidently, my place was not with this group.

At the French Socialist's office I was received by a Russian Menshevik emigrant who wanted to hear horror stories about the Soviet Union from me. I did not peddle that kind of ware. Fortunately, we were interrupted by the arrival of a young German worker who had fled from the Saar, and as he did not speak a word of French, I offered to accompany him to the French family who was going to put him up.

Soon people began returning from Spain. Among them was the writer Egon Erwin Kisch, who told me that it was too late to go: although the Republicans would hold out as long as possible, the war was lost. After some hesitation I decided not to go to Spain; probably, I had not been really wholeheartedly resolved, torn as I was between a sense of duty and deep-seated abhorrence of war.

I had no doubt that once Spain had fallen Hitler would soon start to move. I concluded that the only countries in Europe likely to remain neutral were Sweden and Turkey. I was attracted to both of them, and also to Mexico, but finally decided that the United States was my best bet. I recall that somebody once mentioned Canada. But as I, like most Europeans, thought of Canada as a paperback edition of the United States, I did not give it serious consideration.

The us consulate did not look with favor on a fellow who had lived seven years in the Soviet Union. However, I could show that I had lived three years in God's Own Country without shooting the president; so with the aid of my sister and brother-in-law and of the Jewish Agency, I was finally accepted. However, every time I called, I was told that the quota for the month was filled and to come back in four weeks; this happened five times.

There was an additional problem. I did not want to ask for a visa to be stamped in my self-extended passport; I feared that this might get me into trouble, immediately or later. So I asked the French authorities to give me a six-month permit of residence. They countered that I should try to get my passport extended at the German embassy. I refused, and they finally agreed that I might request extension by a registered letter to the embassy. I sent the letter — an empty envelope — and showed them the registration. It still took some talking to persuade the French bureaucracy that, in order to get rid of me, they had to give me a permit to stay. But I finally succeeded, and I got my us visa stamped on an immaculately pure document.

Had I not obtained that visa, my name would just be an infinitely small addition to the list of millions of Hitler's victims. Strange world, in which human lives are just appendices to scraps of paper.

I was awaiting a visit from Gertel on the occasion of an exhibition of her work in Paris, but the opening date was deferred. In September I decided to hire a bicycle for three days to explore the cathedrals and many other monuments of the Ile-de-France. My strongest impression was Laon — its cathedral remains my favorite, apart, of course, from the incomparable Chartres.

When I returned, I found a note saying that Freundlich had called to inform me that Gertel had arrived several days ago. Freundlich had delayed calling because in his bitter poverty he did not have the money at the time for the pay telephone. I rushed to Freundlich's atelier and from there to the Gallery Zaks, only to learn that Gertel had left the night before. I was desolate. However, Gertel came to Paris again in the following spring. We talked for hours, walking or sitting in cafés or restaurants. On the last day she said we might still live together permanently some day. I shook my head sadly; I knew it was not going to be. Two years later Gertel died.

I had visits from relatives and friends. German Jews were not allowed to travel to the Paris World's Fair, so Olga came only at Christmas. I urged her and her brother to leave Germany without delay. I said that Hitler would soon start a war, would lose it, blame the defeat on the Jews, and massacre all of them. Olga wept; how could I say such terrible things? However, she left the following year, just before the "Crystal Night"; so she could take some of her — and my — belongings with her to New York. Her younger brother lost his bank and was in jail for a while, but then was allowed to leave for London. During the panic following the fall of France he, like all Germans, was shipped out of the country, and landed in Australia. Her older brother who, as a war invalid at that time still enjoyed a measure of protection from the army, was not arrested, stayed as long as possible to act as lawyer for the Jewish community in Hamburg, and arrived in the US in June of 1941.

In the fall I moved into a mansard room in an equally cheap but nicer hotel in one of the oldest quarters of Paris, the "Mont de Paris" behind the Panthéon, right next to the "Place de la Contrescarpe," where I took my breakfast in a café which at that time was frequented mainly by casual workers from the nearby market and by pimps. Many years later, in reading *The Snows of Kilimanjaro*, I learned that I had followed in Hemingway's footsteps. Today this café has succeeded Montparnasse and Saint-Germain-des-Prés as a meeting place of Paris intellectuals.

As I could not risk working illegally, I had much time on my hands. I spent days at the World's Fair and in the streets, parks, churches and museums of Paris and its environs. I also did a lot of reading, including both Michelet's and Jaurès' histories of the French Revolution.

Exploring France

In the spring of 1938 three of the architects of the May group whom I had met in Moscow came from London to Paris: Wilhelm Schütte and Grete Schütte-Lihotsky, and Albert Löcher with his wife. Together we made a week's excursion to the castles and towns on the Loire.

When my wait for the US visa began, I decided to use the monthly waiting intervals to explore more of France. In June I hired a bicycle and rode though Normandy and Brittany all the way from Pont-de-l'Arche, above Rouen, to Brest. There were the towns, cathedrals, and monasteries of Normandy; the miracle of Mont-Saint-Michel longed for since my childhood vacation in Paramé — the wild cliffs of the coast of Brittany and its villages with their touching cemeteries. One night in Brittany I stayed in a peasant cottage with two old women who spoke not a word of French, only Breton. I had not been aware of Breton nationalism. In a tavern a pleasantly drunk worker explained to me that it was not the French who had won the war; it was "la petite Bretagne et la Grande Bretagne" (Great Britain). So much for world history.

I came back by train, stopping at Le Mans and Chartres. I should have done it the other way round, because every day out I had had to contend with a strong westerly wind.

In July, I thought I might cope better with the heat by hitchhiking. This was a mistake; actually the air movement in bicycling cooled the skin most effectively. I traveled down the Loire Valley to Tours, then to Poitiers, a fascinating old town. There I hired a bicycle for three days, visiting the great Abbey of Fontévrault, among many other sights. I continued through Angoulême to Périgueux in the Dordogne, which I explored by bicycle, discovering the marvelous Romanesque sculptures of Moissac and Souliac. I continued as far south as Toulouse and Albi, to return via Cahors and Limoges. On this trip I visited two old "New Towns": Montpazier, built in the twelfth century, and Richelieu, in the seventeenth. Both were stillborn and have therefore completely preserved their original form.

My third trip, again by bicycle, took me from a point about 100 kilometers southeast of Paris all the way to Toulon on the Mediterranean, through Burgundy, the Massif Central, and Provence. With the natural and man-made beauty of Provence, it was the most enjoyable of all. I returned through Dijon, using the train for part of the way.

Apart from boat trips, bicycling is really the most enjoyable way of travel. It is just the right speed to see a country; hiking is a bit too slow, and car driving and other means of mechanized travel are much too fast. France is a beautiful country, immensely rich and varied in landscape, cities, and architecture. I count the sixteen months I spent there among the best of my life.

THE GREAT BETRAYAL

While I was enjoying the beauty of France, I was aware of the growing danger of fascism and war. It could still be prevented if all those threatened stood together to defend mutual security, as the Soviet Union insisted. But the Western powers continued to be blinded by what Thomas Mann called the greatest folly of the twentieth century: obsessive anticommunism. When Sir John Simon was asked at a meeting in Oxford why his government had not carried through with sanctions against the invasion of Ethiopia, he replied that this would have led to the overthrow of Mussolini by the Communists in Italy. The leaders of the West were not unaware of the aggressive nature of the Berlin-Rome-Tokyo "Anti-Comintern Axis." But rather than "quarantine the aggressor," as Roosevelt advocated at one point, they tried to turn him East. They had looked on as Hitler and Mussolini destroyed the Spanish Republic. Now, in the spring of 1938, when Hitler annexed Austria, they again did not move. There remained one bolt that kept the gates of war closed: Czechoslovakia, allied to both France and the Soviet Union, the link between East and West. Hitler threatened it by demanding the "liberation" of the Sudetenland. The Soviet Union declared that it would fight to defend its ally. But France, under the pressure of Britain, of the international banks who had pushed their spokesman Georges Bonnet into the post of French foreign minister, and of the US ambassadors in London and Paris, Kennedy and Bullitt, acceded to the betrayal of Munich. When French Prime Minister Edouard Daladier returned to Paris, deeply depressed about having agreed to this shameful capitulation, he was flabbergasted by receiving a hero's welcome.

Certainly, people felt relieved that the bombs had not started to fall. But it was not love of peace that had motivated the architects of Munich; it was an attempt to channel Hitler's aggression in the direction of the Soviet Union.

The German antifascists in Paris had hoped that the West

would resist. The leaders of the German Popular Front offered to mobilize a regiment of German volunteers to fight against Hitler. They were told that Germans who wanted to fight should join the French Foreign Legion. It was a bitter disappointment: we wanted to fight for the liberty of our own people, not for the domination of others, such as the Algerians or the Vietnamese.

CHAPTER VIII

The U.S.A.
1938 – 1955

IN GREATER NEW YORK

At the end of the same month of October which had seen the Munich betrayal I finally received my US visa. After a visit with my cousin Elsbeth and her husband, Fritz Oppenheimer, in London, I embarked for New York. During the passage we received the news of the "Crystal Night," the start of the final destruction of the Jews of Germany. I arrived on the evening of the sixteenth of November, the last day of validity of my French residence permit. My brother-in-law, Alfred Plaut, was at the pier and drove me to his home in New Rochelle, over the just-completed Westside Highway. I was happy to see my sister and my nephews, who had grown from babies to teen-agers. Olga Solmitz was also there. She had finally left Germany, just in time to be still permitted to take some of her possessions with her. She had included part of my library which had been stored in the farmhouse on the common Solmitz-Blumenfeld property in Gross-Borstel near Hamburg. The balance went up in flames a few years later, ignited by bombs dropped by the Royal Air Force.

There were other relatives and friends whom I met again in America after many years. A cousin remarked that I had not changed at all in ten years; I countered that this was an obvious sign of complete sclerosis. In my first week in my sister's home, at a party at the house of neighbors, a lady told me that she had just met another German refugee architect by the name of Konrad Wittmann. Wittmann had been the only friend whom I had found among my fellow students in Munich, in 1911 and 1912; I had last seen him in 1913. We renewed our friendship. He was an excellent architect and an outstanding human being. After some difficult early years he became a teacher at the Pratt Institute, greatly loved and admired by his students.

America had changed in the twelve years since I had left it. In the twenties, in the days of Calvin Coolidge, the Americans whom I met had talked only about jobs, money, spectator sports, cars, and girls. As to more important subjects, this "New World" seemed satisfied in theology with the concepts of the seventeen century, in politics with those of the eighteenth, and in economics with those of the nineteenth. The depression had shocked Americans out of that kind of complacency; they had begun to question and to think. Also, the arts — in the twenties regarded as a ladies' parlor game, unworthy of the attention of respectable men — were now taken seriously. America had become a much more interesting country.

The negative side of the depression was also apparent. I was shocked to see the many gray, tired, worn faces in the subway. I never had that depressing experience in the subways of Paris or of Moscow.

Lucky as I was to have the support of my relatives, I still needed a job. Would I be able to find one in the depressed economy of 1938? Would I be able to hold one? I had been out of regular work for three years, and out of competition in the Western world for more than eight. At the age of 46 I had to start from scratch.

Again I was lucky. A German colleague in Paris had given me the address of his friend in New York. From him I learned about the recently established trade union of architects and engineers, the FAECT. I went to their headquarters and was well received. They directed me to an office which was designing a big model for General Motors to be shown at the New York World's Fair. To my pleasant surprise, they regarded my Soviet experience as an asset and took me on. It was a huge project employing several hundred architects and designers under the direction of Norman Bel Geddes. My immediate boss was Melville Branch, who has remained a friend. There I also found Albert Löcher, a talented collaborator of Ernst May, whom I had met in Moscow and subsequently in Paris.

I designed the harbor and the central park of the big city which was the core of the model, generating freeways which spread all over the landscape. It was fun, but it lasted only three weeks; I had come in at the tail end of the design stage.

What next? I figured that there were three ways for an unknown architect to establish himself. First, win a competition. But I was a very poor draftsman, so that was out for me. Second, find a job in an office and gain appreciation for my work, possibly to the point of becoming indispensable and being taken in as a partner. This could happen but was a matter of luck. Third, write and publish. This seemed the most promising way in my case.

I had been interested for years in the question of sunshine in housing. I found that the existing literature was limited, dealing only with one or two aspects of planning for — or against — sunshine. I wrote a study with a number of illustrations which explored orientation and distance from other structures, together with shape of rooms, as well as location, size, and shape of windows. Overlays were developed to indicate the floor area covered by sunshine in any room at various latitudes and seasons.

I presented copies to several persons. They found the study interesting but hard to publish — too short for a book, too long for an article. However, James Marston Fitch, then editor of the *Architectural Record,* liked it enough to invite me for a talk. He commissioned me to write an article on "the coordination of natural and artificial light." I plunged into the subject, found it fascinating, and produced a lengthy article which actually dealt primarily with the relation of lighting and seeing. It was published in two sections in the *A.R.* in 1940 and 1941 and received favorable comment.

At that time the USA had just embarked on its program of "Public Housing." The FAECT strongly supported it, and I went out to meetings of other CIO unions to "sell" it. I got a lukewarm reception. "We are not eligible because our wages are above the specified maximum," was the reaction. I concluded that the program could only be a success if it was broadened. I had learnt that at that time the United States Housing Authority raised money on short term at extremely low interest rates and lent it to the local agencies on considerably higher long-term rates. I estimated that rents could be reduced, without direct subsidies, to a level accessible to most workers if the local agencies received loans from the Federal Authority at the rates which it paid to its short-term creditors, and if the projects remained exempt from local taxes. I developed a proposal for such a program in a short pamphlet entitled *Housing Union Labor*. It was published, in mimeographed form, by the FAECT and subsequently also by the New York CIO. The New York architect-planner Albert Mayer, to whom I had given a copy, expressed satisfaction that a refugee architect, rather than talking about his achievements in his old country, had tackled a problem of his new one.

In Paris, Max Raphael and André Lurçat had given me letters to the art critic Meyer Shapiro, whom I found very interesting, and to the architect Simon Breines. Breines took me to a meeting at the Metropolitan Museum where Robert Moses presented his program of "urban redevelopment." We both were shocked by this ruthless proposal for wholesale demolition. Subsequently I joined a study group of the New York Citizens Housing and Planning Council which attempted to prepare redevelopment legislation. It was a very interesting group; its members included Clarence Stein, Henry Churchill, Fred Ackermann, Clarence Perry, Bill Vladeck and Carl Feiss. I did not share their enthusiasm; I warned, "Whatever good urban development may do, it will certainly worsen the housing situation of low-income groups." I insisted that it should be recommended only if accompanied, or better preceded, by rent control and by a large-scale program of subsidized housing.

It has always been a puzzle to me how persons of eminent good will and high intelligence could favor "slum clearance." At a later date I put it this way: "If you want to help a fellow who has worn out his pants, you buy him a pair of new ones or repair the old ones; you don't just tear off his pants." It is really as simple as that.

Breines hired me for a week to help with working drawings for the installation of the Soviet pavilion for the New York World's Fair, but otherwise I was unemployed during the first several months of 1939.

In the spring the FAECT directed me to the firm of Kelly & Gruzen in Jersey City, which wanted a site planner for a small public housing project in Harrison, NJ. I developed the site plan, which later received official praise from the New York chapter of the AIA. More important, when I later asked the opinion of a tenant, he said, "It is nice; every court is different." That is exactly what I had tried to achieve.

Gruzen kept me on for other work, first on details of this project and later on other commissions. When work ran out in the fall, he promised to call me back as soon as a commission came in.

I had moved to Jersey City. First I rented a furnished room, but the landlady threw me out because I made her house look disreputable by pulling down one shade, which was hit by the afternoon sun, and not the other, which was shadowed by the next house. I then rented a furnished cold-water flat. By every definition it was a slum dwelling. The bedroom was windowless, but I used it only for storage, sleeping in the "living room." The bathroom was shared with another apartment, but nobody lived there. So it was really quite adequate. Its great attraction was the view from the bay window; from the edge of the Palisades, it swept across the flats to the Hudson River, the bay, and the Manhattan skyline. I stayed until the end of the year, when the winter cold drove me out.

All the time the approaching war was on my mind. Late in 1938 my sister took me to a meeting of German anti-Hitler intellectuals, mostly from the New School for Social Research. As I had lived in Russia, I was asked about Soviet policy. I said that the popular feeling was, "A curse on both their houses," and favorable to neutrality, but that the leadership was fully aware of the deadly danger of fascism and would continue to do its utmost to arrive at a firm commitment to mutual security. However, if the Western powers continued to reject their proposals, they would turn to neutrality. My analysis was questioned by many of those present, but strongly endorsed by Paul Tillich, the theologian.

When the West again looked the other way while Hitler marched into Prague and liquidated Czechoslovakia, Stalin finally warned publicly that the Soviet Union still wanted to preserve peace by collective security, but was not willing to go to war to pull the West's chestnuts out of the fire. We now know — from disclosures at the Hiss trial — that a full year earlier, when Austria was annexed by Germany, the Soviet ambassador in Paris had conveyed the same message to the French foreign minister, Yvon Delbos. It had been ignored then; it continued to be ignored, despite the warnings of Churchill and others who advocated acceptance of the Soviet proposals.

The public statement by Stalin prompted the Nazi government to seek an accommodation with the Soviet Union. The Soviet government kept the door open for mutual security; only shortly before Hitler marched into Poland did it sign a nonaggression pact with Germany. This was followed by a so-called "Treaty of Friendship," actually an agreement by Hitler to consult the Soviet Union on his actions in Eastern Europe.

I had wondered for some time how long Soviet patience would last. Depressed as I was by the pact, I could not blame the Soviets; it was the only choice left. It bought time and territory; had they not been able to move their boundary 200 miles to the west, they could not have succeeded in stopping Hitler short of Moscow and Leningrad. And, by leaving the West to face Hitler alone, they forced them to face reality. Had they acted otherwise, Hitler would have been able to defeat first the Soviet Union and then the West. In fact, by agreeing to the pact, Hitler signed his own death sentence. The pact never was an alliance, as it is now often referred to. The Soviets gave no aid to Hitler, neither military nor economic. Their only concession was to restore normal trade to the same conditions which had always been, and remained, open to the West. Their attitude actually was "neutrality malevolent to both sides" — a rather natural response to the malevolent attitude of both sides toward them. What bothered me during this period was not their deeds, but the words by which they tried to reassure Hitler.

We know now, from the testimony of the Hungarian prime minister, Count Teleki, and the Italian foreign minister, Count Ciano, as well as of German witnesses, that Hitler was firmly convinced that Britain would continue not to make war on him. He was not entirely wrong; war was declared but — except at sea — not waged; it was rightly called a phony war until Hitler decided to make it real.

I remember the start of the Second World War; from my window I saw the *Bremen* sail out of New York Harbor. It was the second piece of deadly news in a few months; four months earlier Gertel had passed away. A period of my life had come to an end.

There was no dramatic change; the US was still neutral. I rented a furnished room at the corner of Riverside Drive and 142nd Street, with a view over the Hudson River. Once more I returned to my old love, the history of cities. I spent my days at the marvelous Avery Library, the architectural library of Columbia University. Through Carl Feiss I had joined the newly founded Society of Architectural Historians. When I discovered in my studies at Avery a peculiar feature of the ancient Indian city of Mohenjo-daro, I published it in their journal in January 1942. It was my second publication in an American professional journal. It was followed by an article on "Regional and City Planning in the Soviet Union," published in the third issue of *Task,* a journal founded by young teachers and students at Harvard and MIT. I learned that this article had been discussed at a meeting of the American Institute of Planners. I was beginning to get a reputation — but not a job. During the entire year of 1940 I had only four weeks of paid work, at Albert Mayer's office.

Given the insouciance and insolence of my unshakable self-confidence, this did not bother me too much. I lived frugally but happily on borrowed money, digging into the treasures of Avery Library. In studying the beautiful publication by Hulot and Fougères on the ancient Greek city of Selinus, I got caught up again by that question which had arisen in my mind in the spring of 1927 when I contemplated the Temple of Concordia in Agrigento, Sicily: was this a synthesis of two independently existing building types, the "naos" (cella) and a ring of sacred columns on their stylobate, the latter symbolizing the trees of a sacred grove on a mountain?

I have spent more time on this question of the origin of the Doric peripteros than on any other problem which I have ever researched. Several times in 1940 and 1941 I felt close to writing down my tentative conclusions, but I always deferred it. I finally wrote a fragmentary summary in 1985 which is still unpublished.

In the fall of 1940 I participated in a seminar on planning given by Carl Feiss and Raymond Unwin at Columbia University. I had admired Unwin's book since 1912 and his work at Hampstead since 1924; his person fully lived up to my expectations.

PHILADELPHIA
It was also on Carl Feiss' recommendation that the Philadelphia Housing Association asked me to present myself for a job as a research assistant. After a talk with the director, Edmund N. Bacon, I was hired to start in February of 1941. For reasons still obsure to me, Ed insisted on reducing my modest demand for $200 a month to $2000 a year, after three trial months at $150.

I have often thought that I have cheated educators of a model deterrent by not dying at that time. Just imagine: here was a man with many gifts by nature and education, with all conditions for a brilliant career, but he always refused to listen to his betters and pigheadedly went his own way; where did it lead him? To end up in his fiftieth year as a research assistant at $2000 a year in an obscure little organization. Let this be a warning to you, young man.

I had been just two weeks in Philadelphia when I got a call from Sumner Gruzen asking me to come back to work on the site plan for an army camp. I decided to stay with the Housing Association, but did come over some evenings to help in developing the site plan. I recommended Albert Löcher to Gruzen; it worked out very well. Löcher stayed with Gruzen as chief designer for several decades until his premature death; during this time the firm became one of the well-known architectural offices of New York.

I found the work with the Housing Association interesting. I extended our annual survey of housing construction, conversion, and demolition from the city to the entire metropolitan area. I found many previously overlooked aspects and correlations significant for housing; some results of my research were published in the association's annual reports or in special pamphlets. I found that the city could be analyzed in terms of concentric zones, characterized by predominance of demolitions, conversions, no change, and new housing construction, respectively. In analyzing the census of 1940, I found that racial segregation had actually increased. I wrote up my findings at the request of a black student activist — he later became one of the leading reporters of *The Baltimore Afro-American* — and he included them, with reference to their source, in a militant pamphlet which he wrote. When Ed Bacon saw it and called me in, he was livid, fearing some backlash which actually never occurred.

One of our board members, Scholz, a professor of economics, questioned the qualification of an architect for a job of socioeconomic research. So I took a course in statistics, during which I learned a lot, and Scholz' seminar on economic planning. He was very interested in what I had to say about Soviet planning and became one of my strongest backers.

I also met the architect Oscar Stonorov and his then practically unknown partner, Lou Kahn, who became and remained a close friend. They were among the members of an organization of reform-minded Young Turks which had been formed to bring about the adoption of a city charter for Philadelphia. The charter was backed by a majority of Philadelphia voters but rejected by the Pennsylvania legislature. After this defeat the group decided to pursue the more limited goal of establishing an active city planning program in Philadelphia. A City Planning Commission had been appointed many years ago, but it existed only on paper, without funding and without a staff.

Ed Bacon and the Housing Association were deeply involved in this campaign. The focus was to be the annual meeting of the American Society of Planning Officials to be held in Philadelphia. The key speaker on Philadelphia's needs was Hugh Pomeroy; I was charged with supplying him the relevant information on the city's housing conditions.

Hugh, who had started as a Baptist preacher and had subsequently been a member of the California legislature, gave a true fire-and-brimstone speech. Using my material, he thundered that Philadelphia had the worst slums in the nation. The mayor, who had been scheduled to follow Hugh on the platform, got redder and redder in the face and left without giving his speech.

Ed Bacon was desperate, but I told him that the cause was by no means lost. The mayor was to receive a citizen's delegation on the following day which would submit a detailed proposal for a well-staffed planning commission. I recalled my trade union experience in Hamburg. I anticipated that, after the rantings of that "wild radical" Pomeroy, the proposals of the delegation would sound most moderate and reasonable. It worked like a charm. There was support from the banks which handled the city's bonds and were disturbed about the way in which contracts for public works were handed out to friends of the political machine, and also from the city's chief engineer, an able and dedicated technocrat.

A new City Planning Commission was established. Its chairman was Edward Hopkinson, head of the bank of Drexel, Biddle, & Co., the city's main creditors. He handled his task very well. Robert B. Mitchell was appointed director and began to lay out a program and assemble a staff. He had the benefit of the advice of Professor Sweeney, the wizened and experienced head of the Institute for Local and State Government. He gave Bob Mitchell two tips on how to ward off attempts to cut his staff. First, do not ask for research; there was, instead, a division for "Planning Analysis" — evidently an indispensable activity. Second, never give the same title to more than one staff person; when the cutting starts, you can always counter, "This is the only man I have who can do this job."

The United States was at peace, but war was going on in Europe. When Poland collapsed, its government fleeing, and Hitler's armies by-passing heroic Warsaw to advance far to the east, Soviet armies moved west and the Germans retreated. Western correspondents who interviewed Russian soldiers at the time ridiculed them as naive when they said that they had come to save Poland from the Nazis. But history has proved them right. Even in the short run, they were not entirely wrong. In Lvov and other places, Ukrainian fascists had already started to massacre Jews and Poles. The Soviet armies put an end to this. Subsequently, before and during Hitler's attack on the Soviets, they saved the lives of hundreds of thousands of Jews by evacuating them to the interior. Similarly, many Rumanian Jews were saved when the Soviet Union recovered Bessarabia, the homeland of my Russian grandmother.

In the West the events of that period were — and still are — seen as a carving up of other nations by a Hitler-Stalin partnership. Knowing something of the history of that area, I did not share that view. Like Bessarabia, the Baltic Provinces — "baltic" is an adjective — had been part of the Soviet Union at the time of its foundation, different from Poland and Finland, whose independence the Soviets had recognized from their first day. The territories which the Soviet Union recovered from Poland were east of the Curzon Line which the Western powers had established as Poland's eastern boundary — with two significant exceptions, Bialystok in the north and Przemysl in the south. I remembered those names well from the First World War; they were the two main boundary fortresses, Russian and Austrian respectively. The meaning of their occupation by the Soviets was clear: they were battening down the hatches against the threat of a German attack.

The same was evidently true of the Baltics. It was well known — described in detail in the American journal *The Nation* by its military expert, Max Werner — that the plans of the German General Staff were based on an attack on Leningrad on both sides of the Finnish Gulf. The south side, Esthonia, was no longer available; what about the north side, Finland? The Soviet Union asked Finland to oblige itself by a treaty to allow no foreign forces to land on its territory and, in case its defense was not strong enough, to call on Soviet aid. This was quite different from the Soviet proceedings toward the Baltic republics. In fact, it was identical with the treaty under which Finland now exists as an independent free Western-style democracy.

It was not interpreted that way at the time. The Finnish government replied with a flat refusal, backed by mobilizaton and blackout. The Soviets made a second proposal. If Finland could not guarantee that hostile guns would not be installed within range of Leningrad on the Mannerheim Line, then that line must be moved back. In exchange for the territory involved, the Soviets offered to cede an area three times as large further north.

Finland sent a negotiator, the head of the Conservative party, Paasikivi, who later became its postwar president. He was inclined to accept the exchange of territory, but balked at a Soviet demand for a naval base at Hangö. After two months and a break for consultation at home, he returned with new instructions: no change in the status quo. After warning that this was not acceptable, the Soviets attacked.

What had happened in these two months? We know that the Finnish government sought the advice of Berlin before it ended the war. Did it also seek its advice at its start? Was it advised to drag out the negotiations until arctic darkness decreased the effectiveness of the Soviet Air Force? The Finnish resistance gained the well-deserved admiration of the world, but it could not hold once daylight returned.

Did the Finnish government also seek advice from London, and what was the answer? I am convinced that the history of the Finnish war has still to be written. There is no doubt that strong forces in both Berlin and London believed that Hitler's miscalculation had unleashed the "wrong" war; support of Finland by both could turn it around in the "right" direction.

I could not avoid such thoughts in interpreting the strange image presented by the American press. Britain and France, the countries most vitally important to the United States, were in a state of war with a deadly enemy. But this was hardly ever mentioned. The Finnish war dominated the news as if there were no greater danger to Western civilization.

It may seem absurd to speculate now about these events almost half a century after the fact. But for me it meant that I found myself once more in the role of the nonconformist, in a general climate of anti-Sovietism.

When Hitler invaded France, eight months after the declaration of war, Britain had sent fewer troops to the Continent than she had in eight weeks in 1914; but she was preparing to send some 100,000 troops to help the Finns fight the Soviets.* France had sent the man whom they considered their best military leader, General Weygand, to Syria and was preparing to bomb the Soviet oil fields in the Caucasus.**

After Hitler marched into France, Weygand was recalled; the government of Daladier and Bonnet was replaced by that of Reynaud and Blum and, in Britain, Chamberlain and Halifax were replaced by Churchill and Eden. Too late! Had those changes occurred twenty months earlier, there would have been no Munich betrayal and Hitler would not have dared to start a war. The death of fifty million human beings in World War II was the terrible price mankind has paid for the anticommunist obsession which blinded the "men of Munich."

As soon as France was faced with German soldiers, the French Communists started to organize the resistance. The same was true in Denmark and in every country invaded by the Nazis. Nowhere did the local Communists wait for Hitler's attack on the Soviet Union to fight for their country.

Nor did the Soviet Union have any illusions about the increased danger to itself resulting from the collapse of France. They immediately stepped up industrial production by extending the workday from seven to eight hours and the workweek from five to six days, and they transferred arms factories with hundreds of thousands of workers to the Urals and to Asia. Public opinion in the West remained blind to all these signs and continued to regard the Soviets as enemies.

That changed almost overnight when Hitler unleashed his "blitzkrieg" against the Soviet Union. It was indeed lightning out of a clear sky. I cannot blame the Soviet Union for being taken by surprise. So was I; I did not expect Hitler to be mad enough to commit suicide. I was convinced that he would fail. When Ed Bacon asked me how long I thought the Russians could hold, I replied that the question was how long the Germans could

* *The Penguin Hansard, 1, From Chamberlain to Churchill* (London: 1940), 51-53.

** *Recalled To Service: The Memoirs of General Maxime Weygand* (London: Wm. Heinemann Ltd., 1952), 40 and Alistair Horne, *To Lose A Battle: France 1940,* (London: Macmillan & Co. Ltd., 1969), 115-118 incl.

hold — probably through the next summer. He did not reply, but his looks reflected some doubt about my sanity.

I well remember the day the invasion started. As I often did on weekends, I had gone to New York to stay with Olga. Her brother Robert and his wife had arrived the day before — among the last Jews allowed to leave Germany. I read the comments in *The New York Times* of June 24, 1941; one of them shocked me profoundly. It read, "If we see that Germany is winning we ought to help Russia, and if Russia is winning we ought to help Germany. And that way let them kill as many as possible, although I don't want to see Hitler victorious under any circumstances. Neither of them think anything of their pledged word." I had not previously heard the name of the author; it was Harry S. Truman.

Fortunately, most other Americans reacted differently; the work of the American-Russian Institute expanded rapidly. Among the architects I met in this work were Christopher Tunnard and Hermann Field, both of whom became good friends. I wrote several articles on various aspects of Soviet planning and housing for the journal of the institute.

Less than half a year after Hitler's attack the Japanese repeated his folly by attacking the United States. At that time the Soviets had already turned the tide by throwing the Germans back at the approaches of Moscow, Leningrad, and Rostov. Apparently, the Japanese had not understood the significance of this defeat of their ally. It did not mean that he had lost the war — that was decided at Stalingrad — but it meant that he could not win it. There is a parallel here with the First World War. Germany lost the chance to win it at the battle of the Marne, although the certainty of defeat came only much later, probably at Verdun. The parallel is no accident. In both cases Germany wagered all on the card of a rapid first strike, because in a two-front war it was indeed its only chance against a coalition with superior resources.

The war made me technically an "enemy alien." But the controlling office in Philadelphia, in contrast to that in New York, was very liberal and gave me unlimited permission to visit both New York and the Atlantic Seashore. I also visited Princeton, where both Ervin Panofsky, the art historian from Hamburg, and the philosopher and historian Erich Kahler, whom I had known in Munich and Vienna, had settled.

The war also created new housing problems in the USA which modified the work of the Housing Association. Rent control was introduced, but sales were not controlled. The consequence was that the owners of rented row houses, the predominant type of workers' housing in Philadelphia, sold their houses and evicted their tenants. This set off a chain reaction: the evicted tenant, unable to find a row house for rent, bought one and in turn evicted its tenant. I argued that it was absurd to attempt to control the cost of housing in one form, rent, but not in the other, sale, and proposed a moratorium on evictions. The proposal got nowhere; nor did another proposal to ease the housing shortage: a progressive tax on "surplus" rooms, defined as exceeding $n + 2$, n being the number of occupants. The tax would be moderate on the first surplus room, but increase steeply for each successive one. The occupants affected by the tax, owners or renters, would have three ways to avoid it: move to smaller quarters, share their dwelling with friends or relatives, or sublet rooms. All three ways would help to relieve the housing shortage. I still think it is a good idea. But my trade union contact on housing problems did not like it; he lived with wife and child in a six-room house.

I was a member of the office workers' union and one of their alternate delegates to the CIO Council. At one session the question of the liquidation of the *Record* came up, the only one of the three Philadelphia newspapers which favored the Democrats and the New Deal. The discussion turned exclusively on the question of the jobs of the *Record* employees after its takeover by the *Bulletin*. I proposed that the CIO and the AFL, who worked closely together in Philadelphia, buy the *Record* and continue it as a prolabor and pro-New Deal paper. I was laughed out of court; labor could not dream of raising the money. This stunned me; in Germany the labor movement, Social Democrat or Communist, had been able to support its own press. In the Philadelphia area there were over half-a-million union members. Because of the wartime no-strike policy, huge sums had accumulated in the union treasuries; individual workers also had bigger savings than ever. Yet they could not afford to publish a newspaper; the workers, the vast majority of the population, were excluded from any control of the press. What kind of democracy was this?

Ed Bacon joined the navy and Dorothy Schoell-Montgomery succeeded him as director of the Housing Association. She was a long-time housing activist whom I admired greatly. I used to say that there were only three red-blooded he-men in the somewhat wishy-washy North American housing movement: Elizabeth Wood, Catherine Bauer, and Dorothy Schoell.

Bob Mitchell wanted to have me on his staff at the Planning Commission, but for this I had to be a US citizen. I had taken out my "First Papers" on my arrival in late 1938, so I was eligible after five years of residence. I had not been sure that I wanted to take that step. I thought of returning to Germany after the defeat of Hitler, anticipating the formation of a broadly based Popular Front government. But now it looked doubtful whether there would be a German government; and I was offered the kind of work in the States which I had wanted to do all my life. So I applied; I knew I might be rejected if I were asked if I had been a member of the Communist party, as I would have to answer in the affirmative. But the question was not asked and I became a US citizen in 1944.

As the war drew to a close, the Pennsylvania legislature established a Postwar Planning Commission to prepare urban redevelopment legislation. It was headed by Abraham Freedman, legal counsel to the Housing Association. I became his associate; my assistant was Margy Ellin, a young sociologist from New York. When I explained to Freedman my misgivings about the negative effects of urban redevelopment, he asked, "Should we recommend against it?" I said, "No, some such legislation will be enacted in any case; we better frame it so as to minimize the damage." We devised a two-step process: first an "area" had to be defined and its intended future use confirmed by the City Planning Commission; and second, specific projects within such areas, again subject to approval by the Planning Commission, had to be submitted.

I also devised a clause stipulating that occupants could be displaced only on condition that the Housing Authority certified that safe and sanitary housing was available to them at the same rent and with equal accessibility. Evidently, if such housing had been available, the slum dwellers would already have moved into it. So it meant that slums could only be "cleared" if an equal amount of subsidized public housing were built for all displaced persons; but, in practice, the Housing Authorities were not that scrupulous in giving their certification.

I broadened the definition of "blight" to also cover vacant and nonresidential areas and wanted to divorce "redevelopment" from "slum clearance." But Abe Freedman objected that slum clearance had been recognized by the Supreme Court as a "public purpose" and was the only legal basis for expropriation for redevelopment. The legislation was enacted pretty much as we had drafted it.

I was first in the civil examination for senior planner in the Land Use Division of the City Planning Commission and started work early in 1945. The division was headed by Ray Leonard, a most lovable man. My responsibility was to develop the general plan of land use distribution and major transportation facilities. We agreed that the plan had to cover not only the territory of the City of Philadelphia, to which our jurisdiction was limited, but the much larger Metropolitan District, hoping that the logic of our proposals would persuade other jurisdictions to adopt and implement them.

I remember discussing the question of the basic form and structure of our metropolis with Bob Mitchell. I felt that it was far too large to allow for the traditional approach as a system of streets and squares. It had to be organized as an urban landscape of districts of different character, built up or open. I did not believe in the then predominant preference for "decentralization" into satellite towns, nor in the "linear city" propagated by others, but felt the best general solution was a star-shaped pattern, with development radiating from the existing core along main transportation lines, and "wedges" of green open land between the radiating districts approaching as close as possible to the core. Such a scheme had just been adopted for Copenhagen under the name of a "Finger Plan." Of course, it would have to be substantially modified for our jurisdiction, as for any urban area, to fit the existing natural and man-made topography.

In 1947 a meeting of the American Society of Planning Officials celebrated the fiftieth anniversary of Ebenezer Howard's book *To-Morrow,* in which he had developed his proposals for new "garden cities." The notion of channeling urban growth into new towns of predetermined size, designed once and for all to be neatly balanced, was hailed as the answer to the vexing problems of the unpredictable "chaotic" big city. I was the only doubting Thomas. After asking my audience to ponder why in half a century "To-morrow" had failed to become "Today," I noted that, difficult as it had proved to initiate the growth of a New Town, it would be far more difficult to stop it. If successful, the New Towns would soon grow beyond their preplanned size, reproducing all the problems from which the planners hoped to escape. I concluded by sketching alternative forms of metropolitan growth. My presentation, subsequently published, was the first in a series of essays devoted to understanding the metropolis as a new form of human settlement, radically different from the big city which had given it birth.*

Ray Leonard gave priority to the planning of a comprehensive system of freeways. I agreed, but insisted that we also develop plans for the extension and improvement of rapid rail transit, by both subways and suburban railroad service. Some of our proposals, adopted at the time, have not yet been carried out. On the other hand, my proposal to connect the suburban terminals of the Pennsylvania and Reading railroads, rejected at the time as completely unfeasible, is now being realized.

Public opinion favored redevelopment, in particular of the badly decayed oldest section of Philadelphia next to the Delaware River. I wrote a short article entitled "The Waterfront, Key to Redevelopment," stating that redevelopment could succeed only if the commercial piers as well as the wholesale food market, both generators of heavy truck traffic, were relocated. Everyone thought this was a quite impractical "far-out" idea, but several years later it was done. I had encountered the problem once before. When, shortly after my arrival in New York, I talked to Robert Weinberg, an excellent architect then working with the City Planning Commission, I told him that I considered it urgent to eliminate from Lower Manhattan the obsolete piers which obstructed access to and enjoyment of the waterfront to over a million downtown workers and residents. He was shocked by such a radical proposal; it has now been carried out.

Later, I went through the same experience with the "Old City" waterfront in Montreal. I have come to realize that it is a worldwide problem, resulting from the historical fact that so many cities originated as harbors. As they grow, both city and harbor must expand and, inevitably, collide. The city center can be relocated only at tremendous cost, if at all. Relocation of the harbor

---

* My principal papers in the city and regional planning field have been collected and published in two books: *The Modern Metropolis* and *Metropolis . . . and Beyond.* The first was published in Boston by MIT Press in 1967 and simultaneously by Harvest House in Montreal; the second volume was published by John Wiley & Sons of New York in 1979.

is a great gain in terms of land incidentally made available for loading, storage, and transportation. Harbor relocation is occurring in city after city, but usually only after long and costly delays.

Because of the complexities of the situation, redevelopment of the central waterfront had to be deferred, but applications for many other areas came in. I was now stuck with administering the law which I had drafted; I had to make recommendations concerning the establishment of "redevelopment areas." I soon realized, as did others, that designating an area for redevelopment caused its further decay because it discouraged investment. I could think of no other remedy than to declare the entire city, except its newest areas, a "redevelopment area." This was not accepted at the time, but by now practically all old sections of Philadelphia have been so certified.

I did succeed in turning attention to the redevelopment of two nonresidential areas. One, the largest ever tackled in America, was an area at a level too low to be served by sewers. Despite this fact it had been subdivided, on paper, and many lots had been sold; most of these had reverted to the city for unpaid taxes during the depression. Redevelopment involved raising the level of the entire area by landfill and replanning it, primarily for residential development; the residential area was to be separated from a major trucking highway, rail line, and airport by a belt reserved for industry. The development has had a checkered history but has in the main followed the original concept.

Another smaller industrial area contained a number of soap and rendering plants whose penetrating stench was felt as a severe nuisance. As the chemical composition of the gases and the nature of the processes producing them were not known, we contracted with the Franklin Institute, a prestigious research establishment, to investigate this problem. The discussions which the institute's scientists had with the engineers and managers of the plants prompted them into action in order to avoid expropriation, which could be undertaken since their sites had been declared part of a redevelopment area. A few small plants moved out; most corrected the nuisances. As a result, the area, without further government action, "redeveloped" into a sound industrial area which attracted other plants, in particular truck terminals.

As far as existing poor residential areas, officially called "blighted" or "slums," were concerned, I stuck to my view that it was better to rehabilitate them than to tear them down. The question had come up earlier, while I was still with the Housing Association. One day Ed Bacon asked me to select an area of Philadelphia suitable for clearance and redevelopment. I objected for two reasons: first, wholesale clearance was socially destructive, and second, a project built on a man-made desert would look the same everywhere, regardless of the site or city. I suggested instead a project for rehabilitating an existing area in South Philadelphia. Ed had been somewhat secretive about the reason for his request; it turned out that it was destined for the city planning exhibition which he and Oscar Stonorov were planning and which was successfully implemented in Philadelphia after the war. Lou Kahn, at the time still associated with Stonorov, took up with enthusiasm the idea of rehabilitating the area in which he had grown up, and his proposals, presented at the exhibition, attracted nationwide attention.

Significant experience in rehabilitation was gained in a small project initiated by the Quakers, who operated a community center in a large designated "redevelopment area" inhabited mainly by blacks. During the depression the Quakers had successfully organized several self-help cooperative housing projects. They now suggested clearing the block around their community center and rebuilding it by a similar project. I noted that it was not economically feasible to replace four-story buildings by self-built cottages, but that it might be possible to organize a cooperative for rehabilitating the block. They took up the idea and started to enlist members for a racially mixed housing cooperative.

Several unanticipated things happened. The Quakers had been worried that they might have to evict the present tenants. That did not happen; by the time the cooperative took over, the landlords had relocated their tenants into other slum dwellings which they also owned. Another worry arose when the organizers scrutinized the names of the white applicants for membership in the racially mixed housing cooperative; they found that most of them were known for Communist sympathies. Later, when the members got together for their first meetings, the white intellectuals dominated the discussion, and the blacks observed an embarrassed silence; when it came to work with tools, the roles were reversed. The rehabilitated apartments, designed by Oscar Stonorov, were attractive; but very few of the previous occupants could afford the cost.

One day an unexpected request came from City Hall: the city invited the United Nations to establish themselves in Philadelphia, and we were to propose a suitable site, immediately. I suggested a large plateau in Fairmount Park which overlooked the city, and my suggestion was accepted. The commission charged by the UN with recommending the most suitable city and site came to Philadelphia. Le Corbusier made a presentation, followed by a discussion.

The staff of the Planning Commission drove the visitors around to show them the site and the Philadelphia area generally. As I spoke some Russian, I was charged with taking care of the two Soviet delegates, together with the Polish delegate, who rode in the same car. He was Mathew Novitzki, a highly creative and cultivated architect of outstanding sensitivity and intelligence.

After completion of the UN project Novitzki stayed in America, and I saw him several times in New York. Subsequently, he went to Raleigh, North Carolina. On the occasion of a visit to Chapel Hill, friends drove me to Raleigh to see him. Mathew showed me his project for the "Cow Palace." I did not immediately grasp the novel concept. While he was trying to explain it to me, my friends came to drive me back. So Novitzki said, "I will explain it to you the next time." There was to be no next time. On his return flight from Chandigarh he perished in a plane accident. It was an irreplaceable loss.

At the Planning Commission there were personnel changes. My assistant was Martin Meyerson. When he told me that he had become engaged to my former assistant Margy Ellin, I asked, "Am I responsible?" He answered, "Oh no, I met her years ago in New York — and I did not like her at all." It has become a very happy marriage.

After the end of the war Ed Bacon, who had served in the navy, returned and became my colleague as senior land planner. Soon after, Robert Mitchell resigned and Ray Leonard became director. An internal competition was arranged for the vacant position of chief of the Division of Land Planning, in which Ed Bacon came first, I second, and Paul Croley, a very capable administrator, third. A few months later the unexpected and tragic death of Ray Leonard again orphaned us. Ed Bacon succeeded him. I was temporarily put in charge of the Division of Land Planning. Shortly before, Harold M. Mayer, who had headed the Division of Planning Analysis, had left for the University of Chicago. I had worked closely with Harold in preparing the general plan, and he told me that he would like me to take over as his successor. However, the division was temporarily headed by its senior staff member, Harlan Loomer, an able sociologist and demographer.

I felt entitled to succeed Ed Bacon as head of the Division of Land Planning, but he did not want me to occupy that position. When, in the course of our discussion, I mentioned Harold Mayer's wish that I should succeed him, Ed thought that was an excellent idea. I objected that I did not want to push aside Harlan Loomer. When I talked to Harlan — who did not get along too well with Ed — he said that he realized that he had no chance to be appointed as chief and would rather work under me than under someone else. So I accepted the position as chief of the Division of Planning Analysis with the condition that the work on the general plan which I had started would be transferred with me.

I was, however, still interested in the Division of Land Planning. So, when a nation-wide competition for chief was opened, I applied. Out of about two dozen applicants, fourteen were admitted to the second stage, the design of residential development for an existing, still rural, area of Philadelphia. Only two competitors survived, I and Thomas Schocken. Curiously, both of us were German architects of Jewish descent, and both of us had worked in the Soviet Union. Moreover, while I had intended to fight in Spain, Tom had actually done so, as one of a few Social Democrats who had joined the International Brigade. Even more curiously, our two projects were so similar that some people suspected us of collusion. At the final stage, the oral interview by a committee of three, Tom was nervous, while I felt very much at ease. So I won the competition.

This put Ed in a bit of a quandary. He did not want to appoint me, and he could not appoint anyone else. The only way out was to cancel the competition and call a new one six months later. This time one had to design a project in a closed one-day session. Given my poor draftmanship, I knew that I could not win that one, but I still participated. The winner was Willo von Moltke. He did a good job as chief of the Division of Land Planning. We worked together well and became good friends.

Ed Bacon was primarily interested in urban design and specific projects and left the development of the general plan pretty much to me. When the board at one meeting asked him to present a progress report on the general plan, he was surprised that I produced it in time for the next board meeting. Subsequently, several aspects of the plan — on population, industry, housing, etc. — were published.

One of the important aspects of the plan was, of course, a study of the economic base. Right at the beginning, after extended discussion by the senior staff, we had decided not to use the then fashionable approach of starting with the so-called "basic" industries, i.e. those producing for export, and derive from the employment in these the employment in the so-called "nonbasic" or "service" industries, and finally the total population. After our report, written by our staff economist, Maxine Woolston, was published, I was asked frequently by colleagues why we had not used the standard approach. I felt that my answers were inadequate and tried to clarify my thoughts. The result, almost ten years later, was an article entitled "The Economic Base of the Metropolis." It was the longest article I have published and probably the one that touched off the greatest amount of discussion among economists as well as planners.

Increased income and the end of wartime restrictions led to some changes in my personal life. When I first came to Philadelphia, I had rented a garret in an old rooming house within walking distance of the office of the Housing Association. One of the association's main activities was to put the heat on the city's Building Inspection Department to enforce the Housing Code. The code outlawed occupancy of rooms above the third floor without a fire escape. One day officers of the department appeared and closed the one in which I lived. Fortunately, I got help from Karoline Solmitz, the widow of my murdered friend Fritz. She had come to America with her four children and had established a boardinghouse, with the aid of the Quakers, in Bryn Mawr. A friend of Karoline's, a professor of German at Bryn Mawr College, had a room to rent in her house on the campus. The first night I slept there I was enchanted by the cool evening breeze which came into my room, in contrast to the stifling heat of my old abode. I realized how great the climatic differences can be within an urban area.

It is really absurd to call the climate of the northeastern United States "temperate." It is intemperate in both directions. For a while an Indian engineer worked at our Planning Office. He complained about the heat; it was never that hot in Bombay, he asserted.

I bought a bicycle and rode the country roads. People laughed at me; I may well have been the only adult in Philadelphia who rode a bicycle at the time. I discovered a beautiful swimming hole in an old millpond and struck up an acquaintance with some local fellows. When I asked a young lad who had just finished school where he worked, he answered, "In a drugstore in Wayne." That gave me a shock. In my studies of the region I had divided it into a number of areas and identified for each of them the ratio of jobs to resident labor force. My young friend lived in the Schuylkill Valley, where there was a great excess of jobs; he worked on the Main Line, where there was an even greater deficit! The following year I asked him whether he was still working in the drugstore. No, he was now working in a factory. Ah, I thought, finally economic rationality has prevailed. Where was the factory? In Bryn Mawr, one of the very few small factories to be found on the Main Line.

It dawned on me that shortening the journey to work may not be the determining factor in the choice of location of work and residence which planning theory assumes. This was later confirmed by an experience at the Planning Commission. During the war a settlement of about 600 houses had been built for workers of the Budd plant, about thirteen miles from the center of Philadelphia, surrounded by open fields. We wanted to learn something about life in such an isolated community. One group of questions covered the journey to work. Only three men worked close by, at the Budd plant. Two of them, who did not have a car, complained, "It is a long walk, and there are no sidewalks." There were few complaints among the others. One answered as follows: "Where do you work?" — "At the Navy Yard." (18 miles away) — "How do you get there?" — "I take a bus, the subway, another bus." — "How long does it take?" — "About two hours." — "Is it inconvenient?" — "Yes, I have to walk so far to the bus!"

When I became a municipal civil servant, I had to live within the city limits. I was fortunate in finding furnished accommodation, consisting of a living room, a small bedroom, and a bathroom, as big as both of them combined, on the second floor of the house of a retired businessman. Their maid kept my rooms and bed neat and clean, and I had my meals in a drugstore nearby. The house was located in a large garden at the edge of the Wissahickon Park. I often walked or bicycled in the beautiful, deep, and heavily treed ravine of the Wissahickon Creek. When my host died and I had to move, I found a furnished room in the neighborhood.

Philadelphia was at that time run by a Republican political machine; the boss of my ward prided himself on running a tight ship. His colleagues hit back by pointing out that a well-paid city employee in his ward had registered as a Democrat. Some well-meaning colleagues of mine who had heard of this advised me to change my registration if I wanted to keep my job. I refused; nothing happened.

In the summer of 1947 I spent a month's vacation in Mexico. Before leaving, I took some lessons in Spanish; I did not learn very much, but enough to move around independently. I was and remain fascinated by Mexico. It is unique in having three cultures: the pre-Columbian Indian, the Spanish-Colonial, and the Modern, all highly creative in the visual arts, still alive and intertwined in many surprising ways. I also found, as I had in my childhood in St. Moritz, that I feel and function best at an altitude of 2000 meters.

At that time the air of Mexico City was not yet polluted; but I also visited by bus, rail, and bicycle other parts of the country, so rich in Pre-Columbian ruins and Spanish-Colonial churches, monasteries, and entire towns. From Oaxaca I went via Veracruz to visit the great Mayan architecture of Chichén Itzá and Uxmal, to return via New Orleans. It meant much to me that I had once more been able to stroll through the streets of beautiful old towns.

Germany after Twenty Years

In 1949 Sam B. Zisman, who at the time headed a citizens planning organization in Philadelphia, called me. He had been asked to serve as a "visiting expert" on city planning to the United States Military Government, and to propose a second person to serve in the same capacity; was I interested? I certainly was. I very much wanted to go to Europe, but I had hesitated to apply for a passport because it might bring up my past membership in the Communist party. Now I decided to take the chance — and my usual luck held once more. I had to apply not at the State Department, but at the Pentagon. It so happened that a few months earlier Gordon Clapp, then general counsel and later chairman of TVA, had asked for a visa to Germany and had been refused. That of course became a public scandal, and the colonel responsible for the gaffe had been sent away on sick leave. It was his first day back at his desk when I dropped in at the Pentagon. He certainly did not want to repeat his mistake; so — from his point of view — he erred in the opposite direction. I immediately got my passport, with no questions asked.

My contract provided for ninety days in Europe, of which only sixty had to be workdays. This left me free to make visits on my own outside of Germany. I looked forward eagerly to this trip, but not without some misgivings. I feared that I might live as a "pukka sahib" among hungry Germans; and I feared seeing the destruction of cities which I had known and loved. My fears proved to be unfounded. West Germany was already on its way to recovery. The sight of ruins, sad as it was, affected me less than I had expected. What really came as a shock, unexpectedly, was to find a desert where I remembered beautiful trees, as in the former "Biedersteiner Park" in Munich, now gone forever.

After a few hours' stop in the Azores, a military plane took me to Frankfurt. As the sun rose, I could see the beloved small-scale nongeometric pattern of European fields, and then the unchanged beauty of Paris, flying right over the Panthéon. In Frankfurt, I was put up in the Baseler Hospiz, the same hotel where I had stayed several times with Gertel. I took it as a good omen. It showed me the negative side as well: the hallway stopped midway at a gap where the other half of the building had been before the bombings.

On my first evening out on the street, somebody called my name. By one of those totally unlikely coincidences which sometimes occur, my cousin Siegmund Warburg had arrived from London that same day for his first postwar visit to Germany.

The "visiting expert" business is pretty much of a racket, rarely worth its cost to the taxpayers. The most worthwhile part of our activity was selection of people for a term of study in City Planning at the University of North Carolina. Planning in Germany was regarded as an extension of architecture, but I insisted on including at least one economist. I found him in the person of Dr. Olaf Boustedt, who worked at the Bavarian Statistical Office in Munich. Most of our interviews were held in Munich by a group consisting, in addition to Sam Zisman and myself, of a diplomat, Dr. von Herwarth, and a woman member of the German Trade Union Federation. As her knowledge of planning and

Sam's knowledge of German were limited, the task of selection fell mainly on von Herwarth and me. It was surprising that our judgments always coincided, given the difference in background and political philosophy. I believe we selected a very good group. I later held a two-week seminar with them in North Carolina, and several of them have remained good friends.

I visited planning offices to discuss their problems with my German colleagues. I encountered old acquaintances and made new ones. I also spoke at universities and conferences; at the annual meeting of the German Federation for Housing and Planning in Nürnberg, I put aside my prepared notes on regional planning when I noted that the main concern of the participants was the refusal of the newly formed federal government to grant any credits for housing construction. I talked about the various forms of state support which even the government of the rich United States had found necessary to guarantee an adequate supply of housing. My statement was met with great interest and may have contributed to the subsequent change in policy which led to the extensive German program of "Social Housing Construction."

However, more deeply engraved in my memory are the experiences outside my official mission. One taught me something about the perception of architecture. I revisited two of my most beloved interior spaces: the great hall of the Augsburg City Hall, built in the beginning of the seventeenth century, and St. Anne's church in Munich, built a century later by the great baroque architect, J. M. Fischer. In both of them the rich decoration was an integral part of the architecture which I could never imagine without it. Now only the bare walls and ceiling were left; but both were still the magnificent spaces which I remembered.

On my first weekend in Frankfurt I took an early train to Sommerau, where I had been with Gertel in that unforgettable summer of 1920. At the very moment that I entered the courtyard of the old castle, the sun broke through the morning mist. It was too early to arouse the present occupant, the local doctor whom I had known. I left and traveled on to revisit the old towns on the Main River, Miltenberg and Wertheim, unchanged since the Middle Ages. When I hiked from Wertheim to the old monastery of Bronnbach through the beautiful landscape of farms and forests, it seemed inconceivable that this soft and lovely country could have given birth to the horror of Nazism. Nothing is more mysterious than the unlimited potential of human beings for both good and evil.

Sam Zisman and I also attended the Congress of the CIAM in Bergamo, a beautiful old town near Milan. I had been close to the modern architects who had formed CIAM, but had never attended any of their meetings. Now it was a great joy to meet many old friends after years during which I did not know if they had survived. In looking at the exhibits put up by the various groups, it struck me that all of them, after presenting an excellent and sensitive analysis of widely varying local conditions, ended by proposing the same huge multistory slabs of apartment houses. I felt that there must be other solutions. I have since come to the conclusion that there is nothing wrong with tall buildings nor with long ones, provided that one can still see trees and the sky either next to or above them, but that a building which extents both vertically and horizontally so far as to fill the entire field of vision is felt as oppressive.

I met Lotte in the charming Alsatian town of Colmar, where I showed her Mathias Grünewald's altar paintings, the greatest achievement of German art; I also visited her later in Paris. I visited other friends in Switzerland and Austria, Denmark and Sweden, as well as in many German cities, including Berlin, both West and East. My old Communist friends in East Berlin wanted me to come there to help build a socialist Germany. Much as I sympathized with their hopes, I could not quite see myself working in Berlin. I still felt strong ties to my hometown of Hamburg.

It was twenty years since I had last seen Hamburg. I knew that it had been very heavily bombed. When I visited the former workers' district of Hammerbrook, where everything was razed down to street level, a stream of slimy white bugs crawled out of a cellar and across the sidewalk. I suspect that all these years they had been feeding on human bodies buried under the rubble.

But the image of the city had been preserved, because it is largely built around the Alster Lake, which was not a likely bomb target. The neighborhood where I had grown up, consisting largely of single-family houses with large gardens, also had suffered little damage. The house in which I had lived from my third to my eighteenth year was, and still is, standing. It was occupied by a Danish military mission, and they allowed me to visit it. It is strange how some details suddenly evoked memories which had been buried for almost forty years. On the occasion of a later visit I found that a little hotel-pension had been established in the similarly undamaged house next door. Now, when I visit Hamburg, I stay in the pension — at home.

Perhaps this could be construed as an expression of the currently fashionable "search for one's roots" or identity. I don't believe in that kind of navel gazing. Roots thrive only buried in the dark of the earth; if they are pulled up to be inspected from all sides they wither away; and I feel that the identity of my person, as of any other, is uniquely determined by heredity and environment, and is not dependent on identification with one or another "community."

In my childhood we had often bought flowers at Petersen's shop in the neighborhood. When I passed that location, the shop was still there, unchanged. It was eerie. Hamburg had lived through the First World War, the revolution, the Weimar Republic, the Nazi tyranny, the Second World War, the bombings, the defeat, the postwar hunger — and all the time Mr. Petersen had kept on selling flowers. In a way, this incredible tenacity of daily life was more frightening than the destruction wrought by the bombs.

I met my old friend Richard Tüngel. After the Nazis had dismissed him from his job with the Hamburg City Planning Authority, he had worked as a correspondent for a Swiss newspaper. After the war he had become the founder and chief editor of *Die Zeit*, which became and still is one of Germany's most respected and influential newspapers. Though our political views differed, we remained close friends until his death.

The Hamburg Planning and Building Authority was now headed by Oelsner. He had done an outstanding job under the Weimar Republic in the neighboring city of Altona — now part of Hamburg — and had worked in Turkey during the Nazi period. His deputy was Strohmeier, an exceptionally sensitive architect whom I had known well in the twenties. He expected to be appointed director of the newly founded Academy of Arts in Hamburg. Both he and Oelsner wanted me to be his successor. I agreed to take the job as soon as it became available. As it happened, another old friend of mine, Gustav Hassenpflug, was appointed to the Academy, and Strohmeier remained in his position.

One of the reasons why I had wanted to go to Europe was to talk to my Communist friends about the Stalinist terror. I had, of course, known that many people of whose innocence I was convinced had been imprisoned and even killed. But for a long time I could not believe the stories of beatings and torture; they were incompatible with everything I had seen and experienced in the Soviet Union. Only after the war, when they were confirmed by people whom I personally knew and trusted, I had to admit their truth. How could Communists accept such basic violation of everything they stood for?

By accident I had learned that Sebald Ruetgers, the Dutch Communist whom I so highly respected, had survived the war in Holland. I had raised the question in a letter to him. His answer was that, yes, many mistakes were being made, but that we could never repay to the Soviet people the debt we owed them for liberating the world from fascism. True as this was, it did not answer my question.

I had a long talk with the Swiss architect Hans Schmidt, who had become a good friend in Moscow and was now heading the Communist party in his native Basel. He said, "If what you say is really true, I am of course against it." But he hesitated to believe it. Other old friends in Berlin and Vienna claimed that these things had happened because enemies had infiltrated the security apparatus, but they were now a thing of the past. It was interesting — and encouraging — that of all my Communist friends the only one in a position of power was the one who agreed that something was basically wrong. Albert Norden, I was told, was the man closest to Walter Ulbricht, the Party boss of East Germany. When I protested to him that many people were held in camps without any judicial process, he answered, "Now that we have our republic — the GDR had just been established two weeks before — we expect that the Soviets will soon hand the camps over to us; then we will of course — of course! — immediately dissolve them and either release the inmates or try them in regular courts." He added, "By the way, I can tell you that many Soviet officers think about the GPU methods as you and I do."

I had known Norden first in Hamburg, where he edited a newspaper in the twenties. Subsequently, he became the chief editor of the Party's central paper, the *Red Flag.* After working for several months in the anti-Nazi underground, he had to flee Germany. During the war I found him in New York, where he worked in a factory and also contributed to a German-language anti-Nazi newspaper. We had long discussions about the future of Germany. When the Allies decided to evict all ethnic Germans from the German provinces east of the Oder and Neisse rivers, as well as from Czechoslovakia, Poland, and Hungary — some twelve million human beings — I was profoundly shocked. I felt that the German Communists, as the only party which had consistently opposed the encroachments of German imperialism on the right to self-determination of other nations, had not only the right but the duty to stand up for the same right for their own people. Norden disagreed. He stated that nothing that anyone said could change the decision, but could only feed claims for revenge. He was probably right. The refugees have been surprisingly well integrated in both West and East Germany, and the change accepted.

When the Communists and Social Democrats in East Germany merged into the Socialist Unity party, Norden expected that this would be a powerful stimulus to unity in West Germany as well. I feared that it would have the opposite effect. In this case I was right, unfortunately. Norden was a totally honest and dedicated man, unshakable in his belief in a bright socialist future. When I saw him in Berlin in 1949, he predicted that the population of the newborn republic would, in five years, reach a higher standard of living than they had experienced in the best prewar years. I remained skeptical for years; all the cards were stacked against their great experiment. But they have actually succeeded beyond all expectations.

Another encounter in East Berlin impressed me greatly. In the riding lessons which I had taken during my adolescence, by far the best rider was Irmgard Woermann, scion of a family of wealthy shipowners. I had later lost contact with her, but a common friend, Jack Oldenburg, who had also emigrated to New York, kept up a correspondence with her and had told me her story. She had married a landowner in Mecklenburg by the name of Rosen. During the war her two sons, serving in the air force, had been killed in Russia. When, at the war's end, the Russians occupied Mecklenburg, they arrested her husband and she never learned what happened to him. She fled with her mother and daughter to the city of Schwerin; the mother did not survive the hardships of the flight. Schwerin was full of children who had lost home and parents. Irmgard started to work in an organization that tried to take care of these children. Her fellow workers were working women, Communists or Social Democrats. She gradually came to see the world through their eyes, joined the Socialist Unity party, and qualified as a schoolteacher. When I asked her how she had arrived at her attitude, she said, "In a way, it is like it was on the estate: all work together for a common purpose; but here the difference of master and hired hand is gone. Basically, it is a more humane society." She added that when she had visited her family in Hamburg she found that they had little in common. At the time of my visit, she was taking a Communist party course with a group of metalworkers of a former Siemens plant. When she had mentioned her encounter with me to them, they asked me to talk to them about the peace movement in America. I was impressed by the group; they were the type of the serious, dedicated German workers who had built the Labor Movement in the teeth of Bismarck's anti-Socialist law. They found it hard to understand that I talked mainly of religious groups; did the American labor movement not stand for peace?

THE COLD WAR

The American labor movement did not stand for peace. After a short period of association with the Soviet trade unions at the end of the war, it had broken with them and enlisted in the cold war. Why and when did that war start? In 1941 Harry Truman had said, "If Russia is winning we ought to help Germany." In 1945 the Russians were stronger — and Truman was president of the United States.

Certainly, Stalin's paranoia and the terror inspired by it played into the hands of the cold warriors. There was widespread fear of the Russians and a desire for American protection in Germany and, to a lesser extent, in other European countries. In fact, the Soviet Union, bled white by the war, desperately needed and wanted peace. But, however unfounded, the fear was real. I do not subscribe to the view that history is made by "great men." But I cannot help asking myself what would have happened if Stalin had died in 1945, when Roosevelt did, and Roosevelt had died in 1953, when Stalin did. Recently, two of Roosevelt's sons conjectured that their father would not have dropped the atomic bomb on Japanese cities.* Perhaps we could have avoided our present predicament.

---

* Elliot Roosevelt and James Brough, *A Rendezvous With Destiny: The Roosevelts of the White House* (New York: G. P. Putnam's & Sons, 1975), 421-22 and James Roosevelt with Bill Libby, *My Parents: A Differing View* (Chicago: Playboy Press, 1976), 169-70.

At Teheran the three "superpowers," the USA, the USSR, and Great Britain, had agreed to continue their cooperation after the war. They would try to reach unanimity on how to enforce peace in the world; if they failed to reach unanimity, they agreed to disagree and to keep hands off. This was the origin of the UN charter requirement for "unanimous consent" of the "permanent members" of the Security Council.

The three powers had also agreed about the composition of the postwar governments in Europe: they were to exclude fascists but include all "democratic" forces, which, in this context, meant coalition governments, including Communists. Such governments were indeed installed everywhere. But, beginning in 1947, the Communists were pushed out in one country after another. The response in the Soviet-occupied areas was different: the non-Communist parties remained in the government, but became junior partners in a Communist-dominated "national front." On both sides the change occurred slowly. When I was in Germany in 1949, there were still Communists in some provincial governments in West Germany, and a report which I read in the library of the United States Military Government in Frankfurt confirmed that the decisions of the non-Communist parties prevailed in those East German provinces in which they had a majority in parliament.

However, while the change from East-West cooperation to confrontation transpired only gradually, there is reason to believe that it was decided on even before the end of the war. I recall that in the spring of 1945 one of my friends in Philadelphia, who was close to the leadership of the Democratic party, invited me to a glass of beer and spent over an hour trying to persuade me that we had to take a stand against the Soviet Union. Certainly Truman changed his tone at Potsdam as soon as he knew that the atomic bomb worked.

I must admit that at the time I did not realize what the bombs on Hiroshima and Nagasaki meant. I had reluctantly and — as I now realize — wrongly accepted the carpet bombing of German and Japanese cities as a lesser evil than a victory of the Axis powers. Only later did I fully understand the truth of Einstein's warning statement: "The . . . power of the atom has changed everything save man's mode of thinking, and thus we drift toward unparalleled catastrophe."

The drift might have been stopped at its very beginning by an international agreement to outlaw the production and use of nuclear weapons. The Soviet Union submitted such a proposal to the United Nations — and I hoped for its acceptance. The United States succeeded in derailing the proposal by countering with the Baruch Plan. That plan would have given the United Nations Organization, at that time completely dominated by the United States, exclusive jurisdiction over all forms of nuclear energy, including power production, without any binding provision for the prohibition of nuclear weapons. This was not acceptable to the Soviet Union. So the fatal nuclear arms race began.*

Harry Truman said, "One country, and one country only, stands in the way of peace." He was referring, of course, to the Soviet Union, and the peace he had in mind was a "Pax Americana" comparable to the "Pax Romana" which the ancient Romans had imposed on their subjects. One may understand this mentality, still shared by many Americans, by analogy with that of a self-made multimillionaire who is convinced that he has risen to the top exclusively because of his merits, forgetting the role that luck played in his career. At the end of the war the United States was closer to complete world domination than any nation has ever been. It is understandable that they felt that it was normal and right for "God's Own Country" to lord it over an "American century." If the godless Russians stood in the way of "manifest destiny," they must be put in their place.

There was much talk of a "showdown." This evidently meant an ultimatum telling the Soviets to withdraw their troops from neighboring countries — or else the atomic bombs would fall on their cities. The Soviets had no means of retaliation; not only did they not have atomic bombs, but they did not have a single plane capable of flying across the Atlantic and back. The assumed scenario was that they would try to occupy the territory of America's European allies, until nuclear destruction would force them to capitulate.

But the European allies did not want to be "liberated" a second time, but protected. Britain insisted that its defense had to be not on the Channel, but on the Rhine; France not on the Rhine, but on the Elbe; and Schumacher, the Social-Democratic leader, said

* See Walter La Feber, *America, Russia, and the Cold War, 1945-1980* (N.Y.: John Wiley & Sons Inc.), 42 and 43.

Germany had to be defended not on the Elbe, but on the Vistula. So the "sword" of the atomic bomb had first to be supplemented by a "shield" to defend Western Europe on the ground. The Marshall Plan enabled the Europeans to build the shield.

This was the interpretation of the perspective of the United States Government which I derived from careful analysis of the American press. I still think it was correct. But the "showdown" did not take place.

Two things occured in 1949. First, the Soviets developed their own atomic bomb, years before the Pentagon had expected. Second, China was "lost" to the Communists. Attention shifted to the Far East. It is interesting to read the testimony of General MacArthur on the Korean War before the United States Senate. He saw China as a nationalist threat more than a Communist one, correctly interpreting the policies of Mao Tse-tung as a continuation of those of the Kuomintang. It is no secret that he wanted to hit China before it had time to build its strength. Nor is it a secret that General Omar Bradley, then chief of staff, was opposed. Truman sent his secretary of defense, Louis Johnson, General Omar Bradley, and John Foster Dulles, to Tokyo, to arrive at a decision. Soon Americans could see Dulles peering through binoculars at North Korean trenches and assuring South Korea of full American support. Was this not the green light for Syngman Rhee, who had time and again proclaimed his intention to unify Korea by conquering the North?

It is widely accepted in the West that the war was started by an attack by North Korea "on orders of the Kremlin." There is no evidence for that.* The UN mission merely passed on, without comment, to the Security Council a South Korean report on an attack by the North. North Korea claimed an attack by the South. India proposed that both sides should put their case to the Security Council, in conformity with usual procedure. The USA vetoed that proposal; why, if their South Korean client had a good case?

---

* "I don't think, to begin with, that the Russians had very much to do with the outbreak of the Korean War. I don't know this for certain, but I strongly suspect that the North Koreans had been pretty badly aggravated by attacks by the South Koreans before they ever invaded South Korea." (Rear Admiral Jeffrey Brock, Commander of Canadian Forces, Far East, 1950-1951, in "Defence of Canada," Gwynne Dyer TV series, No. 2, *Keeping the Elephant Away,* February 19, 1986.

Two days after the outbreak of war, *Pravda,* on the occasion of Aviation Day, featured a lead article emphasizing that victory in a modern war depended on superiority in the air. To me, who had learned to read *Pravda,* this meant that the Soviet government warned North Korea that it could not win the war and should be satisfied with maintaining its territory. But when the South Korean forces collapsed, the North obviously could not resist sweeping all the way down the Peninsula until they were stopped at Pusan. I also noted that later, when the Americans marched north, there was practically no resistance to their advance anywhere on South Korean territory, including the Inchon landing, while the North Koreans fiercely defeated the other arm of the pincer, the intended American landing on the east coast of North Korea.

Evidently, at that point the war could have been ended by a return to the previous partition line. But MacArthur insisted on marching through North Korea right to the Chinese border. The Chinese reacted by driving the US troops back to the partition line. This defeat seems to have had a sobering effect on the hawks. After lengthy negotiations partition was reinstated.

The escalation of East-West confrontation by the Korean War also had its effect in Europe, leading to the rearmament of West Germany and its inclusion in NATO, with the inevitable response of formation of the Warsaw Pact, including a rearmed East Germany.* This ended my last hopes for a reunification of my homeland.

The Western powers had never wanted a unified Germany. The British wanted to reinstate the 1866 division into two parts, north and south; the American Morgenthau Plan provided for three parts, and the French proposed five. Possibly because of these divergences, the US and UK accepted the Soviet proposal at Potsdam to establish an all-German administration in Berlin, under the supervision of the Allied Control Council. This was the

* "At the State Department, Dean Acheson told him [Mike Pearson] the secret American strategy [in June 1950]. It was startling. The US didn't see Korea as strategically important, Acheson told him. It was just that war in Korea made it politically possible to get a quick increase in defence spending. What the Americans really wanted was to build up NATO's military strength in Europe; Korea was a side-show." ("Defence of Canada" TV Series, No. 2.)

"Austrian" solution for Germany: a neutral country without major armed forces. It certainly would have been preferred by an overwhelming majority of Germans, East and West. However, when the French, who had not been party to the Potsdam Agreement, objected, the US and UK backed out and refused to establish any German authority for the whole country. In 1948, after long inconclusive haggling about a clearly necessary currency reform, the three Western powers suddenly introduced a new "mark," worth ten old ones, in their three zones and also in their sectors of Berlin. Of course, hundreds of millions of old marks flooded into East Germany and East Berlin, buying up everything that could be moved to the West. The Soviets reacted by clamping down controls on movement between West Berlin and West Germany, the so-called "blockade"; but they did not interfere with the Allied airlift. After a new currency had been established and consolidated in East Germany too, the "blockade" was lifted. Movement between the two parts of Berlin continued unimpeded, but there were now two city governments for the two parts of the city. Subsequently, the three western zones established a common administration, soon to be replaced by the "Federal Republic of Germany," followed by that of the "German Democratic Republic." This was the situation when I left Germany to resume my work in Philadelphia.

The cold war grew more intense. I resisted as best I could. I continued to publish articles on housing and urban reconstruction in the Soviet Union. I joined the International Federation of Scientific Workers. I participated in the debates between adherents and opponents of the cold war in my trade union. I worked with the Progressive party for Henry Wallace in the presidential election of 1948, and I supported the struggle for housing, social security, racial equality, and civil rights and against the increasing persecution of real and alleged Communists. Of course, I was regarded as a "fellow traveler." I received repeated appeals in the mail for financial and moral support from the Civil Rights Congress, which was generally regarded as a "Communist front." As I disagreed with the failure of the American Communist party to admit the evil of Stalin's terror, and as I already supported the Civil Liberties Union, I at first ignored these appeals. But as the Congress had taken up several cases which I considered just and which the Union had not been willing to handle, I sent them some money. When they approached me asking me to sign petitions, and subsequently to join their Pennsylvania board, I had to admit to myself that my hesitation was merely the result of cowardice, and I agreed to serve.

I was never called before the McCarthy or any of the other "un-American" committees, but of course I asked myself how I would best deal with the infamous "trilemma" with which they faced their victims by their standard opening question: "Are you or have you ever been a member of the Communist party?" There were three possible answers. First, take the Fifth Amendment; this would be taken as admission that one was a "Fifth Amendment Communist." Second, refuse to seek the protection of the Fifth Amendment and testify frankly about oneself. But once you waived that protection, refusal to testify about your friends was "contempt of court," punishable by imprisonment for a legally unlimited period. I certainly would not take the third option of delivering innocent friends to persecution. But I also decided against taking the Fifth Amendment. I was fortunate in not having to face an actual prison term, which might have been the result of that decision if some committee had thought to call me.

A few people engaged in housing and planning in Philadelphia had formed an informal group to discuss questions of common concern. When the Korean War broke out and the government initiated a war housing program, one participant suggested that we help in that endeavor. I objected that we should ask ourselves whether this war was worthy of support in any form. After a searching discussion I drafted a statement calling on planners to assume social responsibility for the "know why," rather than only for the "know how" of their work. With the signatures of a few other members of the American Institute of Planners, I took this resolution to their annual meeting in Chicago.

At Chicago Ed Bacon told me that the Philadelphia Planning Commission would dismiss me if I moved that resolution and asked me to promise not to introduce it. I refused. However, when the Chairman of the AIP, Paul Oppermann, whom I respected highly, implored me not to bring the resolution to the floor but to submit it to the board of the AIP, I agreed.

The board was receptive to my concern and proceeded to draft a statement on the social responsibility of planners which in some respects went further than my proposal. It was widely and seriously discussed by the local chapters of the institute, thus largely fulfilling my intention, even though it was not adopted.

In 1951 several members of the Pennsylvania State Legislature, anxious to get on the bandwagon of anticommunist hysteria, introduced legislation requiring a "loyalty oath" from all civil servants. This aroused strong protest from many persons, including myself. The legislation went through a long process of committee deliberation, and it must be said to the credit of members of both parties that what finally came out was fairly harmless. My original reaction had been to refuse to take the oath. But as it contained nothing but what I had already sworn to when becoming first a citizen and later a civil servant, I decided on a different tactic: I signed the oath but resigned from my job, protesting that I refused to be made a second-class citizen. I sent a declaration explaining my stand to the newspapers.

After my resignation I went to New York and stayed with Olga Solmitz. After a few days, coming home from an errand, I was greeted by Olga with great alarm: a letter had arrived from the Philadelphia district attorney. He was Richard Dilworth, who had strongly opposed the law and refused to take the oath. As an elected official he was not obliged to take the oath, but most of his colleagues had volunteered to do so. Now he congratulated me on my courage, as did many others.

I did not really deserve that praise; the motives for my resignation were mixed. After seven years with the City Planning Commission I felt the seven-year itch; the old wanderlust was stirring. The State Department had started to refuse passports to people regarded as "fellow travelers," and I suspected that mine would not be renewed. So this might be my last chance to fulfill my long-deferred dreams to see Greece and Egypt. When a colleague celebrating his sixtieth birthday was referred to by his staff as "the old man," it gave me quite a shock; I was in my sixtieth year; there was no time to lose.

Before leaving, I attended a conference at Yale University, on the invitation of Christopher Tunnard. I gave a talk on "Scale in Civic Design," a subject which had interested me ever since A. E. Brinckmann had discussed it during my student days at Karlsruhe. It was subsequently published in England by the *Town Planning Review*. In later years my ego was flattered when colleagues in Budapest and in Peking told me that they had it translated into their respective languages as required reading for their students.

Once More on the Road

Egypt. Olga and I boarded a ship in New York and arrived in the midst of a lovely English spring. We saw Bath, which is a unique and unsurpassed example of a city created as an urban landscape, and continued to Leamington, near Bristol, to visit Cecil Powell, the renowned physicist, and his wife, the daughter of a close friend of Olga's. I knew Powell primarily as a leader of the peace movement; he was a most admirable and lovable person.

In London I saw my second cousin from Hamburg, Gertrud Bing, now secretary of the Warburg-Courtauld Institute. We had not seen each other for twenty-three years, but there was no gap; it was like continuing a conversation interrupted yesterday. I saw other old friends and found a new one, Percy Johnson-Marshall, whose work in rebuilding a destroyed section of East London I greatly admired.

We enjoyed seeing London and old and new towns in its surroundings, then crossed the Channel to continue to Paris, where Olga stayed with a cousin while I visited Lotte. Olga subsequently went to Hamburg, while I embarked in Marseille for Alexandria. I shared my cabin with two students: an Egyptian, and a Syrian of Armenian descent. We had interesting talks about the future of their countries.

A few weeks before my arrival in Egypt there had been riots in Cairo, resulting in the burning down of the Shepherd Hotel. I found that they had caused more destruction than I had expected. The situation was tense; everywhere there were soldiers and barbed wire. On a taxi ride to the pyramid of Saqqara I was stopped half a dozen times for identification. Tourists stayed away; I was one of few guests in a small Greek-owned hotel, and later found myself as the only one in Luxor.

My Egyptian traveling companion invited me to the home of his family, well-to-do businessmen. We had dinner under an arbor in the pleasant garden. While I could converse with each of the guests in either English, French, or German, I could not follow their lively discussion in Arabic. But from the words flying around — democracia, America, Rossiya, Germania — it was evident that they were passionately searching for a new way for their country. At the other end of the social scale, I found great bitterness about their oppressive poverty. It was evident that Egypt was ripe for a revolution, but I did not see who would carry it out. Four weeks later a group of young officers did.

How much change it has brought about remains a question.

The poverty and human degradation, the swarms of beggars and of desperate people pressing their services on me were depressing. In all my previous travels I would have liked to stay longer. Here I felt I wanted to stay only for the time required to see the heritage of the past which I had come to see. But that surpassed my expectations.

No later building has equalled the awesome grandeur of the pyramids. In some strange way their cold and abstract hostility supplements the richness of life reflected in the treasures of the Cairo museum. Equally important to me was Moslem Cairo, in its daily life as well as in the variety of its beautiful mosques. But the most memorable images I have preserved are from Upper Egypt: the temples of Luxor and Karnak, and even more the tombs of the Kings in the Western Desert, with the colors of their bas-reliefs as bright and lively as if they had been painted yesterday, the magnificent temple of Queen Hapchetsut, and, further up the Nile, at Idfu, the only Egyptian temple, a very late one, which has retained its ceilings, creating a unique spatial experience.

Israel. From Alexandria a boat carried me overnight to Limassol on Cyprus. It was quite a contrast. The people were also poor — perhaps a bit less so than in Egypt — but they had completely preserved their human dignity.

After a night spent in a mountain resort, a bus took me to Nicosia. I went to the Israeli consulate to get my visa. They asked when I wanted to go; I said, "As soon as possible," so they put me on a plane right away. On my arrival in the country which claimed to be my homeland, I was received with greater hostility than in any other country I have ever visited. Obviously because of my Egyptian visa, I was subjected to a body search.

Soon after my arrival in Tel Aviv, I called up Alexander Klein in Haifa. I had met him in New York. Klein had a remarkable career. He had been a well-established architect in St. Petersburg before the First World War. After the Russian Revolution he went to Berlin, where he became one of Germany's leading architects. When Hitler came to power, he started a third career as the leading city planner of Israel, occupying the only chair in this discipline at the Technion in Haifa.

When I asked when I could see him in the following week, he answered, "Don't come next week; come tomorrow." I did.

Scarcely had we exchanged greetings, when he said, "I am going to resign, and I want you to be my successor." — Just like that. I objected that I did not speak Hebrew. He replied, in German, "Oh, that does not matter, I am also teaching in German." In talking to the dean of architecture — who turned out to be a former fellow-student from Karlsruhe, Ratner — and to the president of the Technion, I soon found out that it *did* matter. They wanted me to teach in Hebrew, but were not too worried about it. They would send me to an immersion course prior to my start at the faculty. A definite decision could not be made right away, but in principle we agreed on my appointment.

Haifa, built on an amphitheatric site facing the bay, is a beautiful city. On the Carmel ridge, several hundred meters above sea level, many well-to-do business and professional people from Central Europe had built their houses. There were better examples of the modern architecture of the 1920s here than could be found in Berlin.

I visited Tiberias, Sfad, Akko, and other towns and villages. There, as in Haifa and Jaffa, I found the buildings erected by the Arab Palestinians much more beautiful than those built by the Jewish settlers. It was also evident from the many Arab-built middle-class houses that the image of a population consisting only of feudal beys and miserable fellahin was not true.

I visited my cousin Emmy Melchior-Braun in Jerusalem, where she lived in the house of a cousin who was an ardent Zionist, an impressive woman. Emmy, a former lawyer, had survived the German occupation of France by working under a false identity as a farm hand in the orchards and vegetable fields around Perpignan. Her husband had been caught by the Germans; her boy, then barely 15, had fought in the maquis, and is now a French professor of law. Emmy did not return to law but remained attracted by gardening. She had taught at a school in Ein-Karem, a lovely village on the outskirts of Jerusalem which we visited together, promenading in the old garden of a Russian Orthodox nunnery.

I visited two kibbutzim, which impressed me, as did the architects and planners whose offices I visited and who drove me around to see their projects, including the beginnings of the new town of Beersheba. Everyone tried to persuade me to live in Israel. To my objection that I was not a Zionist, they answered that that did not matter; one man went so far as to state, "Nobody here is a Zionist."

It is hardly an accident that Herzl developed his ideas in the city of Vienna in the dying years of the Hapsburg Empire. People, groping for a national identity, were inclined to accept a "blood and soil" myth: the notion that there exists a permanent, God-given unity between a "people" and a "land," one "belonging" to the other.

I had grown up with the notion that my being Jewish did not mean that I was less of a German, and I was not willing to allow a bum by the name of Hitler to tell me differently. In Moscow in 1933 some German Jews changed the ethnicity marked on their Soviet identity papers from "German" to "Jewish," but I did not. Evidently, I was not just a "German citizen of the Jewish faith"; I did not share that faith. Apparently, many Jews feel uncomfortable that they do not really fit into either of the current boxes of "nation" or "religious affiliation," but to a group or "community" of a different type; the only contemporary parallel I can think of are the Parsi.

If there are common characteristics of this somewhat unique group, the Jews, I can think of three which I value: a respect for learning, stemming from a tradition of "the people of the Book"; a desire for social justice, handed down from the prophets; and cosmopolitanism, resulting from 2000 years of diaspora. In Israel the first two are weakening and the third is fiercely rejected; I am inclined to say that the Israelis, by becoming a nation, have ceased to be Jews.

I can of course understand the passionate desire of the survivors of the Holocaust, who had found themselves a defenseless minority in the countries that had been their home, to have a "homeland" which they owned. But Palestine was not "a land without people." Normally there are no such lands. There were, however, under the abnormal conditions of 1945: the eastern provinces of Germany, from which the Germans were evacuated, to which nobody else could claim an exclusive right. I suggested at the time the establishment of a Jewish homeland in one of them, preferably Pomerania. But nobody listened; the emotional fixation of "the land of our fathers" was too strong.

The best of the Zionists, like Martin Buber and Judah Magnes, recognized the right of the Arab-speaking Palestinians to the same land, and hoped for a bi-national state; so did I. When the 1948 war and the ensuing mutual hostility precluded that possibility, the partition proposed by the United Nations appeared to be the only possible solution. It was not surprising that the Palestinians revolted against giving up the best part of the land, including the only cities: Jerusalem, Haifa, and Jaffa-Tel Aviv. As a result they lost much more.

But they continue to exist, inside and outside the boundaries of Israel established in 1948. Israel must find a way to live with them and with their Arab neighbors. At the time of my first visit I said pointedly, "Israel has a future only as a member of the Arab League."

My friends in Israel did not see it that way. Much as I admired their dedicated work, I was disturbed by their attitude toward the Arabs. When I asked my colleagues in the National Planning Office, after they had presented ambitious plans for many parts of the country, what they planned for a section inhabited by Arabs, the answer was, "Nothing." When I visited a mosque in Akko, Israeli soldiers, entering without taking their shoes off, talked and laughed loudly while some old Arabs were engaged in quiet prayer in a corner. While it may be true that the Arabs in Israel are economically better off, and even that they enjoy more human and political rights, including a free vote, than those in neighboring countries, they are definitely second-class citizens in their native country. Let me add that many Israelis are concerned about the fate of the Palestinians, in contrast to the callous chauvinism predominant among North American Zionists.

Because of my rejection of Zionist ideology, I did not want to become an Israeli citizen, but I was willing to live and work there.

Greece. From Haifa an Italian ship took me to Piraeus.

Finally, after fourteen years, I was in Greece. It was all I had expected — and more. I had longed to see the landscape, the mountains and the sea, the islands and the bays, and the great works of art of ancient Greece. But there were two other unexpected sources of joy: the Greek people, and all they had created in Christian times, right down to the present.

The Greek people share with their "classic" ancestors the interest in the human being, an open-eyed curiosity quite free from indiscreet prying. Because they wanted to know me, we also managed to communicate, though I knew hardly any Greek and many of them had only their own language; quite a number knew some other one, English, French, or German, but mostly Italian. They hated the Italians but, to my great surprise, not the

Germans, whom they rather admired. Generally, I heard this praise with pleasure, for example from an archaeologist talking of German work in his field; but I was rather stunned when a fellow boasted of his collaboration with the Gestapo in tracking down Communists!

However, this was an exception. Generally, I found great honesty and dignity. In Corinth, I, together with an American student whom I had met, climbed up to Akro-Corinth on a scorchingly hot day. On the way a barefoot boy joined us and then spent about an hour showing us the sights, explaining what had been built by the Greeks and what by the Turks. When he left to look after his goats, I wanted to give him some money. He refused; we were his guests.

There are, of course, some famous works of Byzantine art, such as the great church at Daphni with its magnificent mosaics. What I had not expected was the many churches and chapels with all their icons; I could not tell if the buildings or the paintings were from the twelfth century or from the twentieth. Even more surprising was the unfailing beauty of all houses still being built in the villages, in particular on the islands. Greece is — or was in 1952 — the only country in Europe where architecture still existed as a living folk art.

On my first day in Athens I walked up to the Acropolis. It was a hot day, and I was thirsty. I saw two boys sitting in a garden at a table, drinking wine. I was not sure whether this was a private house or an inn, but I entered. It was an inn, and the boys invited me to share their wine. They were high-school students who spoke French. They then accompanied me to show me the ancient theater on the other slope of the Acropolis, and after that a chapel containing the Kastalian spring. It had been a sacred spring in antiquity and was still sacred, now with a Christian connotation. They drank and, after some hesitation, offered a cup to me. In descending, they read aloud the inscriptions on the ancient gravestones. Is there any other country in the world where people can easily read inscriptions engraved two-and-a-half millenia ago?

I continued up to the precinct of the Acropolis. In 1952 it was still free of air pollution and of crowds, and I spent many hours there, but also around the agora and the monuments outside the Dipylon gate, and in the museums. I crossed the Saronic Gulf on a little boat to Aegina to visit the temple of Aphaia on its mountaintop.

I explored other parts of Greece. A crowded bus took me to Delphi, and the remains of that sacred site on the ground and in the museum were doubly impressive against the background of the towering rock of the Parnassus. I have seen many mountains which are much higher than those of Greece, but none more overpowering than the steep cliffs of the Parnassus and of the Taygetos. Part of the beauty of the Greek landscape, the sharp outline of its mountains, is really a result of its tragic history, the hubris that led to their deforestation.

Long bus rides on narrow potholed dirt roads through wild mountain country, a ferry across the narrowest point of the Gulf of Corinth, and further long bus rides took me to Pyrgos, and early the next morning, to Olympia. Even more memorable to me than the extensive remains in the sacred precinct are the sculptures in the museum in their unmatched perfection. After a visit to Sparta and the medieval monasteries of Mistra in the foothills of the Taygetos Range, I explored the Argolis: the charming port city of Nauplion, the impressive ruins of Tyrins and Mycenae, and, above all, the unique theater and sanctuary of Epidaurus.

Soon after my return to Athens I took a boat to Mykonos and Delos, at the time still completely unspoiled. On the voyage back to Piraeus, I met two Belgian students who told me they were on their way to Thera (also known as Santorin). I said, surprised, that I had wanted to see that island, but did not know how to get there. They informed me that a ship would be leaving at midnight from Syros, where we would be stopping. So I changed my plans. My little old German guidebook told me that the boat would enter a circular bay, a former volcanic crater, with the village of Thera crowning the top of the rim. I got on deck at dawn; the boat entered a round bay. I saw a white village on the top of the hill, so I climbed down the ship's ladder into a rowboat which took me to the quay. I sat down for a cup of coffee, wondering if the other passengers were still asleep. To my surprise the ship left, and I asked, "Where is it going?" — "To Thera." — "And where am I?" — "In Ios." — "When is the next boat to Thera?" — "In two days."

I count the two days on Ios among the most wonderful of my life. I found a very simple but clean room at the little inn on the quay, and roamed all over the island. It is not small, and several hundred people lived there, but there was not a single wheel on the entire island; all movement, of goods as well as of persons, was on foot or on muleback. In the village, up on the hill, people whitewashed many times a year, not only their houses, but the joints of the large gray slabs of their street pavement.

I was the only *xenos* on the island and was met with friendly curiosity. I found that many of the terraces, built and maintained over millennia by patient toil, were now decaying. I discovered a smooth, paved circular space, enclosed by sloping hillsides, and concluded that this must have been the orchestra of the ancient theater. But then I found two more quite similar round paved places. There could not have been three theaters; it dawned on me that the places must be threshing floors. What was more natural for the peasants, once the threshing was done, than to dance on the threshing floor? It is known that the ancient Greek theater had its origin in the feast of Dionysus, the god of fertility and of the harvest. It seems to me evident that the "orchestra" of the Greek theater is nothing else but a threshing floor; but I have not found this notion in literature.

I also thoroughly enjoyed, as I did throughout my trip, swimming in the clear waters of the Mediterranean and lying in the southern sun.

After two days I proceeded to Thera. To me, Europe is the most beautiful of all continents, Greece the most beautiful of all countries of Europe, the Cyclades Islands the most beautiful of all parts of Greece, and Thera the most beautiful of all the Cyclades. This was before the earthquake. I stayed several days, including a visit to the ruins of archaic, ancient Thera on the top of a rugged mountain.

I went on another boat trip, from Athens to Crete. I was fascinated by the great palace of Knossos, if a bit disturbed by the question, "What here is Minos, and what is Evans?" No such doubts disturbed my enjoyment of the treasures of Minoan culture in the museum in Iraklion.

The boat stopped only twenty-four hours at Iraklion. I regret not having seen more of Crete; it really was the Greece of Greece, the cradle of Greek civilization, as Greece is of ours. We are still guided by the Homeric "Always to be the first and shine before the others," the striving that produced the self-destruction as well as the glory of Greece.

I left Greece on a boat that went through the Canal and Gulf of Corinth and the lovely Ionian Islands to Brindisi, at the "heel" of Italy — it was the last of many days and nights I spent on board

ship during that summer, each and every one of which I profoundly enjoyed.

I recall an amusing episode on the long train ride from Brindisi
to Zürich. A German girl, riding in the same compartment and
looking out of the window, exclaimed, "Ist das erlaubt?" (Is that
permitted?) An Italian, to whom I translated her question, threw
up his arms, exclaiming, "Tutto e proibito, e tutto si fà" (Everything is prohibited and everything is done) — Italy in a nutshell.

In Zürich I rejoined Olga and we visited relatives and friends in
Germany, Denmark, and Sweden. In Hamburg, Oelsner had
been succeeded as director of Planning and Building by Werner
Hebebrand, whom I knew well from Moscow. He wanted me to
take on a new task: to develop regional coordination of the plans
of the City-State of Hamburg with those of the neighboring
states. In my discussion of this proposal with the deputy mayor in
charge, Nevermann, he noted that only German citizens were eligible for civil service positions and, as he did not expect me to
give up US citizenship, he suggested that I act as their consultant.
Assuming, erroneously, that this would involve hiring a staff and
renting an office, I suggested another form which I had known to
exist in Germany, a "special service contract." Nevermann replied that they had not used this for many years, but that he
would propose it to the Senate; however, the Senate turned it
down.

In October, Olga and I went to Italy and celebrated my sixtieth
birthday in Florence. For the first time I saw Urbino, one of the
most beautiful among the many beautiful towns of Italy, with its
Ducal Palace, the most perfect embodiment of the Renaissance.
In Milan, at the Scala, I heard an all-Vivaldi concert by a Roman
chamber orchestra. It was a revelation; Vivaldi had only been a
name to me, connected with Bach; he became a late but permanent love. On the return trip to Germany I stopped over in the
Ticino to see Anna Maria Derleth in her old villa in the mountains, and Hannes Meier in Lugano — both for the last time.

LAST YEAR IN THE USA

In the fall I returned to the United States to a somewhat uncertain
future. I visited Topeka first, where my brother-in-law, Alfred
Plaut, had become chief pathologist of a big veterans' hospital,
while Margaret was teaching Freudian German to the psycholo-
gists of the Menninger Clinic.

When I returned to Philadelphia, I learned that Franklin C. Wood, who had worked with me at the Philadelphia Planning Commission and was now the planning director in neighboring Bucks County, had been looking for me to head a special study of Lower Bucks County. Having failed to locate me, he had engaged Carl W. Wild as consultant for this task. I now became Carl's associate and we worked together very well.

The special study had become necessary because United States Steel had built a huge new plant in Lower Bucks County, which had been followed by a very large new residential development, Levittown, and a somewhat smaller one, Fairless Hills.

Our office was in Doylestown, the county seat, a very pleasant small town in a beautiful landscape to which I commuted from Philadelphia by train.

Bob Mitchell wanted me to join his department at the University of Pennsylvania to do planning research. As there was an interregnum between two university presidents, the appointment had to be decided by the university senate; after several hours of debate, during which both Bob Mitchell and the dean of architecture, Holmes Perkins, strongly advocated my appointment, the senate turned it down for political reasons.

The first task for which Bob Mitchell had wanted me was a study of Levittown. The federal government had encountered several social problems in the "New Town" of Oakridge and wanted to know if similar problems had been found in Levittown, and how they had been dealt with.

The appointment went to Gerald Breese, who immediately hired me as his associate. "There is more than one way to skin a cat," said Bob Mitchell in making this arrangement. We found that most of the Levittown residents were not steelworkers, but worked in Philadelphia or Trenton, where, in turn, most of the steelworkers lived. Problems in Levittown were only those found in any new suburb, primarily a highly abnormal age distribution: young couples with small children, practically no old people and no teen-agers — consequently no baby-sitters.

When my passport expired, I applied for an extension, which was refused. I protested to the State Department, stating that I had no need for a passport right then, but that I reserved my right to appeal. Somewhat later I was notified by the Technion in Haifa that the senate had appointed me head of the Planning School. I asked for an appointment at the State Department, to which I went accompanied by my lawyer. Two gentlemen received us very politely, and then questioned me about membership in a number of organizations on the Attorney General's list as allegedly "subversive." In some cases my answer was "yes"; in some I said, "I do not know if I am a member, but if not, it is an oversight." After a fairly lengthy hearing they thanked me for my frankness. I did not get a passport. The Israelis advised me to go to Canada and board a ship for Israel; but I did not want to become an Israeli citizen, so I refused.

There was a great deal of planning work going on at the time in America. Charles Blessing, who was planning director in Detroit, wanted me to head the work on urban renewal. I warned him that he would run into political difficulties, but he felt confident that he could overcome them. A lady from the Detroit Civil Service Commission came to Philadelphia to give me a daylong written examination. Not long thereafter Charlie asked me to come to Detroit. On my arrival I asked about the political aspect; he said I had to see someone from the Civil Service Commission later in the day; but he was sure that there would be no difficulty and introduced me to his staff. When I came to the interview, the official questioned me about the Korean War, which was still going on, and a fairly heated exchange ensued. My appointment was rejected. I was not surprised, but Charlie was stunned. While we were still discussing the situation, standing in the waiting room, the official called me back in. He was now alone; a lady who had been sitting silently in a corner, and whom I suspected to have been from the FBI, had left. He said, "I cannot tell you how badly I feel about this, but I have a wife and children."

All too many Americans took that stand during the McCarthy period. They included liberals who had been full of contempt for the Germans for not daring to speak up against Hitler. In comparison to the torture and death that threatened those Germans, the risks faced by Americans were minor; perhaps loss of a good job which, in rich America, would not mean starvation.

Many of my left-wing friends — who did stand up — thought the US was already or was rapidly becoming fascist. I doubted their pessimistic assessment. In fact, McCarthyism went out surprisingly fast; the underlying belief of Americans in free speech reasserted itself.

In Philadelphia I had no difficulties. I worked on a large regional transportation study, in close association with Dr. Ernest

Jurkat, a very able economist, to predict future distribution of population. He had been in charge of research for the Berlin Merchants' Association. After Hitler came to power, he had headed the underground organization of the Social Democratic party in Berlin. He happened to live across the street from me, and we became fairly close friends.

Thanks to Henry Churchill, the New York chapter of the American Institute of Architects commissioned me to make a study of "Riverside," the area of Manhattan between Central Park and Riverside Park, from 58th to 110th Street. I found several interesting facts. Because the area had largely lost its former high social status with the conversion of practically all single-family houses into small apartment or rooming houses, it had been assumed that crowding had greatly increased. While there were a number of severely overcrowded dwellings, the average amount of floor space per person was practically the same as at the beginning of the century. I also found the same close correlation between altitude and level of rent which I had identified in Philadelphia — surprising in an area in which the difference in altitude between ground and top floor is much greater than the difference of altitude at ground level. Equally surprising was the finding that the tenants who had moved into new luxury multistory apartment houses, assumed to be highly mobile cosmopolitan people, had overwhelmingly come from the immediate neighborhood.

My general conclusion was that the area needed improved private and municipal maintenance and housekeeping, but that wholesale clearance and redevelopment was neither feasible nor desirable. This was probably not what the architects had hoped for; the study was never published.

While working on this project, I stayed with Olga in New York. At that time the Regional Plan Association had inaugurated a monumental study of the New York region, and I had interesting discussions with the Association's director, Heny Fagin, and with Raymond Vernon, a brilliant Harvard economist who headed the study.

Having lived in New York in 1924 and again in 1939/40, I was of course aware of the social deterioration. However, I was shocked by an accidental occurrence. I was waiting for the light to cross 96th Street at Lexington Avenue, when I noted what I assumed to be a fight between two teen-agers on the opposite side of the street, with a large crowd watching. When I crossed, I saw that it was a fight between two heavyset adult men. One had sunk to the ground, bleeding and semiconscious, but held on to the trouser leg of his opponent, who kept on beating him. I first detached the hand from the trousers, then pulled at the other man's sleeve, shouting, "Stop it; you are killing him." A boy pulled his other sleeve, saying, "Come on, dad, let's get out of here." The man started to leave, but then turned around to threaten me; fortunately, the boy pulled him away. I asked someone to call an ambulance; nobody moved. I went to a drugstore across the street and called the police. An ambulance took the unconscious man to a hospital; whether he arrived dead or alive, I do not know.

Here were about a hundred grown men, about half black, half white, and not one had felt the slightest responsibility for what was going on before their eyes, in their city. What kind of a society was this? It could never have happened in Moscow; there people did consider themselves their brother's keeper — maybe sometimes more than the brother would have liked.

CHAPTER IX

Canada

1955 – 1985

METROPOLITAN TORONTO
PLANNING BOARD
In 1953 the Province of Ontario created
the Municipality of Metropolitan Toronto out of the city and
twelve suburbs. The law which came into force on January 1,
1954 also established a Metropolitan Toronto Planning Board,
extending its jurisdiction over thirteen adjacent municipalities,
for a total area of about 720 square miles.

The Planning Board appointed as director a young political
scientist with a planning degree, Murray V. Jones, and engaged
as consultant Walter H. Blucher, the very knowledgeable and
experienced head of the American Society of Planning Officials.
Blucher recommended me for the position of assistant director.
After an interview I was offered the job and accepted gladly.

The job was very attractive to me for two reasons. First, I had
for years advocated metropolitan planning, considering individual municipalities as unsuitable areas for comprehensive planning. Second, Canadian citizenship would restore my freedom to
travel, of which the State Department's refusal of a passport had
deprived me. A few years later the United States Supreme Court
found this practice of the State Department to be unconstitutional, and I received a passport from the us consulate in
Toronto. But by that time I had decided that I definitely preferred Canada to its big neighbor. For one thing, not being
big — except in territory — it is free from the temptation to play

"Big Brother" to the rest of the world. There was and still is a
sane freedom from chauvinism. At the time I came to Canada, it
did not even have a national flag. Considering all the crimes committed in the name of national flags, I found this an attractive
distinction. Canada has inherited from England a respect for fair
play and a rejection of violence and hysterical swings to the
extreme, which contrasts favorably with the McCarthyism which I
had experienced in the US.

True, the climate of Canada was not exactly my first choice. But
there may be some truth to the claim that it is "invigorating." In
any case, in the almost thirty years which I have lived in Toronto,
I have not been sick for a single day. Another explanation for my
surprising good health is the presumption that I am so full of
venom that no virus can survive in my system.

The chairman of Metropolitan Toronto was Frederick G. Gardiner, a successful corporation lawyer and a true-blue conservative first appointed by the province and subsequently annually
reelected by the council. I came to greatly admire him: I used to
say that he had all of the good characteristics of Robert Moses
and only a few of the bad ones; in particular, he was able to admit
and correct a mistake. As a man of driving energy, impatient "to
get the steam shovel into the ground," he was skeptical of planners and at first treated Murray Jones with contempt; but when he
discovered his ability, he made him one of his trusted advisers. As
Gardiner through his strong personality also dominated the
Planning Board, the work of professional planners was relatively
free from the usual frustrations by the political process.

As the metropolitan council was composed of elected municipal officials, whose main interest was in their local affairs, all
decisions were actually made by the cabinet of very able commis-
sioners which Gardiner had assembled; it was a highly efficient
and effective technocratic government.

The Planning Board had a small but able staff. We had three
operating divisions: land planning, under Ely Comay; research,
under Don Paterson; and transportation, under Raymond Des-
jardins. The inclusion of the specific division for transportation
was a particular strength by comparison with many other planning bodies.

All problems were discussed and usually agreed on by the five
members of the senior staff. My specific responsibility was the
preparation of an "Official Plan" for the planning area. The leg-

islation specified that this plan was to cover the distribution of land use, population and employment, transportation, including public transit, and major public works. Detailed zoning and public works of local importance remained a responsibility of the twenty-six municipalities of the area.

When I arrived in Toronto on August 1, 1955, it was scorchingly hot; so after two days I moved into a little hotel which then existed on the Toronto Islands. I stayed there for six weeks, enjoying my morning swim in Lake Ontario and then commuting across the bay. Toronto, like most North American cities, had sacrificed the enjoyment of its waterfront to railroads and industries. However, God in his grace had given a second open waterfront to the citizens by locating a cluster of islands, covering about a square mile, at a distance of not less than a mile from the shore. In the nineteenth century many city people had built summer cottages on the islands, most of which had gradually been converted for year-round use. I knew about the islands because Jacqueline Tyrrwhitt had sent me copies of studies of her students.

Jackie, as everybody called her, was an English planner whom I had met in New York and Philadelphia. In the academic year preceding my arrival she had established the first city-planning course at the University of Toronto. She had also cooperated with Marshall McLuhan on a journal, the contents of which I found difficult to understand.

The City of Toronto had found it burdensome to service the homes on the Islands, and had transferred them to Metro for use as a park. I felt that this use was completely compatible with continuing residential use. In fact, the presence of homes, gardens, stores and restaurants, and of people, added to the attraction, in addition to giving support to the ferries and other services which were required by the park users. Park visitors mainly used the beaches, which were unencumbered, or walked, or bicycled, an activity more interesting in an environment enriched by houses and gardens. I wrote a report recommending the maintenance and strengthening of the residential use, together with park development.

I had shown the report to Tom Thompson, the parks commissioner, and he had agreed that the houses were an asset more than a liability. However, when my report came before the board, Gardiner remarked that it was counter to the policy pursued for several years, and asked the parks commissioner if he did not prefer to have the entire area for park development. Thompson answered in the affirmative; I felt betrayed.

Most of the houses have been destroyed, but some two hundred remain and have become the object of a bitter thirty-year war involving the city, Metro, and provincial governments as well as the courts.

I had lost my first battle at Metro. But the second one achieved results beyond my expectations.

Like all cities in North America at the time, Toronto regarded as its most urgent need the building of expressways. But Toronto had also been the first North American city in twenty-five years to build a subway. Opened in 1954, it had been a great success. Torontonians were therefore receptive to my consistently pursued goal of maximizing the share of "public" — more correctly called "collective" — transportation in the movement of persons by mechanical means.

In studying the area, both on maps and on the ground, I had noticed that a number of railroad lines branched out from the city center in all directions and had suggested the development of a suburban railroad service. While the inner ring of suburbs, built up or to be built up at intermediate densities, could and should be served by a subway system, the extension of such a system beyond about fifteen kilometers, I considered, would be a mistake for two reasons: first, because of the many intermediate station stops, it would not be competitive in travel time with the private automobile; and second, because the trains would be almost empty on the outer sections of the line. To serve these outer areas, a different system was required, with far fewer trains, proportional to the much lower load, and far fewer stations, permitting higher speeds.

Murray Jones immediately saw my point, and we obtained an interview with the head of the section of the Canadian National Railroad serving our area. His first reaction — not unexpected from a railroad executive — was, "Impossible." When we asked why it was so, he gave as the reason the overloading of Union Station. When I noted that other stations with the same or a smaller number of platforms handled a far greater number of passenger trains, he replied that the bottleneck was not the station itself, but the approaches, which were also heavily used by freight trains. However, after having received our promise to ob-

serve secrecy, he added that our proposal might become feasible
in a few years. The CNR was planning to build a by-pass freight
line and classification yard just north of the metropolitan boundary. Once that was completed, freight trains serving destinations
within the area would move inward from the periphery rather
than outward from the center, as they did now, and would no
longer pass through Union Station. Murray reacted immediately
by offering to facilitate their land acquisition for the by-pass by
keeping subdivisions out of their way. On this basis excellent
working relationships were established between the two staffs.
We obtained some improvements in the detailed alignment of
the by-pass, including the elimination of some grade crossings.

We also had informal discussions with the railroad engineers
on the future railroad service to be established to serve the suburbs along the lakeshore both east and west of the city. I felt that
the line should be electrified and the service extended to the
neighboring cities of Hamilton and Oshawa. The railroad people, while agreeing that this would be desirable, proposed diesel-
driven trains limited to the central part of the line, between its
two junctions with the by-pass. Such a service has now been operated successfully by the Province of Ontario for a number of
years. Recently the province has decided to electrify the service
and to extend it to Hamilton and Oshawa.

The suburban railroad service probably would have been established sooner or later without our initiative. Our most valuable contribution was to bring about a change of the location of
the huge one-by-four-kilometer-large classification yard from the
very midst of the residential areas, where they would have created
a barrier for roads in a corridor of rapidly growing demand, to
open fields stretching away from the developing area. This was
the result of an informal and unrecorded suggestion which I had
made to the railroad engineers.

A few days after I started work in Toronto, Gordon Stephenson arrived. I had first met Gordon twenty-five years earlier when
he visited Giprogor in Moscow, and on subsequent meetings in
the US and England. We had become friends. Gordon had been
the head of the planning school at the University of Liverpool,
but had accepted an appointment to head the prestigious planning school at MIT in Cambridge, Massachusetts. After he had
sold his house and packed his belongings, he was refused entry
to the United States because the FBI claimed he was a "fellow

traveler." In fact, he shared the views of the moderate wing of the British Labour party.

Jacqueline Tyrrwhitt and Anthony Adamson, an unusually perceptive architect-planner, had prompted the University of Toronto to seize the opportunity to invite Gordon Stephenson to establish a city-planning school at the university; I participated sporadically in its work. Unfortunately, after several years we lost Gordon as a result of the blindness of the university government. They refused to upgrade Planning from a diploma to a masters' level, and they did not use Gordon Stephenson to plan the substantial expansion of the campus which was initiated at the time. As a result, Gordon accepted an invitation of the University of Perth in Australia, which has made use of his talents to plan its campus.

The Toronto campus has been developed as a hodgepodge of unrelated buildings. The most accessible parts, at subway stations located at three of its four corners, are given over to low-intensity uses. The intensive uses line two major traffic arteries, and the authorities have failed to seize the opportunity of new building to provide grade-separated walkways for the numerous crossings.

Gordon and I were asked by Mathew Lawson to advise him in developing residential zoning for the City of Toronto. At one point Mathew mentioned to me that he had been charged with preparing the city's submission to the Royal Commission on Canada's Economic Prospects, headed by Walter Gordon. When I asked Murray Jones whether he had received a similar request on behalf of Metro, he took the matter up with Gardiner, who had assigned the task to his finance commissioner, who was, however, glad to leave it to the planners.

The deadline for this report forced us to speed up our estimates for population, employment, land use for different purposes, and all major services, including their capital cost for a planning period up to 1981. We related the capital cost to estimates of regional income, but not to taxes, because of expected changes in the financing of municipal expenditures.

In estimating future population growth I assumed that the postwar baby boom, though it had lasted longer than expected, was a temporary deviation from the long-term trend of decreasing fertility. My colleagues were skeptical and only accepted my relatively low estimates of a 1981 population of 2.8 million for the planning area, of which 2.3 million would live in the municipality of metropolitan Toronto, after much discussion. The 1981 census showed 2.63 million in the area, 2.11 million of whom lived in the metropolitan municipality.

My friends were also skeptical about my assumption that manufacturing's share of total employment would decrease from 38 percent to 30 percent; in fact, it decreased to 26 percent.

The theoretically desirable "finger-plan" form of the metropolis underwent a substantial reduction to three "fingers," east and southwest along the lakeshore, and north along Yonge Street, the latter to be limited in order to reduce water, sewer, and stormwater problems, and to preserve a maximum of farmland close to the city. We opted for gradual growth by accretion as both economically and socially preferable to the creation of detached "instant" new towns or boroughs. Another guiding principle was to minimize the need, but maximize the opportunity, for commuting. Minimization was to be achieved by creating an approximate balance between employment and resident labor force in every major section of the area with about 100,000 to 200,000 population. For this purpose we allocated an ample amount of land for industry. We realized, however, that there would always be many reasons for residents to work at jobs in other parts of the region. From subsequent studies I have arrived at the conclusion that even the best "balanced" job distribution can reduce commuting out of a major section by no more than a quarter.

Thus a good transportation system is vital in order to maximize the opportunity for commuting as well as for purposes other than work. The appropriate technical means for travel, I insisted, depends on concentration of travel demand in space and time. Only the highest concentration, travel to and from work in the city center, can justify the high capital investment of providing a completely grade-separated right of way for rapid transit or suburban trains; once established, these can and do also provide excellent service to many less-concentrated destinations. However, most of the latter will have to be served by a more extensive network of surface vehicles, streetcars and buses, preferably on reserved tracks and lanes. Where trips are even more dispersed in space and time, buses would be practically empty; such trips can be served only by individual transportation which, under present conditions, means the private automobile. With growing dispersion not only of home origins, but even more importantly of destinations for work, services, and recreation, and a growing proportion of nonwork trips, automobile movement is bound to increase, however attractive the service offered by the transit system. Private cars and transit serve different kinds of trips, and can only to a limited extent substitute for one another. It is therefore absurd to pose the question: transit or roads? Roads, of course, are required not only for passenger automobiles, but also for the movement of goods — trucks and delivery wagons — and of services: fire, police, ambulances, maintenance of water, power, and telephone lines, as well as of all surface transit by bus or streetcar.

In the immediate postwar periods the USA, in the absurd belief that the automobile could meet all transportation needs, committed the criminal folly of tearing up streetcar tracks and tearing down elevated railroad lines. Later, with a wild swing of the pendulum, people engaged in the even greater folly of rejecting all urban freeways, thereby forcing all motor vehicles onto city streets. Streets have to serve as access to property and as outdoor living room; these functions are not essentially compatible with through traffic. It is bad enough that we have inherited from the age of horse-drawn vehicles "arteries" intended to serve these two ill-compatible purposes. Transit is one indispensable method to reduce motor vehicle movement on city streets, but it cannot replace vehicles carrying goods or services — which also include not a few passenger cars — nor the many automobiles en route to dispersed destinations. These can only be accommodated by freeways which greatly reduce the total impact of disruption, noise, and air pollution and, above all, the number of accidents produced by cars on city streets. To reject freeways means sacrificing life and limb. It is only their far greater safety which has induced authorities to raise their speed limit and thereby to transform "freeways" into "expressways." I favor a speed limit of 60 to 70 kilometers for urban freeways.

The "stop-the-freeway" dogmatism reflects the same primitive pseudologic as did the "clear-the-slums" doctrine. People perceived a concentration of disease, crime, and delinquency in the slums; ergo, tear them down and these evils will disappear. People perceive concentrations of motor vehicle noise and pollution on freeways; ergo, stop the freeways and there will be no more noise and pollution. In both cases the perceived evils are actually increased and spread by the intended cure.

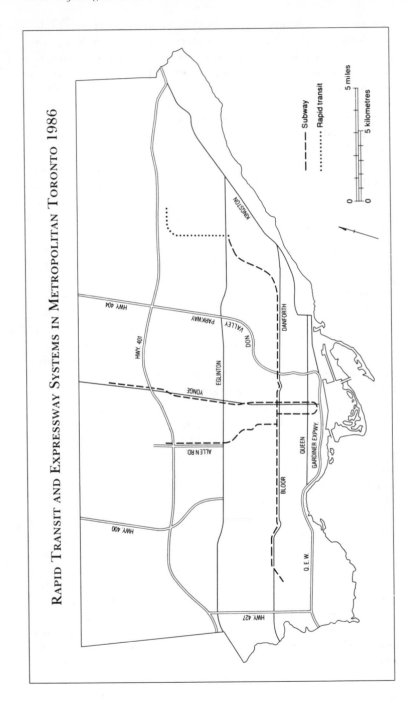

RAPID TRANSIT AND EXPRESSWAY SYSTEMS IN METROPOLITAN TORONTO 1986

It is, of course, difficult and costly to insert a freeway into a developed area, and highway engineers have done much avoidable damage by indiscriminately using the designs which they had developed for overland freeways in an urban environment. Urban freeways should always form a closed system, with every freeway ending in another freeway, never in a city street. Except in purely industrial areas, or adjacent to an existing railroad embankment, urban freeways should be depressed rather than elevated. Their interchanges with the surface system should be handled by ramps rather than by cloverleaves. They should try to avoid cutting through districts, and should form district boundaries. If the only choice is between location in a residential area or in a park, the park location is generally preferable, because some parkland can be reconstituted by decking the freeway.

As to the basic system design, the different kinds of trips to be served by freeways and rapid transit lines require different patterns: radials for subways and a large-scale grid for freeways. At the time work on the official plan started, the province had just built a section of its Detroit-to-Montreal Highway 401 as a "Toronto by-pass," about 12 kilometers north of and parallel to the lakeshore. Along the lakeshore plans for a freeway, later called the "F. G. Gardiner Expressway," were already fairly well advanced. We proposed an additional east-west freeway, called the "Crosstown," at a location intermediate between these two, to be followed by one about 10 kilometres north of 401, at the edge of the urbanized area. In the north-south direction the province had decided to build a freeway (Highway 427) 16 kilometers west of the city center, while Metro decided to build one in the valley of the Don River, some two to six kilometers east of the center. To serve the twenty-kilometer gap between these two, two additional north-south freeways were proposed: one an extension to the south of the 400, proposed by the province; the other an extension to the northwest of Spadina Avenue, one of the very few wide north-south streets in the city, an extension which had been under discussion for decades. In order to minimize disruption in the densely built sections of the city along the lakeshore, we proposed to stop these two north-south freeways at the "Crosstown."

Soon after I had joined the staff, Murray Jones asked me to study the proposal for the Spadina freeway. My immediate reaction was, "Why build a freeway? Why not build a rapid transit line?" On further study I found that the escarpment, which separates the north of the city from the south, was on this five-kilometer-long section traversed by only two continuous north-south streets, each only four lanes wide. I therefore proposed a combined facility, with a rapid transit line located in the center strip of the freeway. Such a combination, of course, greatly reduces construction cost as well as disruption.

As for the basic concept of a radial configuration for a rapid transit system, I found myself in disagreement with the senior consultant of the Toronto Transit Commission (TTC), Mr. Norman Wilson. Mr. Wilson regarded the subway grids of Paris and Manhattan as models. He overlooked the fact that they had been built when these cities had residential as well as employment densities averaging 100,000 persons per square mile. In Toronto residential densities average less than one-tenth of that figure, and comparable employment densities exist only in the central business district. I took a nasty crack at Mr. Wilson, calling him "one of the most advanced minds of the nineteenth century."

The TTC, after having demonstrated the benefits of a subway by the north-south Yonge Street line, now proposed to build a longer east-west line on Bloor Street to replace its most heavily traveled streetcar line. In the report which I wrote for the Planning Board, I strongly supported the proposal for an east-west rapid transit line, emphasizing that transit was the "workhorse" of the transportation system. However, I questioned whether the proposed alignment was optimal, because Bloor Street is located about two and a half kilometers north of the center of the business district. Mr. Wilson proposed continuing the Yonge Street line from its southern terminal to the north by a line on University Avenue, 650 meters west and parallel to Yonge Street, to connect with the Bloor line both to the East and the West. He proposed a complicated operation, with Bloor Street trains alternatively running through from east to west (and vice versa) and turning south to the central business district (CBD) to continue northward on Yonge Street. The operating staff of the TTC strenuously objected that it would not be possible to maintain regular headways during peak hours with such a complicated operation. After thorough discussion, I found their apprehension to be well founded. The TTC staff accepted the proposed alignments on Bloor Street and University Avenue, but insisted on operating the Bloor line and the Yonge-University line separately. This was satisfactory as far as operation was concerned, but it had the obvious disadvantage of forcing all Bloor line passengers bound for the CBD to transfer, with the danger of overloading the stairs and escalators connecting the two lines on this transfer point. I also predicted — correctly, as it turned out — that the University line would be underused even at peak hours and practically empty on evenings and weekends.

I therefore proposed a different alignment, vaguely approaching a radial configuration. The outer sections of the Bloor line would remain, but at distances three to four kilometers east and west of Yonge Street the line would bend to the south, to continue in an east-west direction to the center of the business district on Queen Street, traversing the most densely populated section of the city. The TTC was adamantly opposed to my proposal because it necessitated continuation of streetcar service on Bloor Street.

My proposal was dubbed "U-line," while the TTC's was called "T-line." The planning board approved a study which would simulate, with the aid of computers, the passenger loads to be expected on one or the other alternative routes. The study was carried out by the consulting firm led by Joseph Kates, an outstanding mathematician who later became head of the National Science Council. The simulation indicated that the U-line would provide for only nominally more passenger-miles overall, but would carry about one-third more persons into (and out of) the CBD.

When the question came up at Metro council, Mr. Duncan, the very able general manager of the TTC, who had strongly opposed the complicated operation proposed by Norman Wilson, was asked whether this operation *could* be implemented. His answer was "yes"; it was also "yes" to the next question, *"Will* it be implemented?" It was indeed — for six months. Since that time the two lines are operated separately; congestion at the Bloor-Yonge station has now become a serious problem.

When the U versus T question came up at a meeting of the planning board, Frederick Gardiner said, "The TTC has to operate it; let's accept their proposal." Evidently he had made up his mind long ago, but had used the controversy about the alignment to delay the decision — which benefitted the city — until other decisions benefitting the suburbs had been adopted. But I doubt that even Gardiner had foreseen an even more important effect of the disagreement about the alignment: with everyone's attention riveted on the battle royal between T and U, nobody thought of raising the more basic question, "Is an expenditure of $200 million for a second subway justified?" The first line had cost less than $50 million.

Once the decision on the Bloor line had been made, the TTC agreed to our proposal to extend the University line into the Spadina line, thus providing adequate loads for a continuous north-south line, comparable to the Yonge line.

Thus the system of rapid transit lines has been gradually implemented in conformity with the Draft Official Plan which we completed in 1959. This has, however, not been the case with the proposed closed freeway system.

While the planned freeways were located for the most part either adjacent to existing railroad embankments, or in valleys or open country, some residences were affected. For a short stretch the Crosstown went through an exclusive upper-class area called Rosedale. The threatened residents succeeded in prompting the metropolitan council to eliminate the Crosstown freeway from the plan, without any discussion. When I urged Controller William Archer, whom I knew as a member of our board, to move its reinstatement, his answer was, "Hans, you know that no council will deal with a controversial subject if it can leave the decision to the next council; eventually the Crosstown will be built, even if we have to put it underground." Wise as the first half of his answer was, the following prediction proved erroneous.

Without the Crosstown there was no closed system, just an assortment of isolated freeways with no place to end. When the province decided to widen Highway 401 from four to twelve lanes, we asked for construction of an interchange with the future Spadina Freeway. The province agreed only under the condition that the freeway, at six lanes wide, be pushed two kilometers south beyond its planned termination. In contrast to the balance of the alignment, which touched only a few houses, these two kilometers affected a prestigious residential area as well as the University of Toronto.

Naturally, this aroused protest. By this time the pendulum of opinion had swung to the antiexpressway extreme. A crusade got under way under the slogan "Stop Spadina!" The Manichean fervor was inflamed to white heat by a pamphlet entitled "The Bad Trip," written by David and Nadine Nowlan, a masterpiece of distortion which claimed that the Metropolitan Planning Board's "Report on Transportation" — for which I had been primarily responsible — had doctored its findings to deliberately favor the private automobile! An election was pending. So the very same Ontario government which had been exclusively responsible for trying to push the freeway through a residential area now cancelled the freeway under the slogan "Cities are for people, not for cars!" — a demagogic statement if ever there was one, considering that no car ever moves without a human being at the wheel. So the "Spadina" now ends four kilometers short of its originally designated end, disgorging its load on an already overloaded Eglinton Avenue. Meanwhile, the province is extending its own Highway 400 to dump more cars on the same avenue.

These things happened many years after I had left the planning board. Urban planning is a long-term undertaking — and the politician's time horizon is limited by the next election. In times past dynasties were concerned with a more distant future. Today, the only ones who can afford that luxury are civil servants, the much-maligned bureaucrats and technocrats.

The question can and has been raised whether it makes sense to attempt long-range comprehensive plans, sometimes called "official" or "master" plans, which attempt to project an image of the physical aspect of an area twenty or thirty years in the future. Some planners reject them as "static end-state plans." I was aware of this problem. Early in my Philadelphia days I had formulated it as follows, "In making such a plan, we make three assumptions: first, that we know what the aspirations of people will be; second, that we know what technical means will be at their disposal; and third, that they will use these means rationally to achieve their aspirations. Now we know that all three assumptions are quite unrealistic — in particular the third one." And yet we must make the attempt, because without such a "guiding image" of the future, as the German planners refer to it, it is impossible to anticipate the effects of any present decision concerning one particular element on all other elements. The plan presents a possible and desirable balance between all elements — population, work, services, etc. If any one element develops differently than has been assumed, the plan serves as a frame of reference to indicate what adjustments have to be made in other elements. The plan is not a static blueprint, but a dynamic guide.

Basic to such an image is, of course, the allocation of population and of workplaces to the different areas and subareas of the planning region. This process requires an amalgam of prediction and prescription — as does indeed all planning. We assumed that population density would and should be maintained in the city and increased in the suburbs. The latter goal has been achieved, but density in the city has decreased substantially.

As density is largely dependent on zoning, which was under the jurisdiction of the area municipalities, the question arose how our plan could be implemented. I suggested a clause prohibiting zoning likely to result in a population more than 50 percent higher or 30 percent lower than provided in the plan. Murray Jones rejected this, stating that it would never be accepted by the politicians. How right he was became evident when we presented our draft plan. It was received with hostility; the council members saw it as a limitation to their ability to make deals with developers.

Another objection, raised primarily by the lawyers, was that the text of the plan did not clearly distinguish prediction from prescription; they wanted a clear formulation of legally binding clauses. Until a new draft was adopted, there was no actual "official" plan. However, the draft of 1959 served quite effectively as a guide for a number of years. The final legally binding document was to a large extent a compilation of the official plans of the area municipalities, which had been enacted in the interim.

Our "Draft Official Plan" was essentially a product of what is variously called "informed judgment," "seat-of-the-pants decision," or "intuition." I do not accept the view of reason and intuition as mutually exclusive opposites, as does the philosophy of Henri Bergson which had attracted me in my late teens. I believe that an intuitive judgment is the synthesis of a great number of largely subconscious rational processes.

There was, however, one aspect of the plan which could be tested by explicitly rational methods. The proposed transportation facilities required a capital investment of about one billion. Was the allocation to roads and rail lines, respectively, optimal, or could the people of the area be better served by building either more roads or more rail facilities? This could be tested by simulating the movements to be expected under three alternatives: the proposed "balanced" one, and one each concentrating on either road or rail construction. This study was in the main carried out after I had resigned as assistant director. I worked on it as consultant to the board, and learned a lot from Joseph

Kates and his able associates, Neil Irwin and Hans von Kube, who developed the complex computer programs required for the simulations.

One important result which I should have, but had not, anticipated was the natural balancing process at work. If addition of a rapid transit line attracted people away from driving their cars, the resulting reduction of road congestion made driving more competitive with transit. As a consequence, the differences of modal distribution between the three variants were much smaller than expected.

The results generally confirmed the efficiency of our proposed balanced system. A contemplated rapid transit line on Queen Street was shown to attract volumes justifying only an improved streetcar line.

I greatly enjoyed my work with the planning board and believe that it produced worthwhile results. But, as I was approaching the age limit of 70, I resigned after six years, in 1961.

LIFE IN CANADA

While I was living on the Islands after my arrival in Toronto, I looked for an apartment. I found that most of them had two severe deficiencies: their windows did not open at all, or only to a very limited extent, and there was usually no continuous wallspace for my bookcases. Finally, I found a well-designed one on the eighth floor of the newly built Anndore Apartments. It had the further attraction of a breadth of view comprising the eastern part of Metro, at that time mainly treetops covering low houses, and a portion of the lake. Only later did I realize that it was also ideally located from the point of view of accessibility. After a number of years the Anndore was converted to a hotel, and I was evicted. I found another bachelor accomodation on the twelfth floor of an apartment about a minute away. When my view was shut off by a taller building, I moved across the street to my present abode, a one-bedroom unit on the twenty-fifth floor, high enough to top most of the hundreds of multistory buildings which have meanwhile sprung up east of our block, the same one in which the Anndore is located. So this sample of one confirmed the experience which I had from study of the Manhattan West Side that people tend to move within the same neighborhood.

While I continued to ride my bicycle, I also wished to be able to explore my planning area, Canada in general, and Europe as well, by car. So I took driving lessons and bought a Volkswagen. Having resumed driving in my 64th year, I never became a good driver, and gave it up some years ago. But during the twenty-three years that I did drive, I enjoyed it thoroughly, as it gradually replaced more strenuous forms of movement, such as skating, horseback riding, canoeing, skiing, hiking, and bicycling.

I found both of the entirely different landscapes of Southern Ontario very attractive: the fertile, rolling farmland next to Lake Ontario, and, less than a hundred miles to the north, the forests, lakes, and rocks of the granite "Shield." During my vacation trips Olga joined me — to Quebec and the Maritimes, around the Great Lakes; also once, but not by car, to Vancouver and Victoria, by boat to Prince Rupert, and to Jasper and Banff. Two years later we drove to Vancouver, where the Town Planning Institute held its annual meeting, and returned by way of the Kootenays, Jasper, Edmonton, Saskatoon, and Regina. In Saskatchewan it was oppressively hot, and driving toward Winnipeg on the arrow-straight road through the treeless prairie, I fell asleep at the wheel and the car went into the ditch. I got away with a broken collarbone, but Olga suffered a broken arm which required an operation. I stayed in Regina while she was in the hospital, until she was able, with the aid of a nurse, to fly to Los Angeles, where her brother and his wife nursed her back to health.

On my first visit to Montreal I was surprised to find the French of Quebec so similar to those of France. This was before the "Quiet Revolution," when Quebec still guarded jealously the traditions of the authoritarian, clerical "ancien régime" of 1760; Voltaire was taboo and so was everything in the tradition of the Enlightenment which has shaped the history of France for the last two centuries. The evident conclusion is that all the revolutions and other world-shaking events had not basically changed this strange entity which is the "national character."

In 1956 or 1957 the Town Planning Institute held its annual meeting at Lac Beauport, in the very heart of Quebec. Although at least half of those present were francophones, not a word of French was spoken during three days. It so happened that I had to make a presentation after the concluding luncheon. I gave it in English, but preceded it by a few French sentences thanking our Quebec hosts and apologizing for my subsequent switch to the other national language. For years thereafter, when I met French-speaking colleagues, they greeted me with, "That was wonderful what you did at Lac Beauport." There certainly was plenty of reason for resentment at the arrogant disregard of most English-speaking Canadians for the language and culture of their French-speaking countrymen. That has changed in the last thirty years, and I hope that the Québecois will never make use of their natural right to secede. I think that secession would have three most undesirable results: the English-speaking element in Quebec would be suspected of disloyalty, and so would the French-speakers in the rest of Canada; and the ability to resist American domination would be even weaker than it is now.

In 1959 I took a month of leave without pay to combine it with my annual leave for an extended trip to Europe. In Copenhagen, Olga and I visited my friend Gregersen. I hired a Volkswagen and visited my old buddy from the First World War, Hannes Clausen, and his son, my godson, who now had a son of his own, near Schleswig. Hamburg, by now largely rebuilt, and my birthplace of Osnabrück evoked old memories. We continued through the Rhineland, Belgium, and France, to Spain. I had hesitated to go there with Franco in power, but finally decided not to try any longer to outlive him. I very much enjoyed the rich and beautiful heritage of that country, and was favorably impressed by the dignity and friendliness of the people. We crossed the border at Hendaye and drove through Old Castile to Salamanca. In addition to the joy of the rich "Plateresque" architecture, I was impressed by the simple purity of small "Mozarabe" churches; then by the urban beauty of Avila, Segovia, and Toledo, the almost Egyptian austerity of the Escorial, and the treasures of the Prado, most of all Goya; but even more by the southwest and the northeast of the country, Andalusia and Catalonia, each in its own right. One always fears that such famous sights as Seville, Cordoba, and Granada will turn out to be disappointments, but they are not. The loveliness of the Catalan landscape on a drive from Tarragona to the great monastery of Poblet was a surprise, as was the unique little town of Peniscola on its rock protruding into the Mediterranean Sea.

We then drove to Bonnieux, where Olga for the first time met Lotte; they soon became friends. After a few days we returned to Munich, where I turned in the car. Olga stayed in Germany, while I went to Moscow via Prague.

REVISITING MOSCOW

I arrived in the evening; driving in from the airport, the first thing one saw was the silhouette of the university. Is there another big city in the world where the dominant and most symbolic building is a seat of learning, rather than of state or church power?

I had left Moscow twenty-two years ago; it was now a city of five million. But the first morning I walked along its main street, someone called my name. It was Krayevsky, a Polish architect who had worked with Gropius at the Bauhaus and had gone to Moscow in the early thirties. Through him I also met Rosenberg, who was now in charge of the gardens of the Academy of Agriculture. As both of them are Jewish, I asked them about anti-Semitism. Both said it had appeared but was now past. It was also interesting that both of them were just before or after, respectively, moving to a new and better apartment. A third acquaintance whom I visited, Margaret Kurella, had just moved into a new apartment two months before. The quantity of new housing everywhere was impressive and, judging from the Kurella apartment, fairly well planned. But the new developments were out of human scale. They were, however, well equipped with services; there were no line-ups in the stores, as there were in the city center.

I found some of my old colleagues at Giprogor, and through them also my former "brigade leader," Alexander Mukhin, who was now a member of the Academy of Architecture. He had been an adviser in China and told me that he now had to give many talks on his experiences there. I also visited the Moscow City Planning Office. I asked the very intelligent director if he really believed that they could maintain their planned population limit of five million — which they had already nominally overstepped. He thought they would, and gave a very well-reasoned exposition of the measures they were taking for that purpose. I was not convinced that they could and would enforce them. In fact, now, twenty-five years later, the population of Greater Moscow is approaching ten million.

I saw Obrastsov's marvelous puppet theater, attended a concert by Rostropovich, and revisited the building formerly occupied by the Foreign Workers' Club. I also went to my old apartment; my partners, the engineer Shabadin and his wife, were still living there, in one room. They stared at me as at a ghost when I entered, but then were overjoyed. Their daughter, whom I had known as a little girl with blond pigtails, was married to an engineer in Riga and taught there at the Conservatory of Music; in addition, she was champion woman horseback rider of the Soviet Union. My attempt to cede them my room had failed, and they did not get along with my successors. They hoped to get a two-room apartment within a few months. I asked Shabadin if any of the other people I had known were still living in the apartment complex, and he mentioned the Bauers. They were a couple of architects from Budapest, Party members. Both had been arrested in the late thirties and had been in prisons or camps for many years. But Bauer's sister, a schoolteacher, and his son remained in the apartment, and the boy had completed his education and was now a physicist. The sister was in bed with the flu, and I saw her only briefly, but I had a talk with the son, whom I had known only as a little boy. His parents had returned to Budapest, where his father had been elected head of a borough administration. When he answered no to my question if he was practicing architecture, and I asked, "What is he doing?" he said, with a smile, "He represents the people." Some years later I visited the Bauers in Budapest. He was quite unchanged, as firm a Communist as ever, but with the same great sense of humor, full of jokes over foibles of the Party and government.

The nightmare of the Stalin terror was over. When I asked Rosenberg what people now thought of him, he said, "They try to forget him." When I asked Shabadin what he thought of Khrushchev, the answer was, "He is all right — so far." The Soviet people have learned their lesson; despotism will not return.

But how did it happen? The official explanation, "personality cult," sounds ridiculously inadequate; but it may contain a good deal of truth. The universal reaction to the death of Lenin, "We have lost our father," had shown to the leaders, and certainly to Stalin — if they did not already know it — how deep-seated the need for a father image was among a people that had grown up in patriarchal families. They consciously built Stalin up as the strong, all-wise father of the country, and it must be admitted that it paid off in helping the Soviet people to withstand the terrible blow of Hitler's initial victories.

When other leaders became aware of Stalin's increasing paranoia and tried to eliminate him, it was too late and they fell victims. But it is quite erroneous to assume that the terror was directed against actual or potential dissidents. It was much less rational than that; a large proportion of the victims were and even remained blind believers in Stalin. The apparatus was in motion and its members had to fill their quotas. I understood fully how it worked when I met my old friend Perfanoff in West Berlin in 1949. He had been arrested in 1938 and had been returned to Germany a year later under the Molotov-Ribbentrop exchange. He was subjected to endless interrogations and accused of spying. At one point he lost his temper and, banging on the table, shouted back, "It's a lie, it's a lie, I am not a spy." Thereupon the interrogator got up, looked out of the door and closed it, looked out of the window and closed it, sat down and said, "Citizen Perfanoff, don't get excited. I don't know who you are and you don't know who I am." Whereupon he opened door and window and resumed shouting at Perfanoff.

The terror is gone. But of course that does not mean that opposition has been legalized. At the time of the discussion of the Soviet Constitution in 1935/36 I had noted that the rights which it proclaimed — to work, education, health care, etc. — were indeed vitally important and were really practiced, but that one right was missing: the right to err. I was not familiar with the more adequate English term, the right of dissent. From the point of view of those who deny it, they are opposing error. Indeed, most governments throughout history have considered it not only their right, but their sacred duty to protect their subjects against the poison of wrong doctrines. They have taken it for granted that there is a true doctrine, an "orthodoxy," eternal absolute truth. Only in the last few centuries have people in Western Europe gradually come to take a critical view of that assumption and to recognize that truth can only be approximated by a contest of errors.

I am inclined to believe that this unique development was made possible by the conflict between emperor and pope which undermined both secular and ecclesiastical authority and thereby opened the way for independent thought. The people of the Soviet Union have never lived through that experience; so they replaced Christian — or Jewish or Islamic — orthodoxy with a new one. No one has more strongly rejected the notion of absolute truth than Karl Marx; "Marxist orthodoxy" is a contradiction in terms. That hundreds of millions of people believe in it shows how deep-seated is the human need for certainty, for absolute truth. However, the leaven of Marx's critical thought, together with the whole approach of modern science, is at work to undermine any orthodoxy. The change has taken longer than I had hoped, but it is going on.

Overall, seeing Moscow again after twenty-two years was a positive experience. There were two negative aspects: bad weather and Intourist. As I did not travel as part of a group, I was a "deluxe" tourist, entitled to an interpreter and a car. I did not need either; only twice did I ask for service from Intourist, for visits to the puppet theater and to the university. In both cases, after wasting much time in waiting, they failed to deliver. In both cases I tried on my own and got access without any difficulty. But I can imagine how a non-Russian-speaking tourist would have felt.

I had originally planned to go to Stalingrad and Kiev, but then decided to skip Stalingrad. When I told that to Intourist, they said no, I had to leave for Stalingrad the next morning. I was annoyed and said so to the woman who was in charge of my floor in the hotel. She said, "If you want to stay, don't go." I took her advice, and Intourist supplied me with a plane ride to Kiev two days later.

In Kiev an Intourist car picked me and two other tourists up at the airport. My guide was a charming young Ukrainian woman; she was studying English and was eager to have me correct her. We visited the remarkable monuments of medieval Kiev; the cathedral with its mosaics is indeed magnificent. But modern Kiev is also a beautiful city. It has made the most of its site on a high plateau overlooking the Dnieper and a wide, low plain. On a promontory they had built a very dignified war memorial: a paved platform with an eternal flame at its end, flanked on both sides with flat stones commemorating the victims of each of the nationalities of the Soviet Union, large and small, including the Jewish nationality.

The main street of the city, the Krestchatik, is very beautiful, despite the Stalinist architecture of most of the buildings, thanks to its sweeping curve and its very well-designed cross section and landscaping. I found a similar sensitivity to street design in other parts of the city too. I visited the city planning office — again just by walking in, after Intourist had failed to arrange for an interview. Once more, I questioned their faith in their growth limit of 1.4 million; now the population is over two million. Upon my request, they gave me the address of a new housing development. I found it quite attractive, with four-story brick buildings, and my

Intourist guide thanked me for having shown her a part of the city which she had not seen before.

After I had arranged for my trip to the Soviet Union, I had written to Elena Syrkus, a leading Polish architect, that I intended to stop over in Warsaw for a day or two. Her return letter said, "Do not come for one or two days; come for a week on your return. We will have an international architects' congress that week; enclosed is your registration." So I went from Kiev to Warsaw by train, overnight. In the morning, on every stop in the small Belorussian towns, there were peasants at the stations, selling food to the travelers. In the train from the Soviet border to Warsaw I encountered a group of young East Germans whom I had previously met in the cathedral at Kiev. Interestingly, I found that one young woman was a student of theology. Even more interestingly, she did not hesitate to criticize openly the East German authorities for dwelling exclusively on Nazi atrocities and not saying a word about the misbehavior of Soviet soldiers in Germany.

There were interesting people from both eastern and western Europe at the Warsaw congress, but I was the only representative of the western hemisphere. When I asked whether I should make my presentation in English or German, the answer was, "German or French, but not English." The reasons were purely linguistic, not political; but I found it remarkable that the Poles, only fifteen years after their brutal oppression by the Germans, were willing to accept their language.

Warsaw had been more thoroughly destroyed than any other city, but the Poles have done a most remarkable job in exact rebuilding of historical streets and squares, churches and palaces of their capital. The congress participants were also taken on tours to Gdansk and Krakow. In Gdansk they had restored the houses and churches of the Hanseatic merchants with loving care. The streets and squares are beautiful; however, if you enter a patrician's house and find yourself in a movie theater or a labor exchange, it is a bit of a shock. Krakow has miraculously escaped war destruction and has preserved its beautiful image.

On my way back, I stopped in Berlin and traveled to Leipzig to see Ernst Bloch, the Marxist philosopher whom I had meet in America. Because of his stand in support of the Hungarian revolt of 1956, he had fallen out of favor. He no longer taught at the university, and his writings were no longer published in the East.

But they did not put any obstacles to his publishing in the West nor, evidently, to his emigration two years later to the West, where I again visited him in Tübingen.

In Leipzig he lived in a big, attractive house with his large library, a maidservant, and a car. His wife, an architect, had been expelled from the Party (he had never been a member). She hesitated to show me the children's institution where she had worked; but when we went there, she was received with great cordiality by her former fellow workers.

Bloch, enumerating cases of suppression of intellectual freedom, kept repeating, "I ask, is this Marxism?" He also said, "The socialization of the means of production is the necessary, but not sufficient, precondition of socialism."

In Berlin I discussed the vicious circle endangering East Germany with my old friend from Hamburg and Moscow, the actor and writer Gustav von Wangenheim. That country had started out with an unprecedentedly unfavorable ratio of male labor force to dependents: old and sick, widows and orphans. As the West started to pour billions into West Germany, while East Germany paid billions of reparations to the Soviet Union and Poland, the growing difference in the standard of living enticed more and more skilled young workers to the "Golden West," leaving the old, the invalids, and the children behind. The result was a shrinking labor force forced to maintain a growing number of dependents. The East Germans had enacted severe laws against emigration but could not enforce them because there was no border between East and West Berlin. I told Wangenheim that they thus got the worst of both worlds: hostility because of their laws, and continuing loss of workers. While I would have preferred free movement, I realized that the continuing hemorrhage endangered their survival. Why did they not stop people from going to West Berlin? Wangenheim was indignant; how could I imagine such a thing; Berlin was a city! But two years later they did it, and since then not only has life in East Germany consistently improved, but so have the relations between the two Germanies. Never has the truth of the old saying become so evident that "Good fences make good neighbors!"

That is not to deny that the Berlin wall is horrible. But the horrible fact which it represents is not viciousness of the East German regime, but the suicidal division of mankind into two opposed armed camps.

I had become increasingly convinced that continuation of the arms race will lead to the suicide of the human race, and that all and any other aspiration or effort is entirely futile if we fail to stop it and proceed to universal disarmament. When I had left Philadelphia, an Episcopalian clergyman with whom I had worked at the Civil Rights Congress had given me the name and address of the Reverend Dr. James Endicott in Toronto. I went to see Jim and joined the Canadian Peace Congress and its local constituent, the Toronto Association for Peace. I was subsequently elected to the executives of both organizations; but in those years of relative quiet and general complacency our activities were limited.

FIGHT FOR CITIZENSHIP

I had decided to apply for Canadian citizenship, for which I became eligible after five years of residence, on August 1, 1960. On the same day my American citizenship expired automatically. I had accepted an invitation of the German Public Transit Association to be the main speaker at their annual meeting in Bremen in the last days of September. I told the judge at my citizenship hearing of this invitation, and he had assured me that I would receive my papers in time.

The weeks went by. In mid-September two civilian and civil gentlemen from the Royal Canadian Mounted Police (RCMP) visited me. They were interested in the activities of the Peace Congress and asked for names of members of the executive. When I remarked that we called each other by our first names, they countered, "You must know at least some name." I said, "Mary Endicott"; they did not ask any more questions.

Evidently I was in trouble. I asked Murray Jones to recommend a lawyer, and I went to see Richard Rohmer, who has since become well known as the author of several bestsellers. Rohmer immediately contacted the ministry and felt confident that they would notify him before taking any further steps. However, a few days later I received notice that my application had been refused. Rohmer's efforts to obtain a temporary travel document for me were also turned down. So I had to notify the secretary of the German Transit Association that I could not come. Fortunately, I had sent him my paper and a number of slides. The slides got lost somewhere in the Bremen customs office and were found only later; but the secretary, apologizing for my sudden illness, read my paper, which provoked a lively discussion. Subsequently the association published my contribution, with copies of some of the slides, the discussion, and my response to the discussion.

The refusal of Canadian citizenship was an unexpected setback. I was stateless once more. I could not travel to Europe and, as a one-time member of the Communist party, I was barred from entering the United States by the Walter-MacCarran Act. But once more my good luck prevailed.

Martin Meyerson had been appointed director of the prestigious Joint Center for Urban Research of Harvard and MIT. He invited me to a conference on the metropolis prepared by the center. I answered that I would be able to come only if he could obtain a special permit. Martin went to the State Department. John Kennedy had just been elected president and had put a lot of Harvard academics into high positions in Washington, so Martin was received with great respect. But, said the officials, this is a very difficult situation, and in any case we could not possibly get the permit in time for your conference. "Then we will adjourn the conference," said Martin. . . . I got the permit.

That set a precedent. During the following academic year my friend Kevin Lynch took his sabbatical and wanted me to substitute for him in his course on metropolitan planning. MIT obtained a permit for me for a weekly visit to Cambridge. Subsequently, I repeatedly asked for and received permission to go to the United States for professional purposes.

In Canada my life was in no way affected by my status as a stateless person. Through the mediation of a professor at the University of Toronto I had obtained an interview with the deputy minister. To my query about the reasons for the refusal he answered, "Reasons are never given; you will have to draw your own conclusions. You can apply again in two years." He added, encouragingly, "Maybe there will be another minister." There was. Ron Haggard, whom I had come to know when he had covered the planning board as a reporter on municipal affairs for *The Toronto Star,* brought my case to his attention. But soon thereafter there was an election, and the Conservatives were replaced by the Liberals. I had agreed with Andrew Brewin, who now acted as my lawyer and was also a member of Parliament, that we would try "quiet diplomacy" and had discouraged Haggard from publicizing my case. However, when a year elapsed after my second application and nothing happened, we agreed that publicity could not hurt. Ron Haggard wrote on my case in two subsequent editions of the *Star,* which followed with a short editorial in my favor. Evidently, no government wants to be seen as being pushed around by the press; but three months later I got my citizenship. Apparently, the decision had been made by Guy Favreau; as a result of his sudden death, I received it from his successor — four ministers and three-and-a-half years after my original application.

I was told at the US consulate that I now had to get permission to visit the States from the immigration office in Buffalo. When I called them, the man at the other end of the line said, "I know your case; why don't you apply for a permanent exemption for professional purposes?" I did, and have had no difficulties since that time.

STARTING MY ACADEMIC CAREER AT 70

When I was nearing retirement age, I approached Thomas Howarth, dean of architecture at the University of Toronto, about work in the Department of Urban and Regional Planning. Howarth commissioned me to develop a research program. I developed a fairly detailed one which, however, remained largely on paper because there was nobody to carry it out. But I developed and taught a number of courses over the years. The ones which I repeated most frequently were History of Urban Development and Planning, a kind of cook's tour through five continents and five millenia; and Transportation Planning, in which I dealt with long-distance as well as with "local" transportation, emphasizing its interaction with other aspects of planning. I also developed courses on Metropolitan Planning, on Housing, on Urban Renewal, and, during one term, on Attempts to Apply Systems Theory to Urban Planning.

As I had started my academic career in my seventieth year, instead of ending it in my sixty-fifth as respectable academics are expected to do, I was of course never entitled to tenure or pension, and I could not really fit into any one of the prefabricated cubbyholes of the university establishment.

Not long after I had left the Metropolitan Toronto Planning Board, Guy Legault and Paul Laliberté, employees of the Montreal City Planning Department, visited me to ask me to become assistant director of their department. I did not want to leave Toronto and to give up my work, both at the university and as consultant to the planning board, so we agreed that I would become their permanent staff consultant, coming to Montreal for three or four days at least twice a month.

The work in Montreal was interesting, as the city was gearing up for the 1967 World's Fair. We looked around for a suitable site, and proposed one on the banks of the St. Lawrence. Credit must go to the mayor and his assistants for the better idea of locating it on largely man-made islands; the site we had proposed became the huge parking lot for the visitors.

The city used the occasion of the World's Fair to implement an ambitious program of both subways and freeways. I learned quite a bit from discussions with the very experienced engineers of the Paris subway system. Montreal was fortunate in that the underlying rock formation allowed for exceptionally cheap construction. In discussing various alternatives of subway alignment, I noticed that the engineers were inclined to choose those where there was rock, rather than those where there were people.

I strongly supported Guy Legault's proposal to have each station designed individually by a different architect, pointing out the successful precedent of the Moscow subway. Guy also had the brilliant idea of replacing the customary mezzanine with a few bridges, thus creating a high space over the platforms.

Interesting problems also arose in the design of the freeways, in particular one along the south shore of Montreal Island. The engineer had proposed building an elevated road along the waterfront. We proposed a route farther inland which would be closer to most destinations in the area and would not ruin the waterfront. In the heart of the city is the valley of a former river which, because of poor soil conditions, had attracted no high-value buildings. The highway follows that valley, replacing the stream of water by a stream of cars; because they are below street level, they do not offend the eye and offend the ear less than does heavy traffic on a normal city street. Farther west we could locate the two directions of the freeway at different levels in a steep escarpment — the only location which provides pleasant views both *to* and *from* a road. On a stretch still further west the two directions of the freeway run along the two sides of the railroad. On each side a two-way service road was also needed. With "normal" arrangement the right lane of the freeway would be next to the right lane of the service road which runs in the opposite direction. The interchange between freeway and service road would have required a space-absorbing half-circle. The distance could, however, be reduced to a few feet if the interconnected lanes ran in the same direction. To achieve this, I proposed reversing the direction of the freeway on this stretch. To my pleasant surprise the highway engineers accepted my proposal, and it works perfectly well.

Transportation planning was of course not our only concern. As with most cities of the period, Montreal had adopted a plan for large-scale clearance and redevelopment called, after its author, the "Plan Dozois." I baptized it "Plan Bulldozois." My alternative program involved rehabilitation of existing houses and building small public housing projects, mainly on "infill" sites. In the main, these policies have been followed in Montreal.

Another of my tasks was to help build up the staff of the department, which meant working myself out of a job. I succeeded in persuading Harry Lash to become assistant director, and for a while we worked together on "Montreal 2000," an attempt to get regional planning started which had only limited success.

With few exceptions the staff consisted of French-speaking Québecois. Their attitude to planning differed from that of Anglo-Canadians in two respects: greater emphasis on the role of the state, and more attention to aesthetic aspects.

When de Gaule shouted his famous "Vive le Québec libre!" (long live Free Quebec) from the City Hall balcony next to our office, most of my colleagues were enthusiastic. I consider it a historic moment: for the first time in 175 years a president of the French Republic had paid homage to the lilies of the Bourbons! (The Bourbon lily, in quadruplicate, graces the official flag of Quebec.)

In the mid-sixties the Province of Ontario inaugurated a "Metropolitan Toronto and Region Transportation Study" (MTARTS). On the insistence of several consultants to MTARTS, a study of various development alternatives was included. I considered one of these, providing for two tiers of development paralleling Lake Ontario, divided by a green belt which was to accommodate a transportion corridor, to be neither feasible nor desirable. MTARTS was followed by a provincial study for the development of the region, which unfortunately adopted the "two-tier" alternative. Several years later this plan was revised by a study called "COLUC," with which I was peripherally involved. The second tier has been dropped, but the green belt has remained as an unfortunate inheritance, causing endless acrimonious fights.

When I reached my 80th birthday, my contemporaries began to leave me. Just before that day, my brother-in-law, Alfred Plaut, was felled by a stroke. Gertrud Bing died of cancer in London in the same year. A year later my sister Margaret, without warning, was felled by an aneurism. In the fall of the following year, 1964, Olga suffered a heart attack. When I called her physician in New York, he said there was no urgency. When I called her brother, who had come from Los Angeles the next day, a Saturday, he felt it might be better for Olga not to have too many visitors at one time, and that she was looking forward to seeing me on Monday. But on Sunday she passed away, leaving me a most moving letter. I had left her alone in death, as in most of her life. What saddens me particularly is that she did not live to share my "successes" and "honors," which began to multiply in the following years and which would have meant so much more to her than they did to me.

While I was still working for the Montreal planning department, the University of Montreal asked me to give a course on metropolitan planning, substituting for Benoit Bégin, who was on his sabbatical year. I tried to lecture in French and succeeded better than I had expected.

In the spring of 1968 the university decided to bestow an honorary doctorate on me, together with three other persons. One of these, the head of the French National Railroads, was supposed to give the acceptance speech, but could not come because of the revolts of May 1968, and at the last moment I had to substitute for him. I said in my speech that I was particularly gratified that this honor was bestowed on me, a German, a Jew, and a Marxist, by a French Catholic University. In later years I was made a "Doctor of the Environment" by the University of Waterloo and a "Doctor of Engineering" by the Technical University of Nova Scotia at Halifax. I told the students at Waterloo that all of them should be doctors of the environment and those at Halifax that they should know why they used their "know-how" — to enhance life and not to destroy it by ever more sophisticated armaments.

For several years I taught half time in Toronto and half time in Montreal, but, when my teaching load in Montreal decreased, I decided that it was not worth the time and strain of commuting. However, I did teach a course during one academic year at Guelph and another at Waterloo, both located close to Toronto, again substituting for colleagues on leave.

From time to time I was also invited to give a single lecture or to teach for a few days by other universities or professional societies in Canada and the United States; such invitations also took me to Edinburgh, Paris, and Copenhagen.

PROFESSIONAL ACTIVITIES

I became involved in various professional activities, in particular in the creation of the Canadian Council on Urban and Regional Research (CCURR); the "Regional" was added on my urging. CCURR was being set up as the result of the initiative of the federal Central Mortgage and Housing Corporation (CMHC). This aroused strong suspicion, in particular among university researchers; at a stormy meeting in Ottawa the pun circulated: "CMHC is the tail wagging the CCURR." As a member of a small committee formed at this meeting I found a simple way to diffuse the tension. Because there were to be ten provincial representatives on the council, one for each province, it had been taken for granted that there must be also ten municipally and ten federally appointed members. I proposed to reduce the number of federal appointees to five — and everybody was happy.

Subsequently, I was for several years a member of the committee of CCURR charged with evaluating research projects and developing research programs, a task which involved interesting contacts with other Canadians engaged in urban research.

Much of CCURR's research was funded by the Ford Foundation, where Paul Ylvisaker was in charge of administering the grants related to urban problems. I had known Paul in Philadelphia and asked him occasionally for grants for projects which I considered worthwhile. Once he replied, "Hans, you always ask me for five or ten thousand dollars; come with a demand for half a million, and I'll get it for you." It taught me something about the shortcomings of bigness. Being small myself, I had never really doubted that "small is beautiful" and have often opposed megalomania. But here also the pendulum has now swung too far to the opposite extreme, and I find it necessary to emphasize that "economies of scale" are real and important; and that there are significant problems which require centralized decision-making.

Some time in 1965 I got a telephone call from the *Journal of Liberal Thought* asking me to write about the role of the federal government in urban affairs. I had not been aware of *Liberal Thought;* but I was aware that the government considered following the US in creating a ministry to deal with problems of housing and urban development. I warned the editors that I considered the new ministry a nonstarter; they wanted my article anyway and published it. The government did create the ministry; after a few years it died an inglorious death. However, during its lifetime, government funding for urban research was withdrawn from CCURR, which went out of existence. I was peripherally involved in some of the ministry's research and found it much less cost effective than that funded by CCURR.

I attended meetings of both the Canadian and American institutes of planners, as well as of the International Federation for Housing and Planning. The Federation's meeting in Puerto Rico was the only one attended by a Soviet delegation. Paul Ylvisaker wanted to know how the Soviets dealt with the problem of adjustment of rural migrants to urban life. The Russians did not see it as a problem. "There are schools in the villages, there are machines; what is the problem?" they said. Finally, after a long discussion, the leader of the Soviet delegation exclaimed, "Man is not a cow; he can learn!" It was a characteristic expression of the Soviet faith in human perfectibility, so different from the increasingly pessimistic mood of the West.

At a later date I was invited by the Ekistics Institute in Athens to participate in a small working group on the question of urban densities. Following this I took a boat to Rhodes by way of Crete. A strong bora was blowing and the combination of sun, waves, and wind made me dance with joy. I enjoyed seeing the city of Rhodes, then hired a car to drive through the mountains of the interior to Líndos; I walked up through the lovely streets of the village to the marvelous hellenistic acropolis.

Before leaving Athens, I had an interesting discussion with the founder of Ekistics, Konstantinos Doxiadis. He said that there were really only two choices for a consultant: either to build up a very big organization, as he had done; or to limit oneself to tasks which one could handle personally, without a staff, as I did. However, I frequently worked in association with engineering firms, and also with some of Canada's leading architects: Arthur Erikson, Ron Thom, John C. Parkin and Eberhard Zeidler. I enjoyed the collaboration and learned much from it. Once, when on the way to the office we discussed a problem, my partner said, "Hans, you are talking like an engineer, and I am talking like a planner." I consider this a very positive result of working in multidisciplinary teams.

One day, while I was still working with the Montreal City Planning Department, I was visited by two gentlemen from the Federal Department of Civil Aviation who wanted my advice on how best to protect their flight paths from conflicts of development. They gave me several reports on other major airports, including London and New York. After pondering the problem, I came to the conclusion that our current approach to airport planning is fundamentally wrong: we are creating, on an even larger scale, the same conflict between expansion of the urban fabric and expansion of a major long-distance terminal which had historically developed in port cities and has ultimately forced costly relocation of harbor facilities. I formulated it this way: "A metropolis cannot live without an international airport — and it cannot live with it." It cannot live with it for four reasons: noise, danger, loss of urban land, and interruption of the urban road system. The airport, in turn, also suffers from the conflict: impossibility of expansion and restriction of operations. There is a second, lesser conflict: planes are fast and big, and getting bigger, and pedestrians remain small and slow; the two can get together only by time-consuming and costly movements of planes between runway and terminal and time-consuming and inconvenient walks of passengers between processing and boarding points.

In many airports the movement between pedestrians and planes is mediated by a vehicle of intermediate size and speed, a bus. In some cities buses are also used to carry passengers from an in-city terminal, where they are processed, to an airport terminal where they embark. In London, for instance, a passenger may be carried by one bus from the city center to Heathrow, disembark, wait, and then be carried by another bus to his plane. Why not ride directly from a city terminal to the plane?

If the bus can move on its own reserved right of way at superior speed directly to the runway, the basic contradiction, as well as the secondary one, can be solved — the airport could be close to the city in time, but far in space. When I called up General Motors to enquire about high-speed buses, their answer was, "If you want such high speed, you better think of rail." The vehicle should probably be supported on the line by steel wheels, air cushion, or magnetic levitation, but become a bus for taking on and delivering passengers at both ends.

This was, and is, the core of my proposal, which involves other modifications requiring a much greater length of runways which, in turn, are feasible only far away from a city. My proposal aroused some interest and discussion at the Civil Aviation Administrations in Canada and the United States. However, the only aspect ever implemented was the acquisition of a very large area for the Mirabel Airport at Montreal. As no speedy access to this airport has been provided, it has become a white elephant, and part of the area is being returned to its original owners.

The Civil Aviation Administration subsequently appointed me to a committee charged with finding a location for a new Toronto airport which would permit a gradual phasing out of traffic at the existing close-in Malton Airport. After much buck-passing between the federal and provincial governments, the proposal was postponed indefinitely, and hundreds of millions was invested in new runways and terminals at Malton Airport, exposing a million people to increased noise and danger.

Another job which required frequent visits to the national capital was membership in a committee charged with preparing a report of The Science Council of Canada on urban problems. It was a very interesting group, and we had spirited discussions. In the end I wrote a minority report, which was co-signed by two other members, dissenting on several fairly important points.

However, my strongest ties to Ottawa resulted from my appointment to the Planning Committee of the National Capital Commission. I served on this committee for fourteen years — longer than anybody else; this normally meant one day each month in Ottawa, with occasional additional assignments. The interchange of ideas with the members of the committee, the chairmen of the commission, the staff, and consultants were very rewarding. But whether I contributed much to the improvement of the national capital area is a moot question. Certainly I failed in my two most important endeavors.

Several years before my involvement, the National Capital Commission had acquired a "green belt" encircling the City of Ottawa. When Anthony Adamson, at that time chairman of the commission, asked me what I thought of it, my answer was, "The green is right, but the belt is wrong." The notion of a belt in order to contain the growth of the city is doubly absurd: the aim is in conflict with the goal of having an attractive city, and the means is ineffective, as experience has shown time and again since Elizabeth I tried it in London. The results are higher land costs for those living inside and higher traveling cost (and time) for those living outside the green belt. As much of the Ottawa green belt is neither required nor attractive for recreation, the federal government uses much of it to locate its institutions; as the land is "free," they use it wastefully.

I proposed to transform the green belt into a system of green wedges comprising scenically attractive land; this could be achieved gradually by exchanges with developers as well as by sale and purchase of land. My proposal was repeatedly discussed, but Ottawa still wears its chastity belt.

The second problem concerned the direction of the development of the region. The federal government wanted the national capital to be bi-national and bi-provincial. However, the provinces of Ontario and Quebec had each instituted a regional planning organization to guide development on their side of the Ottawa River. In conformance with established trends, the Ontario side planned extension upstream, to the west, and the Quebec side downstream, to the east. Thus the national capital area will grow more and more apart, instead of together.

Pierre Allard, consultant to the commission, proposed an alternative to reverse this trend. The rapid transit line connecting Ottawa and Hull, then under study, would continue toward the east on the Ontario side and to the west on the Quebec side. As the land in both cases was largely undeveloped, this would also minimize the need for redevelopment. Allard sought my support. I realized that such a radical reversal of trends was beyond the powers of planning generally accepted in Canada. However if — but only if — the federal government was willing to direct its triple powers as landlord, as builder, and as lender toward this goal, it could be achieved. Not unexpectedly, the federal government was not willing, and the two parts of the National Capital Region are going their separate ways.

I was also repeatedly called to Vancouver. The city planners asked for my advice on a proposed second road crossing of Burrard Inlet. I countered with a proposal for a rapid transit line which, using the Montreal technique of tunneling in rock, probably could be built at moderate cost. After serving three stations in the central business district, the line was to continue under False Creek to the city hall area. This area should be promoted for intensive commercial development because it is much more accessible than the eccentrically located historic center.

The city insisted, however, on a study for a road crossing. At one point the proposed route had to be coordinated with a large development undertaken by the Canadian branch of the Grosvenor Estate, the property of the Dukes of Westminster. I was surprised that the head of the office, Mr. John Hardman, engaged me in conversation. It turned out that a young architect working in his office had given him my book on *The Modern Metropolis,* and he had liked it. He commissioned me to make recommendations for the development of a large property owned by the Grosvenor Estate in the Vancouver area. This was the beginning of a very gratifying connection.

Subsequently, I was involved in several transportation studies for the Vancouver area in associaton with several engineering firms; and also, in association with architects, in studies for the redevelopment of the city center and of the False Creek area. To my regret my proposal to transform the basin into a freshwater lake with a constant water level has not been accepted.

However, my most intensive activity in the Vancouver area occurred when Harry Lash was appointed head of regional planning and invited me to assist him in developing his proposals for a "Livable Area." Despite or maybe because of our disagreements on several points, it was a very rewarding experience.

THE VIETNAM WAR

The Canadian Peace Movement which, in addition to the Peace Congress, consisted mainly of church-affiliated organizations, had concentrated on advocating nuclear disarmament, to be followed by general disarmament and the replacement of war by the rule of law as the means of settling international conflicts. When the Vietnam War developed, peace activists from various organizations were discussing their attitudes at an informal meeting. I said, "We cannot be in theory for peace in the future and ignore a real war going on at present." There was agreement that we must actively oppose the military intervention of the USA in Indochina and support the right to self-determination of Vietnam, Cambodia, and Laos.

We participated fully in the demonstrations, delegations, and other activities of the growing movement against the war, trying to strengthen its unity, a sometimes difficult task. Indeed, the developing conflict between the Soviet Union and China endangered the unity within the Canadian Peace Congress. Jim Endicott, its founder and leader, was born and raised in China. After the war he returned there and became closely associated with Chou En-lai and other leaders of the Chinese revolution. It was obviously emotionally unbearable for him to break this association. So, as all of us tend to do in such situations, he persuaded himself that they were right on every question. When Bangladesh fought for its independence from Pakistan, the World Peace Council supported its struggle. Endicott adopted the Chinese thesis that this was aggression against Pakistan by India. The majority of the executive committee, including myself, rejected this interpretation as absurd. Endicott left the Peace Congress. Fortunately, we found an able and dedicated new president in the person of the Reverend John Morgan.

As the Vietnam War dragged on, we tried to find additional methods to oppose it. Frank Cunningham, a professor of philosophy, suggested a large ad in the Toronto *Globe and Mail.* I agreed, but noted that we had to be careful to choose the right moment. When the US unleashed its Christmas bombing on Hanoi, I called Frank. We formulated a one-sentence appeal over the telephone to stop the bombing and started a network of people to collect signatures and contributions to pay for the ad. The movement snowballed beyond our expectations. Within two days we received hundreds of signatures, including those of prestigious persons and leaders of important organizations, as well as pledges sufficient to pay for a full-page ad. In fact, we would not have been able to handle the flood, had not the head of a big advertising agency volunteered to mobilize his staff to sort out and alphabetize the signatures.

Following the publication, John Morgan invited signatories who were leaders of organizations to a meeting. A representative delegation to Ottawa was organized. It received a positive response from the two opposition parties, the Conservatives and the New Democrats, and was attentively listened to by the Honorable Mitchell Sharp, minister of external affairs, and other members of the Liberal cabinet. Subsequently, the government introduced and Parliament passed unanimously an appeal to the United States Government to stop the bombing.

This confirmed the experience which I had found in the planning field that there is no proportionality between effort and result. Large efforts may remain fruitless; and then suddenly a minor effort succeeds beyond expectations.

In the course of the war many American draft resisters and deserters came to Canada, and an organization was set up to help them. I received a letter from a daughter of my old friend Robert Solmitz that a nephew of hers, Richard Riewer, had deserted the army on the eve of being shipped to Vietnam and was now in Toronto. He came to see me, and after he had to leave a couple which had temporarily sheltered him, I put him up in my apartment.

Richard, like most of the American refugees, had entered Canada as a visitor. In order to be permitted to work in Canada, the refugees had to become "landed immigrants." The Canadian support organization had found that the easiest way to achieve this was for the refugees to return to the US and to reenter Canada, applying at the border for landed immigrant status. But when Richard went to the Toronto airport where the US had set up the office controlling entry to that country, he was stopped. He walked out of the office and returned to my place. The support organization advised me that at the border crossing at the Thousand Islands Bridge there was a sizable distance between the Canadian and the US control points, so that I could turn around and approach Canada as coming from the US. So on a cold winter Sunday morning I set out for the four-hour drive to the bridge and proceeded as advised. However, the Canadian immigration officials refused to believe my story that I was returning from Cornell University and had given this young man a ride. I finally managed to reach a lawyer by long-distance telephone, but the only advice he could give me was to drive Richard to the United States. Of course, we were stopped at the border, and the officers took Richard in for questioning while I waited in another room.

I felt very bad. I saw Richard's life being ruined by years in jail. Why had I not chosen the alternative of trying to obtain "landed immigrant" status for him while he stayed in Canada? I knew that it was a difficult, time-consuming, and costly procedure without guarantee of success, but I would have avoided the terribly dangerous situation into which I had put him now.

To my great surprise and immense relief, Richard was released after about half an hour of questioning. Evidently the FBI is not perfect; his name was not on their list. The nightmare was over. There and then I decided that I would do everything necessary to see him through college and to get him established in Canada. After all, under normal conditions I would have had to bring up children; I could easily afford to take care of him until he could stand on his own feet.

I brought Richard to a motel near Rochester Airport and drove back to Canada. From Rochester he flew to Ottawa, where friends put him up. It took months of effort by Andrew Brewin to obtain "landed immigrant" status for him. He has since become a Canadian citizen and has moved to Montreal.

CHAPTER X

Summing Up

TRAVEL ABROAD — WEST AND EAST
With the freedom afforded by part-time
university teaching with its long summer vacations and by more
money than I needed for my style of life, I could more than ever
indulge my love of travel and my urge to see the world. Sometimes my travels also involved professional work, and occasionally participation in peace meetings. Some of the travels I shared
with Lotte, and a few with other friends.

Among the most enjoyable occasions was an invitation to give a
two-week seminar, in English, at the "Università dell' Arte" in
Venice, a small Canadian-Italian institution which had been
founded the year before. I was asked to give the opening address
for the second year. I wrote it in English and read the Italian
translation made by the secretary of the university. The ceremony was held in the Palace of the Doges — no less! At that time
President Kennedy had just made his famous statement, "Auch
ich bin ein Berliner" (I am also a Berliner). So I could not refrain
from proclaiming, "Anch' io sono Veneziano!" (I too am a Venetian), referring to the family legends of both the Blumenfelds and
the Warburgs. In fact, my claim was as questionable as Kennedy's; recent research of the Warburg family has traced our ancestors back to the Middle Ages in Germany.

Lotte later joined me in Venice and we enjoyed the beauty of
that unique city together. One evening we received an invitation
from a member of the board of the university, a count who lived

in a beautiful small palace. As he had been brought up by a German governess, he spoke flawless German. During the Nazi occupation he had impersonated a German officer and had thus been able to supply invaluable information to the antifascist resistance — a most dangerous task requiring unusual courage and self-control.

As the reputation of an "expert" increases by the square of the distance from his house, I was interviewed by the press and asked to put my opinions in writing. The Venetians were concerned about the loss of population of the Island City, as more and more families moved to the mainland, where they could park their cars at their doorstep. I emphasized that the historical cores of all cities were losing population, as families with children tended to move to the periphery and the remaining smaller households absorbed more space per person. As these residents, employees of the cultural, commercial, or government institutions of Venice, or of retired status, were largely of a higher socioeconomic status than those who left, I saw no reason to worry about a purely quantitative decrease.

During the sixties I was repeatedly invited to Israel for consultation, primarily on transportation problems, by various organizations. There is a great deal of national planning in Israel. The Ministry of the Interior, responsible for the pattern of settlements, had a strong ideological commitment to the European pattern of a hierarchical size distribution, including many small towns. But the traditional function of these as market centers for the surrounding countryside does not exist in motorized Israel where the agricultural producers — *kibbutzim* or *moshavim* — deal directly with the big cities. Other ministries — transport, housing, etc. — pursue different policies, and are not much inclined to mutual adjustment, especially if the respective ministers belong to different parties.

I shared my first mission to Israel with Richard Sobermann, a (then) young professor of engineering at the University of Toronto who became a good friend. Much of our work was concerned with the development of the road systems in Haifa and Tel Aviv. I urged greater emphasis on public transportation. The response was primarily in the form of a subway system for Tel Aviv, or even for a rapid rail line between Tel Aviv and Jerusalem, exceeding their means and immediate needs. While I participated in studies for the best alignment for a subway system, I proposed a number of ways to improve their bus system. Not many of my recommendations were implemented.

In Haifa I warned my hosts that they were creating increasingly severe, almost insolvable transportation problems by permitting most of the residential development to locate on Mount Carmel, while places of employment continued to expand at its foot, 300 meters below.

I doubt that my work in Israel has been of great help to them. My colleagues there were highly competent. I enjoyed working with them and some have remained friends. I also enjoyed seeing the country and visiting relatives.

My last visit was in 1969 or 1970. "We now have a big country; it is strange how fast you get used to it," said one of my old colleagues in Tel Aviv. I had been invited for consultation on transportation problems in Tel Aviv, Haifa, and Jerusalem. I had answered that I would be glad to work on Tel Aviv and Haifa, but felt that they had no right to plan for East Jerusalem. When I was introduced to the mayor of Jerusalem, he said, "Whatever the political future of Jerusalem — and of course I hope it will be an Israeli city — it certainly should be able to function as one city." It was hard to argue with that, and my Jerusalem colleagues were so nice and open-minded that I did participate in studying an improved bus system for the entire city.

For the first time I could visit the fascinating old walled city and the Temple Mount. It is truly unique, and so are its two great mosques, the "Dome of the Rock" and Al Aksa, completely different in their architecture, but both equally beautiful.

I was taken, together with two American visiting experts, to the Golan Heights. I was shocked by the chauvinistic attitude of our driver, and equally shocked to learn that all the inhabitants, except the Druzes, had been driven out and replaced by Jewish settlers. It seems to me that the Israelis are their own worst enemies.

More pleasant was a visit with my cousin Emmy Melchior. When, in reply to my question about her activities after her retirement she described them, remarking, "I just like to help people," I countered, "Yes, it is the most enjoyable way to exercise power." She liked the remark.

It is strange, and disturbing, that "power" is always regarded as suspect, if not downright bad ("All power corrupts"), while "freedom" is extolled as the highest ideal. Yet Hobbes expressed a self-evident truth stating that "Freedom and power are identical." Despite the fact that the rational meaning of both terms is identical, we use them with opposite emotional connotations. I think this is very dangerous because it by-passes the question that should be asked: "Freedom for whom and what? Freedom from whom and what?"

During my stay in Israel in the summer of 1967, Lotte joined me. Some of the homeless children whom she had brought up in home-schools in France during or after the war had gone to Israel and had built satisfactory lives for themselves. It was interesting for me to meet them.

Two days after we left Israel for Ankara, the war of 1967 erupted. At Ankara Ernest Jurkat and his wife met us. On the drive from the airport to town I noticed a settlement on a hillside and exclaimed, "What is that? It looks rather attractive." Ernest replied, "I am so glad to hear you say that. It is a squatter settlement. I have a running fight with the Turkish authorities who want to hinder them and tear them down. I tell them that those people are the future of the country, and their children will sit in the seats of power which you now occupy." In Turkish these settlements are called *géshé kondo*, meaning night built. Under Turkish law nobody living under a roof can be evicted. So, when a family decides to move to the city, their friends and neighbors from the village put up the walls and roof overnight; subsequently, the occupant finishes the work. I later had the opportunity to visit some of these settlements in the company of Turkish colleagues. I was impressed by the cheerfulness and energy of the settlers, who tirelessly enlarged and improved their houses and planted vegetables and fruit trees around them.

Ernest Jurkat, who worked in Ankara for the United Nations, was very helpful. He got us a car, with a driver who spoke good English and had a delightful Turkish sense of humor, to explore the interior of Anatolia, impressive by its grandiose landscape and the witnesses of its long, checkered, and often tragic history. We saw the labyrinth of caves where time and again the inhabitants had hidden themselves from invaders, and the incredible scenery of Göreme with its hundreds of rock caves, many of them hollowed out to provide houses and chapels decorated by wall paintings. We visited medieval cities in which traditional Islamic life is still carrying on, in particular Konya, once the capital of the powerful Seldçuk Empire and the home of the great mystic and poet Mevlana. His tomb is now enclosed in an art museum, but the pious still go there to pray at his grave.

From Ankara we flew to Izmir (Smyrna) and visited the magnificent remains of the ancient Greek and Hellenistic cities along the coast of the Aegean Sea. We had intended to spend some time in Greece; but when the Colonels' Putsch occured the day before we left Izmir, we decided to go directly to Italy. However, at the Athens airport, where the atmosphere was tense, Lotte's ticket to Rome turned out to be invalid and we had to defer our flight until the next morning. We did not want to see Athens under the military heel, but finally could not resist the desire to see the Acropolis once more. I was surprised how normal city life seemed to go on, with hardly a soldier or policeman in sight. A surface view of life under a dictatorship can be very misleading.

We spent a week in Rome, hired a little Fiat and drove first to Tivoli and the Alban Hills, and then north to enjoy the beauty of the landscape and the cities of Latium and Umbria. Most memorable was the annual fiesta in the town of Gubbio. The main event, a race of three competing teams — originally representing guilds, but now distinguished only by their colors — carrying images of the Virgin Mary, mounted on heavy floats, to a sanctuary on a hilltop, was opened jointly by the Socialist mayor and the bishop of Gubbio. Everybody tried to give a helping hand to his preferred team in carrying the float. In the evening the whole town was lit up by torches placed on the window sills by everyone. There is much talk among planners about an "urban community." In Gubbio, on this day, I experienced it as a reality.

I made other trips to Italy in company of Lotte, the last one driving all the way to Sicily. Later I traveled with my friend Bent Gregersen from Copenhagen to Northern and Central Italy. My love of the land and people of Italy, in particular of Tuscany and Umbria, has not faded.

Lotte and I also traveled together to other countries in Europe: Holland, Scotland, Norway, Yugoslavia, Hungary. In Budapest we had a very interesting discussion with an economist who had been a fellow student of Lotte's in Vienna and now was one of Kadar's chief advisors. We also visited Noël Field, brother of my friend Hermann, and his wife whom Lotte had known in Geneva. Noël had played, very much against his intentions, a tragic historic role. He had served with the League of Nations and had headed its commission to evacuate survivors of the International Brigades from Spain to France as Franco overran the country. When war came he continued his efforts on behalf of antifascist refugees in the French internment camps, now with the Unitarian Service Committee. Hermann, in the months prior to the war, had similarly administered a refugee escape route via Poland for antifascists caught by Hitler's seizure of Czechoslovakia. During the war years Noël worked with the US Office of Strategic Services and used these contacts to establish liaison between the American forces and the anti-Nazi underground in the countries of Eastern Europe.

When the cold war developed, suspicion, strengthened by misinformation placed into the hands of the secret services of the Eastern countries by the CIA, grew in the paranoic mind of Stalin to the point that he believed Noël Field was the linchpin of a vast anti-Soviet conspiracy involving all the leading Communists with whom he had been in touch. The result was the execution of the best leaders of the Communist parties of Czechoslovakia, Hungary, and Bulgaria, and years of imprisonment and torture for others, such as Kadar and Gomulka.

During an architectural visit to Poland in 1949, Hermann was similarly swept up in Stalin's net and, like Noël in Hungary, disappeared without a trace.

With "destalinization" the victims of this madness were rehabilitated. After five years in prison, both of the Field brothers were released. Hermann returned home to his family, but Noël stayed in Hungary. I could not help admiring his attitude. He even excused his persecutors to some extent, stating that his former connection with Alan Dulles, with whom he had shared an office at the OSS, was a valid reason for suspicion. To my query why he had not returned home, his answer was, "I always wanted to help build socialism; fate has placed me in this country, so I try to make my contribution here." He was working on an English-language journal published in Budapest.

In 1969 Lotte accompanied me to a meeting of the International Federation for Housing and Planning in Orebrö, Sweden. After a few days in Stockholm we took a boat to Helsinki, sailing through the islands in the magical light of the midnight sun. In Finland, while we were waiting for the bus to take us from Otaniemi to Tapiola — both works of Alvar Aalto — a young man stopped his car to ask us where we wanted to go. He had studied forestry in the United States, and said that, being a "summer-widower," he had time to drive us around. He showed us not only Tapiola, but much else of Greater Helsinki, including his mother's home.

In their warmth and hospitality — as in their love of strong drink — the Finns are very much like their Russian neighbors, with whom they now maintain good neighborly relations. In this small country, closer to the Soviet Union than any other, there is far less fear that "the Russians are coming!" than in the United States and in countries living under the protection of its "Nuclear Umbrella." Could it be that it is the absence of that umbrella which allows the sun of peace to shine on Finland?

From Helsinki we took the train to Leningrad, with a sidetrip to old Novgorod. In the Middle Ages Novgorod had been a powerful city-republic, Russia's "window to the West," and it has preserved many outstanding works of architecture and painting.

Leningrad was as beautiful as ever. I was also impressed by the subway, which had some ingenious technical innovations. The stations are less overdecorated and more beautiful than those in Moscow. However, because of soil conditions, they are very deep underground. I timed my ride on the escalator: three minutes! Fortunately, some young couples made good use of those minutes.

Some things had changed since my experience ten years earlier in Moscow and Kiev. I was not approached for black-market deals. A church which I visited was so full of worshippers, including many young people, that I could hardly squeeze in. Intourist worked efficiently.

However, in our Intourist hotel, service still dragged out endlessly. I found that it was much faster in restaurants open to the general public.

On the drive to and from Novgorod I observed the Kolchoz fields and the private gardens of the farmers. The status of both varied widely, from excellent to badly neglected, with the extremes even more pronounced among the private plots than among the communal fields.

From Leningrad Lotte went to Moscow for her first and last visit to the city where she had lived for ten years. I took a boat to Helsinki to attend a congress of the World Peace Council.

The debates were interesting and often passionate. It was the last congress in which the Chinese participated. They accused the

World Peace Council of insufficient support of the liberation struggle of Third World nations and of being afraid of the atomic bomb. In the discussion group in which I participated, I said, "I am not afraid of saying that I am afraid of the atomic bomb." After the meeting several young Chinese tried to convince me, eagerly but with great friendliness, that I had misunderstood their position. I also had a long talk with the Albanian delegate, who spoke excellent French. To my remark that it must be difficult for them to have bad relations with all their neighbors, he replied, "We have grown accustomed to that over a thousand years."

A few years later Lotte and I went to Morocco. I was astonished to find such a great variety in a relatively small country. North of the High Atlas one is in a Mediterranean country, south of it in an African one. Landscapes vary widely: in the north the High Atlas, the Middle Atlas, the Rif, and the plains; in the south the desert, fertile valleys, and oases. But everywhere the old towns and villages were beautiful and full of traditional Islamic life. ·

I was surprised to find no trace of resentment of the French. French is being taught in all schools and understood everywhere. We found remote mountain villages in which the people had a working knowledge of three languages: Berber, Arabic, and French. Canadians, please take note!

The mountain peasants told us proudly that their struggle for national independence had rid them of the despotic rule of the local Beys who had been pillars of the French regime. But generally, we found heavy exploitation, including child labor. There could be no doubt that we were in a police state; in most towns the most conspicuous building was the barracks of the Royal Gendarmerie. We drove back in a leisurely fashion to Bonnieux through Spain, now no longer under Franco's rule.

In 1967 I took Lotte to Canada to see the Montreal World's Fair and to show her a bit of my adopted country. We sailed from Liverpool to Montreal on one of the last ships which made that run. I am always happy to feel ships' planks under my feet; I dreamt of being a sailor well beyond my adolescent years.

A few years later I received an invitation from the Inter-American Planning Society to present a paper to their conference in Panama. This served as a welcome pretext to travel with Lotte to South America.

We flew from Paris to Lima. At that time General Velasquez

had become president of Peru and had, unlike most military dictators, initiated a far-reaching program of social reform. Lotte knew a couple of French journalists in Lima who were ardently for Velasquez, and a Viennese woman doctor and her family who were equally ardently against him. So we got the views of both sides. I have no basis for an independent judgment, but I was impressed by the high level of discussion in the local newspapers. I was even more impressed by the fact that there was nowhere an image of the president. I became curious to find out what the man looked like; but the only time I saw his face was in a group photo of his visit to a small town high in the Andes, hanging on the wall of the town hall which also served as a museum.

But the main purpose of our visit to Peru was to see the natural and man-made beauties of the country, including the treasures in the museums of Lima, Cuczco, and Arequipa. The highlight was Machu Picchu. I know of no other city which grows so beautifully out of its natural site. The tall, steep mountains on which Machu Picchu is built have been transformed into narrow, steep terraces by the unceasing labor of the Indios. The terraces are in turn transfigured into layers of houses, crowned by the sanctuaries.

We proceeded to Quito, which we found particularly pleasant. A colleague in Lima had given me an introduction to an architect in Quito. When we entered his house, we found the walls covered with views of Prague. He hailed from Lotte's hometown, and they found they had many acquaintances in common. Thanks to this man we also saw much of the villages and of the high mountains of Ecuador. It was strange to experience a snowstorm at the equator in midsummer.

After two equally interesting days in Bogota we went to Panama. The conference was a strange affair. Although the society has many members in the English-speaking Caribbean countries as well as in the US and Canada, the proceedings were exclusively in Spanish. It was so badly organized that I never found the registration desk and only with great difficulty found the room where I was to speak. I didn't; an Argentinian gave an oral translation of my paper, leaving only a few minutes for discussion.

Resentment of the "Colossus of the North" runs deep everywhere in Latin America, regardless of position in the political spectrum. When I was in Mexico City in 1947, I was invited to give a talk to the Mexico-USA Friendship Society, their members by definition more friendly to the "gringos" than most of their countrymen. I overheard a conversation among the Mexican members sitting at the head table, discussing a reform which they considered desirable but which could not be implemented because of the opposition of "usted save quien" (you know who). The bitter tone of this *usted save quien* is still in my ear.

From Panama we flew to Caracas, where we were well received by Gertrud Goldschmidt, sister-in-law of my old friend Robert Solmitz and niece of the renowned German art historian Adolph Goldschmidt. Trained as an architect, she had become a successful sculptor under the name of GEGO. She and her companion, also a talented artist of German descent, helped us considerably to see and understand Caracas. It is a strange city, a Latin American Los Angeles. In addition to its fair share of horrors, it contains two noticeable achievements of modern architecture, the university and the Museum of Modern Arts.

In Caracas, as in Bogota and Lima, we visited squatter settlements. In Peru, they had at long last recognized them and had rebaptized them *pueblos jovenes* (young villages). They are indeed young, both because they were born recently and because they are inhabited mostly by young people. The Peruvian authorities supplied them with bus services, electricity, schools, and water delivered by tank trucks. In all three countries the inhabitants displayed great initiative, not only in improving their homes but also in developing a thriving "informal economy" of workshops, retail stores, and even restaurants. In one of them we were served a decent meal in a spotlessly clean dining room.

In addition to these voyages with Lotte, I also made many alone. For a number of years I have spent and still spend at least two months in Europe, traveling around and then resting a month at Lotte's place in Bonnieux, on the slope of the Luberon mountain in Provence. Lotte has transformed the near-ruins of a huge rambling peasant house into a most attractive and livable home. There, in the shadow of a hundred-year-old Linden tree, I have been writing these lines. I have met Lotte's many friends there, including many young people who have also become my friends.

This lovely region has become a second home for me. It is incredibly rich in visual delights. Each one of the old villages has its own character, one more beautiful than the other. The landscape of vineyards, orchards, and groves of deciduous trees, their greens enlivened by small patches of ocher, is incredibly varied; one walks a hundred steps and sees a different image.

A few months after I wrote these lines, I received notice that Lotte had died in Paris. It leaves a great void in my life.

During the sixties and early seventies I traveled by car. After the age of 85 I gave up driving. Having learned to drive only in my sixty-fourth year, I was always a poor driver and a menace on the highway. The time had come to eliminate this threat to myself and others. Since that time I have used an Eurorail pass. Trains in Europe are very comfortable, fast, on time, and, most importantly, frequent. I still enjoy looking out of the window as much as I did more than eighty years ago.

As I grow older, my desire is shifting from discovering new sights to revisiting those which I had come to love in my youth — primarily in Southern Germany, Austria, and Italy — and from seeing sights to seeing people.

TRAVEL IN ASIA

This does not mean that I am not interested in visiting places which I have never seen before. Since adolescence there had been two countries and two cities which I particularly wanted to see: China and Peking, and Iran and Isfahan.

In 1979 I joined a most congenial group of Canadian architects and planners for an eighteen-day tour of China. The tour, starting and ending in Hong Kong, covered Canton, Shanghai, Nanking, Sian, Peking, and the Great Wall of China; upon our insistence our hosts added a side trip to the gardens of Soochow and interviews with professional colleagues in Shanghai and Sian.

What impressed me most in China was the enormous amount of human labor applied to careful cultivation of the soil. The people were cheerful, friendly, and intensely curious to watch us exotic animals, in particular in Sian, where not many foreigners had been before. They looked healthy and adequately fed and clothed, but housing, both new and old, was extremely crowded and without heating facilities, even in Peking and Sian, where winters can be severe.

The complex of the Imperial City in Peking surpassed my expectations. As one proceeds along the great axis, the impression changes from awe to splendor. One ascends to the three great halls, the middle one sheltering the imperial throne. Then one enters the more relaxed ambiance of the residential quarters. In my view this complex represents the highest peak ever achieved by the art of urban design.

Having waited over eighty years for my first visit to China, I expected to have to wait another eighty for my second one. But in January 1980 I received an invitation from the Chinese Association of Architects. A friend of mine, a talented young Chinese-Canadian architect in Vancouver, Bing Thom, had persuaded the Chinese authorities that they could get good advice from me and Fritz Gutheim of Washington, DC on city planning, and from Arthur Ericson of Vancouver, BC and another expert on hotel building. So this "Gang of Four" was invited.

I gave talks and had interesting discussions with groups composed of municipal officials, architects, and planners in Peking, Shanghai, and Tsientsin. The whole affair would have been a complete catastrophe if I had been forced to rely on the official translators. Fortunately, Professor Chen Zhan-kiang, a leading Chinese architect and planner who had worked for several years with Sir William Holford in London, volunteered to translate both ways. Last year, I had the pleasure of meeting Professor Chen again on the occasion of his visit to Toronto.

Some changes had occured in the seven months between my two visits to China. The first time the scapegoat was the "Gang of Four," the second time it was the "Cultural Revolution."

On both trips to China I stopped over in Japan for a few days. My impressions were much more favorable than I had expected. Different from China, the traditional high aesthetic culture is still very much alive, expressing itself in the surroundings and implements of daily life — admittedly side by side with mass-produced kitsch. Also, contrary to the horror stories about the ruthless pushiness of the Japanese, I found them to be extremely friendly and helpful. Any time I stopped on the street, uncertain which direction to take, someone, man or woman, came up to offer help in broken English, often accompanying me for some distance.

On my first visit to China, I had not returned across the Pacific, but had completed my round-the-world voyage via India, Iran and France.

Not the least benefit of being a university teacher is the fact that one finds former students all over the world. One in Hong Kong met me at the airport and introduced me to his large family, which took me to its bosom. My friend in Isfahan had been a well-known architect before coming to Toronto to study city planning. Some time after his return to his hometown he had become deputy-mayor of Isfahan. Just three weeks before my arrival he had resigned that job in protest against the constant interference from Teheran in the affairs of the municipal and provincial governments. This gave him time to show me much of Isfahan and its surroundings. Isfahan has beautiful mosques, palaces, and gardens. Its great bazaar and labyrinth of alleys are typical of Islamic cities. But quite atypical are the city-planning creations of Shah Abbas, the seventeenth-century founder of the Sefevid dynasty, the fourth great creative period of Iranian history. His long, straight, tree-planted streets and the huge rectangular central square, surrounded by regular two-story arcades — the second story being purely decorative — may have been influenced by Europe or, more likely, by India. But completely original are the great two-story bridges which combine to serve the needs of traffic as well as of recreation, providing platforms and pavilions for the population to enjoy the coolness of the river.

My friend also introduced me to his father, a master craftsman, the best goldsmith in Iran. He was a very likable person, as was his daughter, who lived with him in a simple but pleasant house with a garden.

The same friend recommended me to an architect in Shiraz, a city famous for its gardens. He was equally helpful, showing me the city and driving me to the magnificent ruins of Persepolis. When I found many Iranians at the mausoleum of the great medieval poet Hafiz, I asked, "Is the Islamic prohibition of alcoholic drinks no longer taken seriously?" When he answered that it was taken very seriously, I wondered how they could venerate a poet who had glorified drunkenness. He replied that the drunkenness was an allegory of the overwhelming joy of contemplating God. I had never before heard this interpretation.

A few months after I had left Iran, the revolution broke out. Contrary to my experience in Egypt in 1952, I had not expected it. The country was relatively prosperous; hundreds of thousands of workers had immigrated from Pakistan and Afghanistan to share that prosperity. While there was of course poverty, I saw no outright misery; my friend confirmed that nobody in the country was in danger of starvation. The only complaint which I heard repeatedly was about the neglect of agriculture; they considered it a shame that Iran, famous through millenia for its large herds of sheep, now imported frozen lamb from Australia. But the revolution erupted not in the countryside but in the cities. The Iranian experience confirms the thesis that revolutions are the product of rising expectations rather than of lasting misery.

I worry about what may have happened under the present regime to my friend in Isfahan and to his sister, who had also been my student and whom I saw in Teheran, where she had married into a rich upper-class family. But I do not dare write to them for fear that it might endanger them.

On East Germany and on Marx

Over the years I have also paid half-a-dozen visits of one to two weeks to the German Democratic Republic (GDR). Except for my last visit, in 1980, which was limited to East Berlin, I drove all over the country. As a Canadian I did not have to obtain a visa prior to my trip; I received it without difficulty at the border crossing point.

Of all the Communist-governed countries, the GDR is the closest, but probably least known by North Americans. It is closest to the West not only geographically but, more importantly, in its level of development. While average income per head is still lower than in West Germany, it is much more evenly distributed, and is equal or slightly higher than in the United Kingdom. This is really a greater "economic miracle" than the justly famous one of West Germany, if one is aware of the formidable handicaps with which East Germany was faced. It started out as the slightly poorer and much smaller part of the divided country, having depended on West Germany for 42 percent of all goods — including 99 percent of steel — compared to 16 percent in the other direction. For ten years billions of dollars worth of reparations flowed out of East Germany into the Soviet Union and Poland, while billions flowed into West Germany from the West. As I have already mentioned, East Germany started out at the end of the war with an extremely unfavorable ratio of dependents to labor force, in particular male workers, which was further deteriorated by the "brain (and muscle) drain" to the West, stopped only in 1961. Since that time the level of living has increased annually by about 4 percent, under conditions of full employment and stable prices.

I was surprised how freely my many chance acquaintances,

hitch-hikers and people met at eating, drinking, and other public places, talked to me. Several volunteered information about things they had done which, if reported, could have landed them in jail.

Over the years there has been a subtle change in the attitude of the population. In the fifties the majority felt nothing but hatred and contempt for the regime, and identified with West Germany. Now they probably still do not identify with their government, but they strongly identify with the great progress of the country which they have achieved under its leadership, which they have come to respect, if not to love, and they resent the arrogance of the West Germans. The great universal complaint is, of course, against the severe restrictions of travel to the West. Equally understandable complaints against the suppression of public or organized dissent I heard only from intellectuals, including not a few members of the ruling party.

There are, of course, many gripes because of recurrent shortages of this or that, but most of them do not last long and are a nuisance rather than a hardship. The "Market" and the "Centrally Planned" economies — the terms used by the UN — have exactly opposite problems. The great problem in the "West" is the threat of demand not keeping up with supply; for the entrepreneur or manager to sell his goods or services, and for the worker to sell his labor power; in the "East" the problem is supply not keeping up with demand. In the "West" the managers fear bankruptcy of their firms because they cannot find a market, and the workers fear losing their jobs. In the "East" managers fear their inability to fulfill the plan, because they cannot find the required inputs of goods and of workers, and the workers fear not finding the goods they need or want. In the "East" the lines form at the retail outlets; in the "West" they form at the labor office and the factory gate.

Every person who has worked in both the "East" and the "West," mostly emigrants, to whom I have presented this definition of the difference between the two economic systems has immediately agreed with it. But in the public discussion, on both sides, it is obscured by futile semantic quarrels whether the "Eastern" system should be called "socialism," or "state capitalism," or whatever fancy terms verbalizers can think up.

I am not interested in these semantic exercises. To me capitalism is unacceptable on moral grounds. It is based on the principle

of buying in the cheapest and selling in the dearest market —
which implies that the other fellow has to sell in the cheapest and
buy in the highest market. It is the exact opposite of the principle,
"Do unto others as you would have others do unto you"; the
principle which Christianity calls *caritas* and socialism calls
solidarity.

It seems to me that the GDR has a stronger claim to being a
"Workers' Republic" than the Soviet Union, Poland, or Hungary.
The gap between workers and intellectuals appears to be smaller,
not only in level of living, but also in education and lifestyle.

In Warnemünde, which is both a seaside resort and the seat of
a big shipyard, I tried in vain to determine, on the beach and in
the cafés and restaurants, who was a vacationer and who was a
shipyard worker.

In driving out of Berlin to Warnemünde, I picked up a young
fellow. Our conversation is worth recording.

"What is your occupation?" — "I am a student."

"What are you studying?" — "Theater Science."

"How much of a stipend do you get?" — "115 mark."

"That is not much." — "It is not much, but one can live on it."

"You live with your parents?" — "No."

"You live in a dormitory?" — "No."

"Where do you live?" — "I share an apartment with a friend."

"What is the rent?" — "30 mark a month."

"You probably made some money during your vacation?" —
"Yes."

"How much did you make?" — He did not answer directly, but
said, "If one works well, one can make 600 mark; but that is not
enough for that heavy work."

So, he considered 115 mark adequate for studying an esoteric
science, but 600 not enough for heavy physical labor!

When, in the following year, in Provence, I met a French girl
who had worked several months in a factory in the GDR, and I told
her that story, she replied, "That does not surprise me at all. My
German boyfriend worked in a factory during the day, and in the
evening he played in a jazz band in a restaurant. He said to me, 'It
is not just; my work in the factory is harder than my playing with
the band, and I get paid less for it.' "

Both these young men felt that their view, which I wholeheartedly share, was in no way in conflict with the Party line; it was just
one of those things which needed improvement.

Admittedly, most of the members of the "professional-managerial" group in the GDR do not share this view. They object strongly if one regards the quite substantial advantages which they enjoy as "privileges," noting that they are the result not of property rights, but of the just recompense for the "higher" quality of their work.

Certainly, property has been and still is the main instrument of exploitation, but it is not the only one. I consider it exploitation if one man, by whatever means, exchanges one hour of work — or none — against ten or a hundred hours of the work of others. This does not mean that I favor equality. Human beings vary enormously in their development and potential, and consequently in their needs for development. Yehudi Menuhin needs a Stradivarius violin; to give one to me would be unpardonable waste.

I am interested in attempts to "build socialism" in any country, and in particular in my native one, because I, as a born and re-born Victorian, adhere to the philosophy of that great Victorian thinker Karl Marx. "Dialectical materialism" means to me that the "material" world as defined by science on the basis of our sensual perceptions — the world of "pure reason" in Kant's terms — is real; that the essence of reality is movement; that movement, as the ancient Greek Eliatic philosopher already recognized, is a paradox, is inherently contradictory; and that this unending contradictory movement constantly creates genuinely new phenomena rather than merely a cyclical "eternal return."

"Historical materialism" means to me that existence, the life experience of human beings, determines their consciousness. How else could consciousness ever change? The human brain, as a part of organic nature, inherently tends toward homeostasis, the maintenance of the status quo. All human beings are conservative, as observation of child behavior confirms.

The consciousness of a tribe which supports itself by gathering plants and hunting animals does not change. But the very success of their hunting and gathering economy results in multiplication to the point where it can no longer support all its members. If they are to escape this "Malthusian" dilemma, they have two choices: they can develop new forms of production, such as cultivating plants and raising animals; or they can move to a different natural environment, where they can again survive only by modifying their means of production. They are also likely to encounter other tribes with a different consciousness.

Certainly, once this process gets under way, consciousness increasingly reacts on existence. However, the most profound and lasting changes of consciousness probably continue to result from changes in actual "material" existence.

As means of production develop beyond the hunting and gathering stage, they increasingly call for "modes of production" which assign different roles to different classes of the population. Their different life experiences result in different aspirations. The conflict between these different aspirations, the "class struggle," is the basic determinant of political action. Conscious political action changes "existence" by changing both the means and the modes of production. The relation of existence to consciousness is progressively reversed. The logical conclusion of this process would be a state of society in which human beings reorganize production so as to optimize the conditions of development of every individual. Marx called such a state of society "communism"; I see no need for another word.

Does this "materialist" world view leave any room for the moral law, Kant's "categorical imperative"?

Kant had recognized that the world of "pure reason" is strictly deterministic, leaving no room for "free will"; but he also stated that causality, which governs that world, is an "a priori" concept of our mind. He postulated that our equally "a priori" concept of "free will," and its corollary, responsibility, was an equally valid approach to ultimate reality, the forever inaccessible *ding an sich* (thing in itself), not an illusion.

I, as a materialist, believe that the world of "pure reason" is ultimate reality and that, consequently, "free will" is indeed an illusion. But this illusion is both inescapable for the mind of any individual and indispensable for the survival of any human society.

The inescapable conviction of one's own freedom of will and of responsibility for one's own decisions appears to be part and parcel of our genetic endowment. A certainly very complex combination and interaction of genes, including those enabling rational thought and generalization, probably is the basis of the moral law. I am inclined to think that it is the result of natural selection among thousands of generations of our anthropoid ancestors; those poorly endowed could not integrate themselves into the herd and perished before they could produce offspring. I can, of course, not prove this hypothesis, but I know of no better one.

Max Weber distinguished two forms of ethics: *verantwortungs* (responsibility) and *gesinnungs*. There is no exact English equivalent of *gesinnung;* it implies "ethics" as well as "mental attitude" — *verantwortung* and *gesinnung* — pragmatic and dogmatic ethics. In their extreme forms, *verantwortungs* signifies that "The end justifies the means"; *gesinnungs* implies "N'importe, si le geste est beau" (It does not matter, if only the gesture is handsome); or worse, "Fiat justicia, pereat mundus" (Let justice be done, may the world perish).

The famous sentence, "The end sanctifies the means," was first formulated by the Jesuits. My Protestant schoolmates in Hamburg quoted it to justify the suppression of the Jesuit order by the Kaiser's government. It did not take me long to realize that the sentence is purely analytical: it correctly defines the relation of means to ends. Means have no value (or "justification" or "sanctity") in themselves; we employ them in order to achieve desired ends. Everybody does this every day. Most of those who wax indignant over the famous sentence accept "just wars"; almost all go along with depriving human beings of their freedom by putting them in jail. All approve labor as a means of supporting life, even if it is dull, painful, often dangerous, unhealthy, or degrading, and almost always an impediment to the full all-around development of the human potential of the working person.

But does the sentence mean that its followers are willing to commit any crime to achieve their ends? And therefore can never be trusted? This is the accusation leveled at Jesuits — and Communists.

Certainly the sentence has often been used to justify crimes. But that is a narrow, mechanical, and incomplete interpretation. Every cause has more than one effect; every human action has not only the intended effect of achieving (if successful) the desired goal, but other effects as well. A criminal action always corrupts the actor; almost always, except in the very rare and always uncertain case of being permanently hidden, it corrupts those who hear of it; and it undermines the moral law.

The Jesuits were well aware of this and developed the doctrine of the "proportionality of ends and means" now fully adopted by the Catholic church.

The proportion of ends to means varies, of course, from case to case. The Jesuits therefore developed "casuistics." They have been blamed for this. They should be praised for taking the moral law seriously and for studying its application to real life situations.

The ethics of "responsibility" obliges one to study and weigh all possible consequences of one's actions. That is a demanding intellectual task. Worse, the weighing always will be incomplete and leave torturing doubts. It is much easier to adopt *gesinnungs* morality in a dogmatic form: "Thou shalt not . . ." (lie, steal, kill, etc.), regardless of the consequences. But it is irresponsible — and therefore basically immoral.

Of course, I also react emotionally against the sentence, "The end justifies the means," like every other person, but I distrust that reaction. Does this mean that I reject emotion? Certainly not; without emotion there can be no motion. Without heat to produce steam a steam engine cannot work. But the steam should not produce an explosion, and as little as possible should be used just "to blow off steam." It should be used to drive the engine of rationally conceived purposeful action.

Marx said, "The philosophers have only interpreted the world differently; what matters is to change it." I must admit that my temperament is different; I have always been more interested in understanding the world than in changing it; in the "vita contemplativa" than in the "vita activa." If I have become an "activist," it is because my understanding of current human behavior tells me that it is rushing toward catastrophe, and the moral law bids me to try to change it.

Central to Marx's program of action was the concept of the proletarian revolution to overthrow capitalism. But in the 137 years since *The Communist Manifesto* that revolution has not occurred. The only two attempts, in France in 1871 and in Central Europe in 1918-19, were defeated within a few months. There is no reason to expect that other attempts will be more successful, or indeed will be made.

But since 1944 there have occurred revolutions of a different type, which have indeed overthrown capitalism in several countries. In chronological order they are Albania, Yugoslavia, Vietnam, China, and Cuba. Essentially all of these were national anticolonial peasant revolutions under the leadership of a small group of professional revolutionaries, which in all cases except the last one, Cuba, was the Communist party. All occurred in countries in which incipient capitalism was combined with earlier forms of oppression and exploitation.

With the wisdom of hindsight one notes that the Russian Revolution was not, as its leaders as well as all observers, friend and foe, believed, the proletarian revolution predicted by Marx, but a revolution of the second type. Certainly, in Russia the industrial proletariat played a greater, and national liberation a lesser, role than in the later revolutions. But the mass of its fighters was supplied by the army and navy, 80 percent of its members being peasants, and its leadership by Lenin's Bolshevik party. The organizational forms, strategy, and tactics by which Lenin led the October Revolution to victory are probably still relevant for the "developing" countries, though they certainly cannot be copied. They have no relevance for "developed" countries.

What then are the prospects for the "West" — apart from the most likely one, nuclear suicide? I see two potential scenarios. It is possible that there will be permanent stagnation as a result of unwillingness to change, as happened in Spain after the sixteenth century. The other alternative — which I hope will become reality — is a nonviolent transfer of political power to the working class, followed by a systematic transformation of the socioeconomic pattern into a socialist society.

There are many indications that Marx in his later years, after 1871, questioned his theory of the proletarian revolution and thought of the potential for revolution in "protocapitalist" countries such as Russia. It is certain he considered that in democratic countries the working class could conquer power by peaceful means; he specifically said so in discussing Great Britain, the United States, and the Netherlands.

The great difficulty for any transition to socialism is not the political or military, but the economic power of capitalism, provided by its international mobility. The working class cannot overthrow a procapitalist government by a general strike, but the big bourgeoisie can overthrow a prosocialist government by a general strike, a massive withdrawal of capital. The inevitable consequence is a radical deterioration of the level of living, undermining the popular support of the prosocialist government.

Perhaps the only way to avoid this danger is the employment of "Fabian" tactics, taking one relatively small step at a time. Each such step will of course disturb investors, but not enough to abandon their investment. The political form of such a long transitional period is a "popular front" government, an alliance with other democratic forces, which may favor "free enterprise" but is strongly opposed to the dominance of multinational corporations. In some countries such a popular front may be constituted within a social-democratic or labor party; in most it will require a coalition of several parties.

ON DEMOCRACY

I do not see any contradiction between socialism and democracy. On the contrary, my years of work in the Soviet economy have convinced me that suppression of dissent and, in particular, obsessive secrecy are serious impediments to its progress.

We can never have "definite" knowledge of the truth because of constant change both of reality itself and of our knowledge and understanding of reality; we can only approximate it, and this can best be done by a conflict of errors. I therefore consider any restriction of the right to err — or dissent — however well intentioned, as dangerous. The "right to dissent" is currently called "democratic." A more correct term is "liberal," because throughout history that right has been respected as much (or as little) by monarchies or aristocracies as by democracies.

"Democracy" has become one of those "good" words, like "freedom" and "justice," which everybody endorses because everybody interprets them to suit himself. In contemporary North America it is often even identified with capitalism. Considering that contemporary capitalism gives to the heads of big corporations — elected by nobody and responsible to nobody — the right to destroy the lives of thousands of families, of entire communities, and even of nations by closing or relocating "their" plants, this is stretching the term democracy rather far.

The ancient Greeks, who coined the term, gave it a double meaning. First, it meant rule by the majority of citizens (who actually constituted only a minority of the adult population, often a small one). Second, it meant direct decisions by a people's assembly. A system under which the people delegated that right to representatives whom they considered best suited to make decisions, the Greeks called "aristocracy."

The rationale for this kind of "direct democracy," or "citizen's participation" was stated two thousand years ago by Julius Caesar; stuck in a forlorn town in Spain, he said, "Better here the first than in Rome the second." Citizen participation creates many small ponds which allow many individuals to become big fish. As man is a political animal, he is frustrated if he can never act as such.

The rationale for majority rule was given by Frederick II of Prussia in his statement that "God Almighty is usually with the stronger battalions." The majority certainly is not always right, but it is always strong. It is much wiser — and cheaper — to test the strength of two contending parties by the ballot than by the bullet.

The "man in the street," if asked what he meant by democracy, would probably answer, "equal opportunity." Under this definition, the claim of the Communist-ruled countries in general, and of the German Democratic Republic in particular, must be taken seriously. There may well be no other country where the life-chances of an individual are less dependent on sex, ethnicity, place of birth, or socioeconomic status of parents than the GDR.

BECOMING A "KNOWN PERSON"

The Russians use the term *znatnye lyudy* (known people) for people whose names are more or less frequently mentioned by the mass media. This aspect of life indeed only began well after age 65 for me. I cannot deny that I enjoy it; but there is the drawback that I always have to be on my best behavior. I shudder when I think of what might have happened if it had hit me in my younger years.

In 1965 I got a telephone call from the architect Paul Spreiregen. I had not heard his name before; I found that he was a nephew of Sam Zisman, with whom I had worked in Germany in 1949. He proposed to edit a book consisting of a collection of my articles, to which I agreed.

I dug up out of my filing nonsystem whatever I could find, including a few previously unpublished papers. Paul came to Toronto and we spent several days together going through the mass, or mess, to make our selection. As the articles had been written at different times for different journals, they contained many repetitions. We spent several days together in Washington, cutting and splicing texts.

Paul took upon himself the two most onerous tasks of editing. He translated my mostly very poor sketches and photos into brilliant line drawings, and he took care of the entire business end. The book was published in 1967 by MIT Press in the USA and by Harvest House in Canada under the title *The Modern Metropolis*. After several thousand hardcover copies had been sold, it was issued as a paperback. Over the years a total of both editions of about 15,000 copies has been sold. There has also been a Japanese edition. I cannot check the translation and do not know how many copies have been sold, but it certainly looks very handsome.

I have also learned that several planning schools have made my book "required reading" for their unfortunate students. I never "require" any reading from my students. I recommend to them a list of books and articles, indicating the content of each, and leave it to them to choose these or others according to their interest.

In 1977 Paul Spreiregen suggested an enlarged second edition of *The Modern Metropolis.* However, after we went through the papers which I had written in recent years, we decided that it would be more appropriate to use them, together with a few earlier pieces not included in *The Modern Metropolis,* to make a second book. In order to keep costs down, we omitted illustrations.

Whether because of the lack of illustrations, or of the rather stiff price, or of poor promotion, the book, published in 1979 by John Wiley & Sons, New York, under the title *Metropolis — and Beyond,* has not been a commercial success; only about one thousand copies have been sold. The only country where it seems to have found some response is India. I received two long letters which contained interesting and flattering comments from university teachers in Delhi and Calcutta.

Since that time I have continued to write occasional articles and book reviews on various subjects related to planning. Unrelated to planning was an article which I submitted to the *Journal of Architectural Historians;* it dealt with the Pantheon in Rome. As is well known, the design of the coffers of the cupola of that great building varies from tier to tier. The literature states that this was done for reasons of perspective effect — without saying what effect. When I was last in Rome, I posted myself in the center and looked straight up at the cupola. After a while a strange change occured, comparable to the mutual switch between figure and ground frequent in the contemplation of two-dimensional ornamental patterns: I saw not a cupola, but a huge cylinder, the opening at the top apparently as large as the diameter of the building, and the coffers all identical, square, and strictly symmetrical. This cannot be an accident, but must be the result of calculated design. Considering that the Pantheon is certainly one of the world's most extensively studied buildings, I assumed that this was known. However, in studying the recent exhaustive work on the Pantheon by Williamson, I found no mention of it; I subsequently received a communication from him expressing interest in my observation. I received confirmation from my friend Harry Lash, who found a photo taken from the same central point; most people looking at that photo also dis-' covered the cylinder.

My communication to the journal had also referred to an earlier observation which I had made in the tholos at Mycenae, misnamed the "Treasury of Atreus." The entrance to this building is through a hallway with sloping walls; the lintel is shorter than the threshold. However, as the walls of the tholos slope inward toward the top, the lintel is closer to the center than is the threshold, and therefore appears longer than it is. Seen from the center of the building, this apparent difference compensates exactly for the actual difference, so that the opening appears to be strictly rectangular. Here too, I am convinced that this is the result of a deliberate "perspectival" design.

The use of perspectival design in the Parthenon had been amply documented. My two observations indicate that the Greeks employed it both before and after the "classical" period, through one and a half millenia. Maybe we would produce better architecture if we designed our buildings not exculsively in terms of horizontal and vertical orthogonal projections, plans, sections, and facades, but from a perspectival viewpoint.

THE STRUGGLE FOR PEACE

Be that as it may, my main activity has been increasingly devoted to the struggle for peace.

Shortly after I had become a Canadian citizen, I joined the New Democratic party (NDP), which is comparable to the British Labour party. It is a social-democratic rather than a socialist party, but it has ample room for socialists of various hues. All party members agree on three tasks: struggle for immediate improvement of the lives of working people; education about the nature of capitalism and of socialism; and support of the liberation struggles of "Third World" people; they differ in their evaluation of the relative importance of each. I was and am also in agreement with the foreign policy of the NDP, but felt in the federal election campaign of 1979 that they did not sufficiently emphasize their demand for an independent Canadian foreign policy promoting disarmament. I attended several "all-candidates" meetings in order to raise the question. To my surprise, I observed that "fringe" candidates were allocated as much time as those of the major parties. I concluded that this offered a unique opportunity to reach people who had never been reached by the peace movement. So, when a few months later the fall of the Clark government led to a new election, I decided to run as an independent candidate on the single issue of peace and disarmament, in the riding in which I live.

The NDP candidate, aware that he had no chance to be elected, did not object to my running. I got support from the Toronto Association for Peace, and from some former and present students, as well as from some people previously unknown to me who volunteered their services. We distributed leaflets door to door and I spoke at all-candidates meetings.

One pleasant aspect of this campaign was the attitude of the candidates of the two main parties. The incumbent, Conservative David Crombie, the former mayor of Toronto, was sure of reelection. At one all-candidates meeting, at which he followed me, in alphabetical order, on the platform, he praised me as an outstanding citizen. At another meeting, his Liberal rival took my hand and whispered into my ear, "If I were not running myself, I would vote for you."

I was aware that not many voters in my riding shared her feelings. I predicted that I would get 200 votes; I got 197.

For a number of years I served on the executive of the Canadian Peace Congress and am still acting as chairman of its local branch, the Toronto Association for Peace, participating in the usual activities such as organizing meetings, distributing leaflets, gathering signatures for petitions, and marching in demonstrations. I also drafted their main statement, entitled "A Time For Disarmament," and other pieces of literature and correspondence. I feel, however, that the peace movement spends too much time preaching to the converted. I therefore frequently write letters to the general press, and have had the satisfaction of seeing most of them printed in the Toronto *Globe and Mail.**

In the sixties the conclusion of SALT I and of the Helsinki Agreement on Security and Cooperation in Europe seemed to indicate that the USA had finally accepted the necessity of peaceful

---

* A collection of my letters to the press on disarmament questions is being gathered and edited by Stephen Salaff, Ph. D., of Toronto.

coexistence with the Soviet Union as the only alternative to no existence — recognizing that each side could destroy the other, but only at the price of its own destruction. "Mutually Assured Destruction" (MAD) actually has deterred the outbreak of war. It is sometimes called "equal security"; it is in fact equal insecurity. However, the "balance of terror" is inherently unstable. I remain convinced that in the long run no nation can achieve security by making others more insecure — that is what "deterrence" means — but only by making everybody secure. MAD can at best serve as a stopgap to arrest the vicious cycle of armament arousing fear and distrust, leading to more armament. We must replace it with a disarmament trust — disarmament virtuous cycle, which might be started by unilateral action as well as by negotiation.

The adherence of the United States to the Helsinki Agreement had been hesitant; from the beginning the United States Government — and Canada as well — have disregarded the clause requiring wide publicity of the text of the agreement. The resultant ignorance has enabled the "West" to claim the existence of a "basket" on human rights. In fact, the Helsinki Agreement is not organized in "baskets"; it contains a number of operational sections, preceded by a statement of general principles. These principles refer indeed to human rights, but none of the operational sections mention the right to dissent nor the right to emigrate. The violation of these rights by the Soviet Union, profoundly disturbing as it is, is not a violation of the Helsinki Agreement. By treating it as such, the "West" has transformed the agreement from an instrument of cooperation into a platform for confrontation.

The most hopeful event of the seventies was the unanimous consent given to the Final Document of the United Nations Special Session on Disarmament in June 1978: "Mankind is presented with a choice: we must halt the arms race and proceed to disarmament or face annihilation." But while Trudeau traveled from Ottawa and Giscard d'Istaing from Paris to attend the UN meeting in New York, President Carter stayed in Washington to engineer a fatal move in the opposite direction: a decision by NATO to increase armaments of all its members by three percent annually in real terms.

It is not clear what caused this reversal of US policy, but since that time things have gone from bad to worse. MAD, the balance of terror, has been supplanted by the doctrine of "counterforce," a nice-sounding synonym for "first strike," the illusion that the US can obtain "superiority" and "prevail" in a nuclear war by destroying the opponent's nuclear force. That this doctrine is now based on "Star Wars" fantasies makes it no less dangerous.

The most dangerous step on this fatal course toward the annihilation of mankind, against which the UN has warned, has been the stationing by the US of "theater" nuclear weapons in Europe, in particular the "Pershing II" launchers in Germany. These reduce the "warning time" from twenty to four minutes; their aim is to "decapitate" the Soviet armed forces before they can act by destroying their command and communication structure. They have nothing to do with "balancing" the Soviet SS 20's — which are directed against the same targets as were their clumsier predecessors, the SS 4's and SS 5's — as NATO's commander in chief, General Bernard Rogers, admitted. A "balance" to the Pershing II's in Europe would be Soviet "theater weapons" in America. The Soviet Union tried that once — during the Cuban crisis — though their missiles had neither the range nor the accuracy of the Pershing II's. We know how the US reacted to this threat. In comparison, the Soviet reaction — suspending disarmament talks — has been extremely mild and restrained.

As the Reagan administration openly embarked on a course of confrontation with the Soviet Union, many people all over the world finally began to wake up to the reality of the danger of global suicide. We still talk about "defense" — but there is no defense against thermonuclear bombs carried by intercontinental missiles. We talk of war and peace. War, according to Clausewitz' classical definition, is continuation of policy by other means. But there is no conceivable policy that can be implemented by nuclear arms; suicide is not a policy. The struggle for peace and disarmament is the struggle for survival, survival of every individual now alive or yet to be born.

I do not question the sincerity of the opponents of disarmament; as were my high-school teachers in Germany seventy-five years ago, they, and their counterparts on the other side, are convinced that only armed strength deters the "enemy" from aggression. Can we muster the courage to break out of the vicious circle of distrust and fear? "We have nothing to fear but fear itself," Roosevelt once said in a different context. In the present situation it is truer than ever.

There is indeed no other basis than mutual fear for the hostility between the USA and the USSR. If it were a question of economic competition, the US would oppose Japan or Europe rather than the Soviet Union. It is sometimes said that the hostility is the result of different "values." But the "values" of the China of the Cultural Revolution — not to mention those of Saudi Arabia — certainly differ more from American ones than do those of the Soviet Union. In fact, conflict arises not when states pursue different goals, but when they pursue the same one. I like to illustrate this by a historical example.

In the beginning of the sixteenth century, the Catholic church was hard pressed by the advance of both the Reformation and of the Ottoman Empire. But the two most powerful Catholic princes, Charles V of Spain and Germany and Francis I of France, were fighting neither the Protestants nor the Turks, but each other. So Francis was told by his Father Confessor: "You and Charles are Catholic brothers in Christ and should be of one mind." "But," replied Francis, "but Father, that is just the trouble; my brother Charles and I *are* of one mind: we both want Milan." The USA and the USSR are of one mind: both want to be top dog! I must, however, modify this statement. There is strong evidence indicating that the USSR understands that in the nuclear age nobody can be top dog; but they will not accept to be underdog; they claim "equality" and disclaim the goal of "superiority." The USA, for understandable historical reasons, still finds it hard to accept a world not reshaped in conformance with the "American way."

As the danger has grown, more and more people have joined the movement for peaceful coexistence and disarmament, and many new organizations have sprung up. I have joined some of them, such as Science for Peace, and have worked for cooperation and common action of all peace groups. In Toronto, as elsewhere, a request was made to put the demand for a nuclear-weapons-free city on the municipal ballot; it was adopted by a vote of 12 to 11 by the city council. However, a second vote was needed to approve the required funds, and supporters of the motion feared that one or the other alderman might change his yes vote to no. The peace movement therefore mobilized supporters to be present during the vote. Not only were all spectator seats in the council chamber filled half an hour before the session, but additional hundreds overflowed the lobby. The effect was amazing: one after another the former opponents, including the mayor, rose to state that they had reconsidered their position. The motion passed 22 to 1. The question was included on the ballot and passed by a majority of 4 to 1.

There is no doubt that the attitude toward the peace movement has changed. Peace, coexistence, and disarmament are no longer dirty words, as they were in the fifties, but are in the mouths of the heads of government, including President Reagan. However, so far deeds do not conform to words; the arms race is not being reversed. As any driver knows, before going into reverse a car must come to a full stop — a "freeze" in the case of the arms race. I believe that this has to be the central demand of the world peace movement. It does not necessarily have to wait on negotiations. It could be initiated by either the USA or the USSR unilaterally declaring a temporary freeze, or "moratorium" of three to six months on the testing, production, and deployment of nuclear arms and means of their delivery. It is to this that I intend to devote my remaining strength.*

In 1978 the Canadian Government, which in 1960 had considered me unworthy to become a citizen, made me an Officer of the Order of Canada. I have no doubt that I owe this honor to Pierre Juneau, the president of the Canadian Broadcasting Corporation (CBC), who had come to know me while he was chairman of the National Capital Commission. At the ceremony I was pleasantly surprised to find that the order included a fairly broad cross section of Canadian society.

My work for peace has also found some echoes in the mass media and has earned me some honors.

The Canadian Peace Congress proposed a banquet on the occasion of my eighty-fifth birthday in 1977. I felt that a round number would have been more appropriate, but they did not want to wait five years. As I had to admit that the banquet would be good public relations for the congress, I agreed. The affair succeeded beyond expectations; several hundred people braved the worst snowstorm of the year to attend. The mayor of Toronto, David

---

* The Soviet Union actually declared a unilateral moratorium on the testing of nuclear weapons which began on August 6, 1985 and will endure until at least January 1, 1987. It called upon the USA to do likewise, but thus far the latter has refused to join in the freeze.

Crombie, now a member of the Conservative cabinet in Ottawa, gave a speech and presented me with a coffee-table book on Toronto in the name of the city.

Five years later, in 1982, the Peace Congress repeated the celebration on a slightly smaller scale. I was particularly pleased that the members of the congress executive agreed to invite my old friend James Endicott, with whom they had not been on speaking terms since his break with the World Peace Council. I used the opportunity to launch the "Franz Blumenfeld Peace Foundation" in memory of my brother, whose death at the front in 1914 prevented him from carrying out his intention to devote his life to peace. The foundation is still struggling for tax exemption.

With the delay which academics consider appropriate to their dignity, the University of Toronto celebrated my ninetieth birthday in the following year. The Department of Geography, to which our Planning Program had been transferred from the Faculty of Architecture after a long and bitter struggle for survival, together with the Centre for Urban and Community Studies, convened a conference on "The Metropolis" in November 1983. They had expected an attendance of 200, but over 500 came, and the papers and discussions were of a high caliber. For me, the best part of it was the opportunity to once more meet old friends whom I had not seen for years, among them Edward Bacon and, in particular, Kevin Lynch. I had engaged in correspondence with Kevin on his last and best book, *Theory of Good City Form.* It was to be our last meeting; a few months later his sudden death deprived the profession of one of its best minds and his friends of a most lovable person.

In 1984 the International Union of Architects honored me by its "Abercrombie" Prize. In 1984 the World Peace Council also made me one of its honorary presidents. But the most unexpected honor was the bestowal in 1985 of the annual award of "Lambda Alpha, Land Economics International." Founded as a fraternity by students of Richard Ely at Wisconsin, it now comprises chapters in all major centers of the USA and one in Toronto. It unites people interested in land planning, economics, etc. with those who have "an interest" in land — developers, real estate men, and mortgage bankers. Our chapter holds three or four meetings each year. After a dinner, which is far more sumptuous and exquisite — and expensive — than those which I cook for myself at home, a member or invited guest makes a presentation, followed by a lively, searching, and well-informed discussion between people of widely varying viewpoints.

What pleased me particularly about this award was that the citation also praised my work for peace — considering that most members of the organization are likely to be supporters of Ronald Reagan.

"KNOWN PEOPLE" I HAVE KNOWN

In the course of my long life I have met many distinguished people in addition to those mentioned in the text of this book.

Lewis Mumford, whom I greatly admire not only for his encyclopedic knowledge and profound understanding of cities, but equally for his clear and consistent stand against the madness of the arms race and other follies of contemporary society, I met in Philadelphia. From his writings I had the impression that he might be a bit pompous; but I found him to be a very modest, friendly, and approachable person. We disagree on many points; he is a prophet, and I am just an analyst and practitioner.

Mumford's most formidable antagonist, Jane Jacobs, I met soon after she moved to Toronto. I had published a rather critical review of her famous book, *The Death and Life of Great American Cities,** but she received me graciously.

I had acknowledged that she had made many acute observations which the "experts" should have made, but never did make, and had debunked many wrong or obsolete planning theories. Unfortunately, though not surprisingly, her own recommendations have become equally harmful shibboleths.

I worked with Jane Jacobs on "Harbourfront," a large residential project initiated by the Province of Ontario and developed by Eberhard Zeidler into an exciting design for a "Canadian Venice." When the ministry in charge changed heads, the entire project silently dropped to the bottom of Lake Ontario. Jane and I also gave conflicting testimony before the Ontario Municipal Board. I regret that I see her so rarely.

I met another famous Torontonian, the late Marshall McLuhan, a few times. I liked him as a person, but I question his theories. He certainly had one of the best heads around, but he used it too

---

* Published under the title "The Good Neighborhood" in *Adult Education* (May-June 1962): 264-70; reprinted in *Modern Metropolis*, 180-89.

often to stand on. His love of paradox vitiated his insights. It is not print, but speech, that is linear. In its written or printed form it is slightly less so, because one can refer back to earlier passages. Reading phonetic script is not a "visual" activity; one uses — and abuses — one's eyes as ears. It is different with a pictorial script, such as Chinese, which is truly visual. It is hardly an accident that among well-known leaders of the visual arts in North America the proportion of Chinese and Japanese names is at least ten times as high as it is in the general population.

Perhaps even more important, being able to read Chinese script, which can be understood in any language, such as Japanese or Vietnamese, equips its reader with two different ways of thinking and feeling. I believe that being "bilingual" is the best way to develop flexible and innovative thinking. Where did ancient Greek thought develop? Not on the mainland; all the "pre-Socratic" philosophers came from the colonies, where they probably were as fluent in the language of their neighbors, with whom they traded, as in their own.

Probably the later development of European thought also had something to do with the thorough knowledge of Latin among the educated classes, in particular as it became more widespread after the invention of printing. Familiarity with mathematical and computer language may be an adequate substitute for the purpose of developing different ways of thinking, but it cannot contribute to understanding alternative modes of feeling.

I will stop name-dropping, but I cannot refrain from mentioning Brian McHarg, the brilliant and innovative landscape architect, because our only encounter is connected with a story which is so characteristic of the two persons involved. After a lecture by McHarg in Philadelphia, some of us accompanied him to have a beer. On the way from the lecture hall to the beer parlor a heated debate went on between McHarg and Jacqueline Tyrrwhitt. When we arrived at the pub, Jackie plumped down on her seat, exclaiming, "Ha, first time anyone ever talked me down!"

I also once met Viljo Revell, the architect of Toronto's new city hall. The city hall is a highly original creation, and Torontonians have taken it to their hearts. It consists of two elegant office towers facing each other, shaped as segments of a circle and enclosing a huge circular entrance hall topped by the equally circular council chamber. The towers have glass fronts on the inside, and unbroken concrete walls on the outside. Being the mischievous little boy which I still am, I made a nasty crack about its functional symbolism: "The bureaucrats look only at each other; they look down their noses at the elected representatives, and they turn their backs on the people."

Over the years I have also come to know many leaders of Canada's three political parties, on municipal, provincial, and federal levels, and also many high civil servants. I have found both groups, the "politicians" and the "mandarins," to be of a much higher caliber than the general public gives them credit for.

THOUGHTS ON PLANNING

Planning is a frustrating activity. The saving grace is that it leads one to the discovery of new problems.

In addition to my courses at the University of Toronto, I have been and remain engaged in occasional lectures and consultations and, in particular, in research and writing.

The title of my second book, *Metropolis — and Beyond,* refers to "beyond" not only in terms of time, but also of space. The definition of "metropolitan area" by the census bureau of the United States and Canada as a "commuter shed" established a very important concept which still remains valid, but decreasingly so. The concept is based on a "model" of places of work and services located at the center and residences at the periphery. As jobs and service centers move increasingly to the periphery of the metropolitan area and even beyond, the concept begins to lose its validity. People living in the "fringe," too far from the center for daily commuting, travel to work and service centers in the periphery of the census metropolitan area. The distinction between that area and its fringe becomes increasingly blurred.

Even more importantly, in a very large fringe, extending as far as 100 to 120 kilometers from the metropolitan center, there are to be found many residents and establishments which would not be there if the center were not there. John Friedmann has called this large unit, including its center, an "urban field." I have used the terms metropolitan "region" or "orbit," to be distinguished from its core, the "metropolitan area" or "commuter shed."

Two kinds of people and establishments are to be found in this fringe. First, residents of the central metropolitan area who use the natural resources of the fringe for temporary or permanent enjoyment, and the sizable permanent population which serves them. Second, establishments, primarily manufacturing plants which use the business services of the metropolitan area, including its airport and its warehouses for rapid delivery of goods, in particular "spare" parts of machinery; and their workers, who use, to a lesser extent, the "higher-order" consumer services of the center.

I have recently published a study on the population changes from 1970 to 1980 in the orbits of all metropolitan areas of the USA with populations of half a million or more, limiting the "fringe" by a circle with a radius of fifty miles for those with populations under two million, and of seventy miles for the larger ones.*

The 72 "metropolises" thus defined contained, both in 1970 and 1980, slightly more than two-thirds of the total population. In the northeastern United States the percentage is much higher; in West-Central Europe and in Japan it probably approaches 100 percent.

Of the much-discussed decreasing share of the population of the United States counted in census metropolitan areas, four-fifths were absorbed by the "fringes" and only one-fifth by genuinely nonmetropolitan counties. The rate of population growth in the fringes was almost four times that of the areas outside of them, and nearly ten times that of their central metropolitan areas.

New and very tough problems are arising in the fringes, requiring new and imaginative planning approaches.

I have come to the conclusion that the entire history of the distribution of human settlements and population since the emergence of towns has been and will be basically determined by four factors, two being permanent and two changing ever more rapidly. The changing factors are the techniques of production and of transportation-communication. The permanent factors are Ebenezer Howard's "two magnets," urban and rural. The rural pole provides access to nature, the urban one to other human beings and their works. Both poles attract in two different roles: as resource and as environment. During the past 250 years revo-

---

* "Have the Secular Trends of Population Distribution Been Reversed? An Investigation of the Metropolitan Fringe in the United States: 1970-1980," Centre for Urban and Community Studies, Toronto, Research Paper 137.

lutionary changes in the techniques of agriculture and mining have reduced the percentage of the labor force required for "on-site" work to exploit natural resources from 80 percent to 5 percent of the labor force. The remaining 75 percent have been attracted by a centripetal movement to urban concentrations. Their growth to population agglomerations of multimillion proportions was made possible by effective techniques of long-distance transportation, primarily steamships and railroads.

But while the rural pole has lost most of its magnetism as resource, its attraction as environment is as strong as ever, if not stronger. Hence the large-scale centripetal "rural-to-urban" movement has been met, during the last century, by a spatially more limited centrifugal "city-to-suburb" movement, made possible by electric traction and the telephone, followed by the motor vehicle and means of wireless communications.

In the most "developed" areas of the world this younger, centrifugal movement has almost completely washed over the centripetal one. Ultimately the entire inhabited world or *ecumene* may be covered by contingent metropolitan orbits.

Another even more vital problem that has in recent years occupied my thoughts is that of ecology, or of the "limits of growth."

It is self-evident that on a limited planet there cannot be unlimited growth of anything, neither of the number of people, nor of the amount of commodities each person consumes, and even less of the first multiplied by the second, gross global product (GGP) of goods. (There is no absolute limit to the growth of services per person, hence of the total GGP).

There can be no doubt that continuation and expansion of our current wasteful and short-sighted ways of production will lead to the destruction of a global environment capable of supporting organic life. What disturbs me in much of the literature warning against this danger is that it regards nature in a mechanical way as a static storehouse of "stocks"; human consumption exhaust these stocks — "and then there are none," and life comes to an end.

That is not the way I understand nature. I see her as a highly complex system of mutually interdependent cycles whose interaction maintains organic life. We are now disrupting these cycles by taking more out of nature than she can reproduce, and putting more into her than she can digest. The first problem is the lesser one, because it can almost always be met by substitution of another resource, albeit at higher cost.

The basic answer to the second problem is contained in the statement which Paracelsus made over 400 years ago: "Everything is a poison, nothing is a poison." In the right quantity, at the right time, in the right environment, any "poison" may have a life-enhancing effect.

For decades I have been preaching that we must discard the concept of "waste" to be "disposed of" as obsolete, and replace it by the notion of by-products to be reused and recycled. That is, of course, easier said than done; it requires a redirection of science and technology from life-destroying to life-preserving goals.

Recycling is the main means to reduce both the plundering and the poisoning of nature. It can, however, never be complete; its cost rises exponentially with the percentage of any material recycled. *The real limits of growth are the limits of recycling.*

Where recycling is not feasible, substitution of plentiful and/or nonpoisonous materials for those presently used must be sought; generally, this will raise the cost of the product. One measure which involves no cost, and therefore should receive highest priority, is world-wide disarmament, which would reduce both pollution and exhaustion of scarce resources by at least 10 percent.

OLD AGE

Old people are pitied as being weak, sick, lonely, and lost in a world which they no longer understand. My experience has been much more fortunate.

Certainly, I note from year to year a decline in physical strength. Probably there is a parallel decline of mental strength, but like most people I am blissfully unaware of it. I am only aware that my inability to remember names and telephone numbers has increased from 90 percent to 99 percent.

As I had to give up practicing one sport after another as my bodily mobility gradually decreased, I learned to drive and to enjoy motoring. After I gave up driving, I presented myself on my ninetieth birthday with a radio-tape player, and now can indulge my love of music more than ever before in my life.

My health has generally improved with old age. Apart from a few days in hospital for treatment of prostate troubles, I have not been in bed for a day during the almost forty years since I came to Toronto. When asked for the reasons for this unusual state of affairs, my answer is, "I am so full of venom that no virus can survive." Certainly, my good health is not due to a regular schedule, which I do not keep, nor to exercise, which I do not do. (The hubris which tempted me to write the preceding sentences has not failed to attract the revenge of the gods. A week after they were written, I suffered a stroke. It did not paralyze me, but it left me enfeebled and with slightly blurred vision.)

I do not feel lonely. As friends and relatives have passed away, one after another, I have acquired new friends in the two following generations, those around sixty and those around thirty. Admittedly, there is not the feeling of intimacy which one shares with those whom one has known since childhood.

I do not feel that I have lost touch with the world in which I live. This does not mean that I understand it; but then I never did. Possibly in younger years I was less aware of this; the main thing one learns in life is to know that one does not know.

It is often said that people suffer "future shock" because change is rapidly accelerating. Change in science and technology certainly is. But for the change that really matters, in social relations and in the thoughts, feelings, and valuations of human beings, it is true only for the "Third World," but not for the "West," including Russia.

I can now look back over about eighty years during which I was more or less aware of the world I lived in. It seems to me that the changes which have occurred between 1904 and 1944 were more fundamental than those from 1944 to 1984. This might be an illusion, produced by decreasing ability with increasing age to recognize change. However, if I project back, I find that 1904 differed more fundamentally from 1824 than from 1984, at least in North America.

Certainly, scientific and technical progress has been rapid during my lifetime. I recall my surprise at seeing a streetcar not drawn by horses, but moved by electricity. A little later the first telephone was installed in our house; our number was 68. I remember first seeing the funny, abrupt movements of people on a movie screen, and hearing the croaking of an early phonograph. The first automobile I saw had electric traction. Somewhat later my family took me to a race track — amidst a crowd of thousands — to see an airplane fly from one end to the other.

It would be tedious to enumerate the many innovations that have come into being since my childhood. But I believe that three new fields of science are of secular importance for both theory and practice: nuclear physics, molecular biology, and cybernetics, including computer science. I am somewhat less interested in rockets and space exploration. I tend to say with Robert Frost, "I am afraid I am a bit provincial."

I have indeed been unusually fortunate in escaping most sufferings of old age. I still enjoy the pleasures of the mind, of eye and ear. Life becomes easier as emotions calm down; as desires decrease, so does the frustration about their lack of fulfillment. But the greatest advantage of old age is that one no longer has to worry about the future, because there is so little of it. I pity the people who worry about life after death. I feel like Shakespeare:

> "For our little life
> is but a dream,
> and rounded with a sleep."

Index

Ashkhabad, 159
Austrian Communist party,
119-20, 163
Austrian Socialist party, 119
Automobile, 103-04, 128, 131,
242-43, 249, 251-52. *See also*
Freeways; Transportation

BACON, Edmund N., 19, 191,
192, 193, 196, 198, 203, 204,
205, 221, 305
Bad Mergentheim, 9-10
"The Bad Trip," 248
Bauhaus, 113, 136, 254
Bavarian Soviet Republic, 64-65
Bayerischer Kourier, 68
Bebel, August, 21
Bergson, Henri, 250
Berlin wall, 259
Bernstein, Eduard, 59
"Biedermeier" style, 28
Bing, Gertrud, 223, 265
Black Shirts, 48
Blau, 68-69
Bloch, Ernst, 258-59
Blucher, Walter H., 236
Blumenfeld, Anna (mother), 13,
16-18, 28, 30, 34, 35, 43, 44,
48, 51, 53, 61, 71, 74, 81, 82,
88, 89, 96, 102, 107, 115
Blumenfeld, Carl (uncle), 11, 13
Blumenfeld, Franz (brother), 14,
18-19, 23, 26, 30, 40, 41, 42,
44, 45, 46, 47, 98, 305
Blumenfeld, Hans: childhood, 23-
26; adolescence, 26-29; early
education as architect in
Tübingen, 33-34; at the
Technical University of
Munich, 35-36; studies design
at Karlsruhe, 36-37; meets
Gertel Stamm, 37-40; joins
field artillery regiment at
Bahrenfeld, 46; sent to the
front in East Prussia, 47; in

Latvia, 48-49; in Rumania, 50;
hospitalized in Nis, Siberia, 50;
in Moldavia, 51; hospitalized in
Bucharest, 52; first prison
experience in Buzau, 52; in the
Crimea, 54-56; exempted from
battle service in Macedonia, 57-
58; joins USPD, 57; participates
in Spartacus revolt, 62-63;
resumes studies in Munich, 64;
establishes legal aid office for
USPD, 66-67; arrested for
participation in murder, 68-69;
prison in Stadelheim, 69-70;
student at Darmstadt, 71;
editor of *Workers' Newspaper for
South-Hesse,* 73-74; purchases
farm at Brunstorf, 74-75; as
member of KPD, 77; prison
in Brixen, 79-80; receives
master's degree from
Darmstadt, 81; first job as
architect in Hamburg, 83-85;
travels in Germany and Italy,
88-95; first visit to the United
States, 97-105; in New York,
100-01; as draftsman in
Baltimore, 101-02; as designer
in Los Angeles, 103-04; travels
through Panama Canal to
Europe, 106; first visit to
Temple of Concordia, 107; as
architect with Karl Schneider in
Hamburg, 108-09; as trade
union activist with Butab, 110-
14; as architect with Frank and
Wlach in Vienna, 114-15; as
architect with Kulka and Loos,
115-16; meets Alfred Adler,
117-18; joins Austrian
Communist party, 119; courier
for "Red Aid," 120-21; as
architect with Second Building
Trust in Moscow, 124-28;
employed by Giprogor, 128;

as city planner for town of Vladimir, 131-36; as member of the Communist party of the Soviet Union, 137; as chairman of German Workers' Club, 137-40; works at replanning the city of Vyatka, 141-43; travels in Caucasus, 144-46; as planner in Makeyevka, 148-51; travels in Soviet Central Asia, 155-59; as head of architectural department with Moscow Province Projects Trust, 159-61; expelled from the Communist party of the Soviet Union, 161; denounced by *Arkhitekturnaya Gazeta*, 163-64; leaves Soviet Union, 172-73; visits Turkey and Greece, 176-77; travels in France, 182-83; writes on "the coordination of natural and artificial light," 187; writes *Housing Union Labor*, 188; as site planner for Kelly and Gruzen, 188-89; joins Society of Architectural Historians, 190; publishes "Regional and City Planning in the Soviet Union," 191; hired as researcher by Philadelphia Housing Association, 191; becomes U.S. citizen, 199; and Postwar Planning Commission, 200; writes "The Waterfront, Key to Redevelopment," 201; appointed chief of the Division of Planning Analysis, 205; serves as visiting expert on city planning to the United States military government in Germany, 208-215; revisits Sommerau, 210; revisits Hamburg, 211-13; works for Progressive party in election of 1948, 220; resigns from

Eisner, Kurt, 64, 68
El Salvador, 105
Endicott, Rev. James, 260,
    271-72
Endicott, Mary, 260
Engels, Friedrich, 123, 126
The Erfurt Program, 59
Ericson, Arthur, 267, 286
Expressways. *See* Freeways

FAECT, 186, 187
Fascism, 161, 183
FBI, 233, 240, 273
Federal Department of Aviation,
    268-69
Feiss, Carl, 191
Ferghana Valley, 155-56
Field, Herman, 279, 280
Field, Noël, 279, 280
"Finger Plan": in Copenhagen,
    200; in Toronto, 242
Finland, 194-95
Fischer, Theodor, 35, 39, 64, 65
Fitch, James M., 187
Five-Year Plan: 126, 139, 148,
    153; and city planning, 129
Ford Foundation, 266
"Form and Function in Urban
    Communities," 81
Franco, F., 174, 178, 179, 253,
    280, 282
Frank, Joseph, 114-15
Franklin Institute, 202
Franz Blumenfeld Peace
    Foundation, 305
Freeways, 201, 243-46, 248-49,
    263-66. *See also* Automobile;
    Transportation
Freud, Sigmund, 17
Freundlich, Otto, 57, 107, 179,
    180
Friedmann, John, 308
Frost, Robert, 313
Fuhrmann, Ernst, 61, 62, 97
Future shock, 312

GARDEN City movement: 129;
    garden cities, 200
Gardiner, Frederick G., 237, 238,
    241, 247
Garnier, Charles, 166
Geddes, Patrick, 119
General Motors, 103-04, 268
George circle, 36
George, Stefan, 34, 36
German Communist party (KPD),
    60, 66, 72, 73, 74, 77, 85, 86,
    96, 110, 111,112, 114, 147,
    178, 179
German communists, 60, 64, 65,
    66, 95-96, 110, 111, 113, 146-
    47, 161, 179, 214, 288-90
German Democratic Republic
    (GDR), 87, 214-15, 259, 288-90
German Independent Social
    Democratic party (USPD), 52,
    54, 60, 61, 64, 66, 67, 68, 69,
    71, 72, 73, 74, 86
German Popular Front, 178, 184,
    199
German Public Transit
    Association, 260
German social democracy, 27, 42
German Social Democratic party
    (SPD), 42, 52, 60, 63, 64, 65,
    67, 72, 73, 74, 86, 110, 111,
    112, 113, 114, 146, 178
German Soviet Republic, 59
Gerson, Hans and Oscar, 83-84
Géshé kondo, 278
Gestapo, 161, 163
Gide, André, 47
Giprogor, 128, 129, 130, 131,
    134, 140, 141, 146, 170, 240,
    254
Gizeh (pyramids of), 103
The Globe and Mail, 272, 300
Goethe, J. W., 9, 155, 177
Golan Heights, 277
Goldschmidt, Gertrud, 284
Gorki, 140, 141, 143, 146